BELIEF AND BEHAVIOR

BELIEF AND BEHAVIOR

Essays in the

New Religious History

Edited by

PHILIP R. VANDERMEER and

ROBERT P. SWIERENGA

RUTGERS UNIVERSITY PRESS
New Brunswick, New Jersey

Library of Congress Cataloging-in-Publication Data
Belief and behavior : essays in the new religious history / edited by
    Philip R. VanderMeer and Robert P. Swierenga.
        p.   cm.
    Includes bibliographical references
    Contents: 1. Introduction / Philip R. VanderMeer and Robert P. Swierenga—
2. Declension, gender, and the new religious history / Harry S.
Stout and Catherine A. Brekus—3. Sinners are turned into saints
in numbers / Gerald F. Moran—4. Enthusiastic piety / Marilyn J.
Westerkamp—5. The spirit in the flesh / Linda K. Pritchard—
6. Sex and the second Great Awakening / Terry D. Bilhartz—
7. Women, feminism, and the new religious history / Margaret Susan
Thompson—8. Religion and immigration behavior / Robert P. Swierenga—
9. Seating and the American synagogue / Jonathan D. Sarna—
10. Religious divisions and political roles / Philip R. VanderMeer.
    ISBN 0-8135-1671-4 (cloth)—ISBN 0-8135-1672-2 (pbk.)
    1. United States—Church history.   2. United States—Religious
life and customs.   I. VanderMeer, Philip R., 1947–
II. Swierenga, Robert P.
BR515.B5135   1991
277.3—dc20   90-47389
                                                                   CIP

British Cataloging-in-Publication information available

To Our Parents,
RAY and HELEN VANDERMEER
JOHN SWIERENGA

CONTENTS

List of Figures   ix
List of Tables   ix
Preface   xi

1   Introduction: Progress and Prospects in the
New Religious History   1
PHILIP R. VANDERMEER and ROBERT P.
SWIERENGA

2   Declension, Gender, and the "New Religious History"   15
HARRY S. STOUT and CATHERINE A. BREKUS

3   "Sinners Are Turned into Saints in Numbers":
Puritanism and Revivalism in Colonial Connecticut   38
GERALD F. MORAN

4   Enthusiastic Piety—From Scots-Irish Revivals
to the Great Awakening   63
MARILYN J. WESTERKAMP

5   The Spirit in the Flesh: Religion and Regional
Economic Development   88
LINDA K. PRITCHARD

6   Sex and the Second Great Awakening: The
Feminization of American Religion Reconsidered   117
TERRY D. BILHARTZ

7   Women, Feminism, and the New Religious History:
Catholic Sisters as a Case Study   136
MARGARET SUSAN THOMPSON

8   Religion and Immigration Behavior:
The Dutch Experience   164
ROBERT P. SWIERENGA

9   Seating and the American Synagogue   189
JONATHAN D. SARNA

10   Religious Divisions and Political Roles: Midwestern
      Episcopalians, 1860–1920   207
      PHILIP R. VANDERMEER

Contributors   235

LIST OF FIGURES

FIGURE 8.1   Provinces of the Netherlands, Showing the
Percentage of Emigration by Religion, 1835–1880, and the
Percentage Over- or Under-represented According to the
1849 Census   169

LIST OF TABLES

TABLE 2.1   Male and Female Church Admissions by
Decade, 1639–1989   27

TABLE 2.2   Church Admissions by Gender and Spouse,
1740–1799   30

TABLE 3.1   Growth of Church and Population in
Connecticut, 1670–1770   45

TABLE 3.2   Connecticut Pulpits Vacant for More Than
One Year, 1650–1740   47

TABLE 3.3   Clerical Tenure in Connecticut, 1640–1740   48

TABLE 3.4   Admissions in Milford First Church,
1639–1774   50

TABLE 3.5   Admissions in New Haven First Church,
1639–1774   51

TABLE 3.6   Mean Admissions in Connecticut, by Date of
Church Founding, 1639–1770   52

TABLE 3.7   Percentage of Women Entering Connecticut
Church, by Date of Church Founding, 1639–1770   55

TABLE 5.1   The Founding of Congregations by
Settlement Decade in the Upper Ohio Valley, 1770–1860   94

TABLE 5.2   Congregations per Capita in the Upper Ohio
Valley, 1780–1860   94

TABLE 5.3   Comparative Congregational and Population
Growth Rates in the Upper Ohio Valley, 1780–1860   95

TABLE 5.4   Religion and Ethnicity in Ohio Counties,
1850   99

TABLE 5.5   Congregational Organizational Motives
in the Upper Ohio Valley, 1770–1860   101

TABLE 5.6   Religion and Economic Factors in the
Upper Ohio Valley, 1850 and 1860   104

TABLE 6.1   Occupations of Caucasian Churchgoers
by Denomination, 1800–1830   120

TABLE 6.2   Estimated Size of Baltimore Denominations,
1790–1830   122

TABLE 8.1   Religion by State, 1850, 1860, 1870:
Dutch Immigrants and Their Children   170

TABLE 8.2   Religion by Year, Total Netherlands
Emigrants, 1835–1880   176

TABLE 8.3   Religion by Geographic Region, Protestant
and Catholic Dutch, 1870   179

TABLE 10.1   Size of Episcopal Congregations in 1905   213

TABLE 10.2   Church Financing Systems in Western
Michigan   217

TABLE 10.3   Occupations of Grand Rapids Vestrymen,
1877–1915   223

TABLE 10.4   Occupations of Grand Rapids Politicians,
1850–1906   224

PREFACE

The origins of this book lie in the developments of the 1970s. The ferment of historical scholarship during that decade reflected tremendous changes throughout the profession—changes in the subjects considered worth studying and in the approaches to doing history. The rise of analytical, theoretical, quantitative, and social histories (which overlapped in all sorts of combinations) had numerous manifestations and consequences. Among the most significant of these was creation of the Social Science History Association. Eclectic in its aims and membership, this organization encouraged interaction among scholars in small subgroups. In particular, the Religion and Society Network fostered both informal discussions among historians interested in religion and convention sessions on religious topics. We have both been involved with this network, as have several other contributors to this volume. Philip VanderMeer served as network convener for seven years, collecting information for the newsletter and arranging convention sessions. This activity revealed how many able historians were working in the field, and it suggested the value of creating a collection of essays on the New Religious history similar to existing collections on the new social, political, and economic history. After some preliminary work, he asked Robert Swierenga to join in the project.

This volume is the result of our efforts to represent the best available scholarship that systematically analyzes religious belief and behavior. Mirroring the perspective of the Social Science History Association, we are not dogmatic in our approach to this subject; we have included both quantitative and nonquantitative works, essays based on large data bases as well as those relying on more traditional sources. We have, however, placed some limits on the types of work we have included. While we appreciate the value of studies that focus on ritual and symbol, or that investigate popular belief systems having no institutional expression, our primary interest is in the systematic analysis of the connections between behavior and belief. The distance between case study and illustration may not always be great, but it is sufficient for our present purposes.

It is also appropriate to note our debt to traditional religious history. Any new venture necessarily "pushes off" from previous work, highlighting differences in order to clarify for both audience and participants the best direction for the future. But while such distinctions are clearly necessary, they may also seem to overstate or neglect the values of more traditional studies—those in the past as well as more recent work. Thus, we may preach a new gospel, but we recognize that inspiration and insight come in different forms and from various sources.

The completion of this volume was aided by many individuals. We wish first to thank our contributors, for their work, present and past, for many invaluable conversations, and, for many of them, their participation in the Religion and Society Network. We also wish to acknowledge Gregory Singleton, whose pioneering work was important to many students in this field, and, except for his untimely illness, would have had an essay in this volume. Harvey Graff expressed interest in this project at an early stage, and James Bratt offered helpful suggestions near its completion. Finally, Philip VanderMeer wishes to thank Mary Ann VanderMeer and Robert Swierenga to thank Joan Boomker Swierenga for sacrificing, as do many spouses, for the "greater glory."

Philip R. VanderMeer
Robert P. Swierenga
October 1990

PHILIP R. VANDERMEER and
ROBERT P. SWIERENGA

1

INTRODUCTION: Progress and Prospects in the New Religious History

The last thirty years have seen the emergence of strikingly new subjects and methods of historical study. Despite continuing controversy over the extent and the desirability of all the changes, their essential characteristics and fundamental importance are clear. Thus, references to the "new history" and to particular subfields such as the "new social history" or the "new political history" are common and generally understood.[1] This book highlights the general direction and some of the significant work in the "new religious history." This nascent subfield shows significant parallels and interconnections with other branches of the new history, but the nature of the subject and the role of religion in American society have given religious history a unique position within the discipline.

In one sense the word "new" rings rather strangely as a description of American religious history, for this is among the oldest and most venerable fields of historical study. As settlers stepped on American soil, they began detailing the development of religious experiences and institutions. This tradition culminated in the multivolume *American Church History Series,* published in the 1890s.[2] During the next several decades, however, the subject of religion virtually disappeared from the mainstream of historical literature.

What explains the rapid demise of this field? One factor is the secularization of American society—reliance on natural and scientific explanations and a focus on immediate and material problems in society.[3] More directly influential were the new, "professional" historians, who reshaped the approaches, methods, and concerns of historical writing in the early decades of the twentieth century. Like their contemporaries in the social sciences and in society generally, these historians focused on material conditions and influences. They saw economic elements, not spiritual or intellectual features, as the important subjects and causal forces.[4] By adopting this perspective Progressive historians effectively reduced the scope of historical inquiry, but their pursuit of professionalism also narrowed the field. Employment in a university history department was a minor and largely symbolic issue. Adherence to the emerging professional canons of historical research was a much more important matter and a legitimate concern. Religious histories, like the many community and institutional histories commonly written in the nineteenth century, were generally commemorative, filiopietistic, and parochial—showing little or no awareness of a larger context or of connections with nonreligious developments, and written more as an act of faith than as a description or analysis of its manifestations. Thus, the basis for religious history's traditional importance was also its weakness and the reason for its downfall.

Over the next several decades a few religious historians produced some useful studies. The most notable were by William Warren Sweet, a careful scholar who used the Turner frontier hypothesis to analyze the development of religion in the West. Despite the appearance of these and several other able studies, however, the basic character and status of religious history changed very little.[5] Most religious histories, even though they were improved in standards of proof and evidence, and some were relatively objective in their approach, remained the product of seminaries, bound to simple, unimaginative descriptions of denominational records and narrow subjects. Within the mainstream of the profession, then, religious history was unread, and religion remained largely an irrelevant subject.

The reemergence of religious history during the 1950s was the product of several forces. The religious revival of that era may have stimulated greater awareness of the potential influence of religion, but historians as a group were also more receptive to this message because of changes in the religious and ethnic composition of the profession. Equally significant was the shift of historiographical interests to greater emphasis on the role of ideas. Most important, however, was the cumulative influence of model religious studies. Perry Miller's reanalysis of the Puritans, for example, revealed the complexity and significance of religious systems of thought. The work of Timothy Smith demonstrated a connection between religion and social reform in the mid-nineteenth century, and a variety of subsequent studies revealed that religious beliefs has been held firmly and had directly shaped attitudes and actions regarding such fundamental aspects of American history as slavery and industrialization.[6]

The publication of grand surveys of religious history further legitimatized and stimulated work in this field. Replacing the earlier denominational histories, which focused narrowly on ministers, buildings, and dramatic events, able historians such as Winthrop Hudson, Martin Marty, and Edwin Gaustad produced general studies of American religion that explained broad patterns and common religious interests. By describing the range of religious groups and their real world context, these scholars suggested the considerable extent of church membership and attendance, and they showed that religious beliefs had directed the perspectives and behaviors of many persons.[7]

Thus, by the 1960s religion became a legitimate historical subject, one with important implications for particular movements and individuals, and one with notable, intellectually impressive leaders. But religious history was still split between the study of theologians and broad trends, on the one hand, and a consideration of specific institutions and reforms on the other. The relationship of denominations to the various national trends in American life was not always clear, and the focus on major religious leaders obscured the vitality and significance of religious organizations. Similarly, while acknowledging, even emphasizing, that the subject of religion was tied to the rest of American history, these works discussed leaders and did not pursue the ways and the extent to which the religious perspectives of most persons were connected to their social, economic, and political lives.

Besides the important works by religious historians, sociologists of religion in the 1950s also produced influential studies, which were notable for their historical analysis, methodology, and use of theory. The first, and in several ways the most striking of these, was Whitney Cross's *The Burned-Over District*. This systematic, quantitative analysis of life in western New York in the antebellum era attempted to explain the religious revivalism of that area as the product of socioeconomic conditions. Several recent reanalyses of Cross's conclusions attest to the continuing importance and attractiveness of this work. A second noteworthy study was Will Herberg's *Protestant-Catholic-Jew*. Building on earlier studies, Herberg developed the notion of a triple melting pot, which stimulated considerable research in the following years. By the 1960s sociologists were filling the *Journal for the Scientific Study of Religion* with debates on Max Weber's theories of religious organization and, especially, Ernst Troeltsch's church-sect typology.[8]

Another influence on the development of a new appreciation of the role of religion in American life was studies of contemporary politics and society. The investigations of Paul Lazarsfeld, beginning in the 1940s, alerted many analysts to the potential effects of religion; Lazarsfeld had a more direct impact on Lee Benson, whose *Concept of Jacksonian Democracy* first demonstrated the historically significant connection between religion and politics. Another influential analysis was Gerhard Lenski's *The Religious Factor*. Lenski's model of devotionalism and orthodoxy was later borrowed by Paul Kleppner and Richard Jensen to explain late nineteenth-century midwestern politics. It was, in fact, Kleppner, Jensen, and other "ethnocultural" historians who devised schemas for dealing with the diversity of religious groups and who first explained the crucial connections between religion and sociopolitical life.[9]

In the last two decades the study of religious history has expanded in various directions. This volume represents the "new religious history," the interdisciplinary trend that began in the 1950s and was further stimulated after 1976 by the activities of the Religion and Society Network of the Social Science History Association. Whether emerging from traditional questions or new interests within religious history, or drawn by contact with historians seeking to explain behavioral patterns in their subfields of political, economic, or social history, these studies share a common approach. Their work is analytical rather than narrative; it employs theory and models; it often (though not always) evaluates quantitative data; and its subjects are recurrent not unique events, groups rather than individuals, and general patterns often examined through case studies. These are the characteristics that define social science history, but our objective here is a basic consensus, rather than a stringent set of criteria, to be inclusive rather than overly restrictive.[10]

The general interests of this history as evidenced in existing work or implied by the direction of its development center on religious institutions.[11] While this may seem a reversion to an older, denominational perspective, it reflects the reality of historical records. It also reflects historical realities: that institutions were vital for developing and perpetuating religious beliefs and behaviors, and that religious institutions had major political and social roles in America. Finally, the analysis typically goes beyond simply denominational and religious boundaries.

By contrast with the focus of earlier studies on ministerial leadership, the new religious history has concentrated on the sources and characteristics of the membership, sometimes using aggregate information but frequently employing individual-level data. Some of the most important findings concern the increased proportions and responsibilities of women, especially during the nineteenth century. The traditional subject of revivalism has attracted interest and offers new insights into the nature of church membership. Changes in church membership—for reasons of geographic or social mobility, because of changing beliefs, or because of expulsion—are now beginning to receive systematic attention.[12]

Important subjects yet to receive major consideration involve issues of commitment and intensity of identification: distribution of leadership, frequency of church attendance, and participation in church rituals. Although church records have not survived as commonly as one would like, there are a significant number of membership lists in manuscript, as several authors have shown. In addition, some published church histories include lists of membership transfers. Other useful sources include biographical collections, occasional public records like the Iowa State Census of 1895, and even published sources like city directories sometimes asked for religious information.[13]

The analysis of church leadership is also an important subject when done as collective, rather than simply individual, biography. In truth, we know very little about lay leadership—whether the distribution varied between denominations, or reflected socioeconomic differences within congregations, or overlapped with political leadership in the community. There is some analysis of the ministry as a profession, but considering the issues and compared with the literature on lawyers and doctors, this needs far more attention.[14] Fortunately, tremendous amounts of information on the clergy are available for analysis. Of course, manuscript church records contain relevant information, but much of this is more readily available in other sources. Published denominational histories at various levels (national, regional, diocesan, and congregational) include clerical biographies. City and county histories almost uniformly printed information about virtually all local clergy.[15] Such sources make it possible to evaluate systematically the recruitment of ministers and especially the role of family background; to consider the significance of education or other forms of preparation; to analyze career mobility and determine whether a hierarchy of churches existed or a system of distributing information within a denomination; and finally, to evaluate the changing levels of ministerial income and status.

The nature of religious institutions themselves also deserves scrutiny. Strikingly, we know more about small sects and denominations than about the major denominations.[16] Many groups originating as sects have become denominations over time, while denominations have altered their institutional arrangements. Although seemingly mundane, these matters relate to basic definitions of clerical and lay responsibility and to the fundamental character of the church. The morphology of congregational development also requires considerably more systematic analysis, for it is closely connected to the founding and growth of communities and neighborhoods. The expense of church buildings indicates not only the ability and willingness of the members to save and contribute funds, it also tied them, at least to some degree, to a particular place. Congregational growth may also have required, depending on the group, a certain gender balance—enough women to provide sufficient church workers, but not so many that would suggest female dominance. Finally, the existence and support of other religious institutions such as missions and convents, provides an additional means of evaluating the nature of commitment and the role of religion in society.[17]

Although one cannot determine the beliefs of each church member, the decisions of congregational, parish, and diocesan leaders are more representative than the writings of theologians. A minister's sermons explicate his point of view, but beyond a certain point they also clarify the religious world of the listener. The existence and success of support agencies like catechism classes or Sunday School, as well as the materials they used, help explain the nature of belief in an institution. Finally, information in congregational records, church bulletins, and devotional materials further indicates the character of religious beliefs.[18]

Despite the increased information about church membership at particular times, relatively little is known about changes in denominational attachments. Such information would have several possible ramifications. First, knowing the prior religious affiliation of new members could help to explain how and why churches changed. Second, revealing a shift, for example, from an ethnically homogenous church to an assimilated or ethnically diverse membership could help to explain the logic of church mergers.

A final consideration is the relationship between religious and nonreligious subjects. An increasing variety of authors have demonstrated the impact of religion on politics—in the early twentieth century, during the crisis of the 1850s, or on the Anti-Masonic party. The connection between religion and family life has been discussed in various forms, including an analysis of family size. The relationship of religion and ethnicity in establishing communities is the subject of increasing analysis. Finally, the role of religion in economic development remains an interesting and controversial issue.[19]

Thus, despite its considerable variety, the new religious history generally seeks the connections between religious and nonreligious elements, and it focuses on the general, the recurrent, and the group. It has moved the study of religion from individual ministers to groups of ministers or congregants, from theology as the pronouncement of theologians to religious belief systems, from an examination of the religious lives of some members to an analysis of the role of religion in the lives of many men and women, and from a consideration of churches as narrow religious institutions to an awareness of their broad social-political significance.

The contributors to this volume address the major topics in American religious history. The first three chapters consider the democratizing effects of the Great Awakening and American Revolution in the eighteenth century, in which the laity came to take a leading part in religious life. The next two chapters explain the impact of economic and social forces on Protestant churches in the Second Great Awakening during the early nineteenth century. Individual chapters follow on feminist struggles within Catholicism and on democratizing changes within Judaism. The final two chapters explain the role of religion in the process of immigration and in political life.

In the opening chapter Harry Stout and Catherine Brekus offer the first findings of an innovative study of church membership records over a period of 350 years at the First Congregational Church of New Haven, Connecticut. Their data challenge Perry Miller's paradigm of "declension," loss of religiosity, and secularization, which themes have dominated Puritan scholarship since the 1940s. Total membership did not decline, but rather kept pace with New Haven's population growth until the twentieth century. There was a structural shift, however, after 1800 when men dropped out as more women joined. The church was feminized but not secularized for another hundred years and more. How could Miller and his followers be so wrong? Stout and Brekus suggest that they focused only on the male elites while ignoring the people in the pew. Moreover, American intellectual and social historians squeezed religion out of religious history because of a "republican point of view," which dictated that Puritans must become Yankees prior to the Revolution.

The deep piety and long-term institutional loyalty that Stout and Brekus found in New Haven existed throughout colonial Connecticut churches, according to the summary by Gerald Moran of available membership records from 1690 until 1740. He discovers that the nearly two hundred ministerial graduates of Yale College fired up the lethargic Congregational churches *before* the arrival of the great English evangelist George Whitefield in the 1740s. The already vibrant churches were growing out of the "loins of the elect," to quote Increase Mather, and by tapping the loyalty of women and the enthusiasm of youth. The Great Awakening, Moran concludes, was not the beginning but the culmination of widespread popular participation in the Connecticut churches.

In Philadelphia, notably among the Scots-Irish Presbyterians, Marilyn Westerkamp similarly finds that the Great Awakening was a lay religious crusade of increasingly individualist immigrants who subsequently wrested control of society as well as the church from traditional leaders. Drawing on insights from Clifford Geertz's anthropological constructs of the symbolic nature of rituals, Westerkamp highlights the spiritual dimension of the Awakening. The most remarkable feature of Scots-Irish ritual behavior, she discovered from local church sources, was its extreme emotionalism. These were an "enthusiastic people" who took religious beliefs seriously indeed; they rent the church asunder when they disagreed and even forced unsympathetic clerics out of office. With remarkable insight, the author traces these ardent ritual practices from Scottish and Ulsterite roots to the Presbyterian churches of New

Jersey and Pennsylvania. In the process of cultural transference, however, the purpose of the revivals underwent a sea change, from communal renewal to individual conversion.

Linda Pritchard explores the Second Great Awakening from without, more than from within, by showing how rapid economic expansion in the early nineteenth century affected churches in the upper Ohio Valley region. Her statistical analysis of economic and demographic factors in new church plantings in twenty-six sample counties in 1850 and 1860 revealed that prosperous commercial farming regions spawned more evangelical churches but industrializing urban areas had more liturgically oriented and non-evangelical churches. Turning from the macro to the micro level, the author offers a case study of church growth in the commercial farming area of Washington County, Pennsylvania, which was a Scots-Presbyterian stronghold where Baptists and later Methodists made strong inroads. The ability to analyze an individual county within its broader regional context is a distinct advantage of Pritchard's innovative methodology.

Terry Bilhartz studies urban religion in the Second Great Awakening and reevaluates the cultural effects of revivals on church membership. Contesting Barbara Welter's feminization thesis, he analyzes Baltimore church membership lists to show that aggressive revival preachers who employed "new measures" gained more male converts than did clerics who clung to traditional forms of worship. The "muscular brand of Christianity," which stressed human accountability and the dangers of materialism and consumerism, appealed to rising businessmen. Thus, the revivals actually increased the number of males in churches from 20 or 30 percent to 40 percent and more. But the gains were temporary, and evangelicals failed to "masculinize" the Christian churches, despite their deliberate attempts to do so.

In contrast to Protestant feminization, the Roman Catholic church remained solidly patriarchal. Margaret Susan Thompson, whose research exemplifies the "new feminist religious history," is the first social scientist to make a detailed study of Catholic sisters during the nineteenth century. Despite a paucity of sources—religious women were undocumented because they lacked credentials and were often volunteers—Thompson uncovered sufficient nunnery records to reveal a startling militancy. Nuns were not submissive, self-effacing, super-spiritual women, but a confrontational lot who were determined to safeguard the integrity of their orders, even in the face of all-powerful male superiors who resorted to "cruel opposition." Under the surface, therefore, friction between prelates and sisters was endemic in American Catholicism in the nineteenth century, according to Thompson.

Not only did the Catholic church struggle over power and place, but Robert Swierenga's chapter, which compares both Calvinist and Catholic immigrants, shows that in Catholic multiethnic parishes the newcomers became Americanized sooner and intermarried far more frequently with non-Dutch fellow religionists. The larger purpose of Swierenga's effort is to describe how religion strongly influenced the entire process of immigration and resettlement. The churches as institutions, their clerical and lay leaders, their societies, and even their theology sheltered immigrants, buffered them from a hostile environment, and gradually eased their adjustment to a new society. The process was slowed in homogeneous church colonies and speeded up in urban mixed parishes. Theologically, pietist Protestant immigrants were more willing to immigrate and adapt to new ways than were liturgicals, who sought cultural maintenance and resisted change.

Jonathan Sarna investigates the specific question of acculturation among Jews by tracing changes in seating arrangements in the synagogues. Such a mundane matter as where people sat during worship, in Sarna's hands, is transformed into an indicator of the extent of Jewish cultural adjustment to the larger American society. The major issue was the controversial shifts first from stratified, designated seating based on rank—the traditional practice—to the rental or sale of pews based on wealth, which occurred during the nineteenth century, and then finally in the early twentieth century the further change to free unassigned seating based on ideals of "classlessness" and democracy. American society clearly impinged on traditional Jewish worship practices and social values, of which seating was a public indicator. Reform Judaism led the way in the free synagogue movement, but realistic revenue needs often militated against idealist reforms and forced synagogues to continue to rent pews.

In the past twenty years no subject has sparked more excitement among political historians than research proving that religion was the key variable in voting behavior throughout the nineteenth century and even until the 1930s, if not later. The move to restore religion to political analysis gained momentum slowly after World War II through the work of the eminent scholars Paul Lazarsfeld, Gerhard Lenski, and Samuel Lubell; and it culminated in the 1960s when historians Lee Benson and Samuel Hays brought the new insights to a generation of young scholars. By the 1970s, this so-called ethnocultural (or ethnoreligious) interpretation of voting behavior had received wide, though not universal, acceptance.

Philip VanderMeer expands the reach of ethnocultural scholarship by concentrating on one liturgically oriented denomination, the Episcopal church. In a detailed study of Episcopalian churches in Grand Rapids and Indianapolis in the years from 1860 to 1920, VanderMeer uncovers internal conflicts over liturgy, pew-rental practices, church governance, and social issues such as temperance and Sabbath-keeping laws. The conflicts essentially pitted Low Churchmen against High Churchmen. The most remarkable finding is that the more evangelical Low Churchmen affiliated with the Republican party whereas the more ritualistic High Churchmen were Democrats. Even within an individual denomination that was predominantly English-American in membership, therefore, a modified pietist-liturgical model has explanatory power.

As this overview of the book shows, the chapters that follow demonstrate new research directions in the methodology and subjects of religious history. Of necessity we have represented this literature as it now exists, which means that the essays do not offer a complete coverage of American religious history. What they do reveal, however, are the new behavioral sources and the types of questions historians have been asking, as well as the answers they have found. Of the missing subjects, the most obvious are investigations of popular belief, studies of religious minorities, particularly racially based churches, and the story of religion in the twentieth century, especially the declining denominational tradition.[20] Fortunately, some historians are already studying these topics, and we look forward to their work and the continuing expansion of this field.

NOTES

1. For example, James B. Gardner and George Rollie Adams, eds., *Ordinary People and Everyday Life: Perspectives on the New Social History* (Nashville: American Association for State and Local History, 1983); and the several articles of the "AHR Forum" in the *American Historical Review* 94 (June 1989): 581–698.

2. Phillip Schaff et al., eds., *American Church History Series,* 13 vols. (New York: Scribner, 1893–1897).

3. Jon H. Roberts, *Darwinism and the Divine in America: Protestant Intellectuals and Organic Evolution, 1859–1900* (Madison: University of Wisconsin Press, 1988); Robert Morse Crunden, *Ministers of Reform: The Progressives' Achievement in American Civilization, 1889–1920* (New York: Basic Books, 1982); and James Turner, *Without God, Without Creed: The Origins of Unbelief in America* (Baltimore: Johns Hopkins University Press, 1985).

4. Richard Hofstadter, *The Progressive Historians: Turner, Beard, Parrington* (New York: Knopf, 1968); Thomas L. Haskell, *The Emergence of Professional*

Social Science in America (Urbana: University of Illinois Press, 1977); John Higham, *History: Professional Scholarship in America* (Baltimore: Johns Hopkins University Press, 1983); and Allan G. Bogue, "A Strange Case of Identity Denied: American History as a Social Science" (Paper presented to 25th symposium, Interuniversity Consortium for Political and Social Research, November 1987).

5. William Warren Sweet, *The Story of Religion in America* (New York: Scribner, 1930); C. Howard Hopkins, *The Rise of the Social Gospel in American Protestantism, 1865–1915* (New Haven: Yale University Press, 1940); Samuel Eliot Morison, *Builders of the Bay Colony* (Boston: Houghton Mifflin, 1930); and Perry Miller, *Orthodoxy in Massachusetts, 1630–1650* (Cambridge: Harvard University Press, 1933). Other exceptions are the works of H. Richard Niebuhr, notably *The Social Sources of Denominationalism* (Cleveland: World Publishing, 1929).

6. Henry May, "The Recovery of American Religious History," *American Historical Review* 70 (October 1964): 79–92; Perry Miller, *The New England Mind: From Colony to Province* (Cambridge: Harvard University Press, 1953); Timothy L. Smith, *Revivalism and Social Reform in Mid-Nineteenth-Century America* (New York: Abingdon Press, 1957); and James Ward Smith and J. Leland Jamison, eds., *The Shaping of American Religion* (Princeton: Princeton University Press, 1961).

7. Winthrop S. Hudson, *Religion in America: An Historical Account of the Development of American Religious Life* (New York: Scribner, 1965).

8. Whitney Cross, *The Burned-over District: The Social and Intellectual History of Enthusiastic Religion in Western New York, 1800–1850* (New York: Harper & Row, 1950); Linda Pritchard, "The Burned-Over District Reconsidered: A Portent of Evolving Religious Pluralism in the United States," *Social Science History* 8 (Summer 1984): 243–265; Will H. Herberg, *Protestant-Catholic-Jew: An Essay in American Religious Sociology,* rev. ed. (Garden City, N.Y.: Anchor Books, 1960); and an analysis of some of the literature in William H. Swatos, Jr., "Weber or Troeltsch?: Methodology, Syndrome, and the Development of Church-Sect Theory," *Journal for the Scientific Study of Religion* 15 (June 1976): 129–144.

9. The latest review of the literature and analysis is Robert P. Swierenga, "Ethnoreligious Political Behavior in the Mid-Nineteenth Century: Voting, Values, Cultures," in Mark Noll, ed., *Religion and American Politics: From the Colonial Period to the 1980s* (New York: Oxford University Press, 1990): 146–171. The pioneer works include Richard J. Jensen, "American Election Analysis: A Case Study of Methodological Innovation and Diffusion," in Seymour M. Lipset, ed., *Politics and the Social Sciences* (New York: Oxford University Press, 1969), 226–243; Lee Benson, *The Concept of Jacksonian Democracy: New York as a Test Case* (Princeton: Princeton University Press, 1961); Gerhard Lenski, *The Religious Factor: A Sociologist's Inquiry,* rev. ed. (Garden City, N.Y.: Anchor Books, 1963), esp. p. 25; Paul Kleppner, *Cross of Culture: A Social Analysis of Midwestern Politics, 1850–1900* (New York: Free Press, 1970), 73; Richard

J. Jensen, *The Winning of the Midwest: Social and Political Conflict, 1888–1896* (Chicago: University of Chicago Press, 1971); and Ronald P. Formisano, *The Birth of Mass Political Parties: Michigan, 1827–1861* (Princeton: Princeton University Press, 1971). The major exception was the work of Robert Doherty, including "Social Bases for the Presbyterian Schism of 1837–1838," *Journal of Social History* 2 (Fall 1968): 69–79; and *The Hicksite Separation: A Sociological Analysis of Religious Schism in Early Nineteenth Century America* (New Brunswick, N.J.: Rutgers University Press, 1967).

10. Lee Benson, *Toward The Scientific Study of History: Selected Essays* (Philadelphia: J. B. Lippincott, 1972); Bogue, "Strange Case of Identity Denied"; and Robert Fogel, " 'Scientific' History and Traditional History," in L. J. Cohen et al., eds., *Logic, Methodology, and Philosophy of Science,* vol. 6, *Proceedings of the Sixth International Congress of Logic, Methodology, and Philosophy of Science, Hannover, 1979* (Amsterdam: North-Holland Publishing Co., 1982).

11. There are several valuable bibliographies of religious history. Rather than duplicating those efforts, this discussion aims to highlight crucial issues and subjects deserving additional analysis, and the references indicate the most recent quantitative work. For further discussion see Jon H. Butler, "The Future of American Religious History: Prospectus, Agenda, Transatlantic *Problematique,*" *William and Mary Quarterly* 42 (April 1983): 167–183; Jay Dolan, "The New Religious History," *Reviews in American History* 15 (September 1987): 449–454; Anne T. Fraker, ed., *Religion and American Life: Resources* (Urbana: University of Illinois Press, 1989); and Dewey D. Wallace, Jr., "Recent Publications on American Religious History: A Bibliographical Essay and Review," *American Studies International* 19 (Spring–Summer 1981): 15–42.

12. See, for example, Gerald F. Moran, "Religious Renewal, Puritan Tribalism, and the Family in Seventeenth-Century Milford, Connecticut," *William and Mary Quarterly* 36 (April 1979): 236–254; the excellent study by Gregory H. Singleton, *Religion in the City of Angels: American Protestant Culture and Urbanization, Los Angeles, 1850–1930* (Ann Arbor, Mich.: UMI Research Press, 1977); Rosemary Radford Ruether and Rosemary Skinner, eds., *Women and Religion in America: A Documentary History,* 3 vols. (New York: Harper & Row, 1981–1985); Kevin J. Christiano, *Religious Diversity and Social Change in American Cities: 1880–1906* (New York: Cambridge University Press, 1987); Kevin J. Christiano, " 'Numbering Israel': The U.S. Census and Religious Organizations," *Social Science History* 8 (Fall 1984): 341–370; Paul Goodman, "A Guide to Church Membership Data before the Civil War," *Historical Methods Newsletter* 10 (Fall 1977): 183–190; Terry Bilhartz, *Urban Religion and the Second Great Awakening: Church and Society in Early National Baltimore* (Cranbury, N.J.: Associated University Presses, 1986); Jack D. Marietta, *The Reformation of American Quakerism, 1748–1783* (Philadelphia: University of Pennsylvania Press, 1984); Henry K. Carroll, *The Religious Forces in the United States,* rev. ed. (New York: Scribner, 1912); George M. Thomas, "Rational Exchange and Individualism: Revival Religion in the U.S., 1870–1890," in Robert Wuthnow, ed., *The Religious Dimension: New Directions in Quantitative*

Research (New York: Academic Press, 1979), 351–372; and two papers presented at the Social Science History Association meeting on 18 November 1989: Ed Tebbenoff, "Religion and Family among the Dutch in Eighteenth-Century Schenectady, New York," and Janet Lindman, "Women, Family, and the Baptists in Colonial Virginia and North Carolina."

13. Donald Parkerson and Jo Ann Parkerson, " 'Fewer Children of Greater Spiritual Quality': Religion and the Decline of Fertility in Nineteenth-Century America," *Social Science History* 12 (Spring 1988): 49–70.

14. Daniel H. Calhoun, *Professional Lives in America: Structure and Aspiration, 1750–1850* (Cambridge: Harvard University Press, 1976); James W. Schmotter, "Ministerial Careers in Eighteenth-Century New England: The Social Context, 1700–1760," *Journal of Social History* 9 (Winter 1975): 249–268; Donald M. Scott, *From Office to Profession: The New England Ministry, 1750–1850* (Philadelphia: University of Pennsylvania Press, 1978); Ronald Balmer, *A Perfect Babel of Confusion: Dutch Religion and English Culture in the Middle Colonies* (New York: Oxford University Press, 1989); Burton J. Bledstein, *The Culture of Professionalism: The Middle Class and the Development of Higher Education in America* (New York: W. W. Norton, 1976); and Nathan O. Hatch, ed., *The Professions in American History* (Notre Dame: University of Notre Dame Press, 1988). On lay leadership, see Marilyn J. Westerkamp, *Triumph of the Laity: Scots-Irish Piety and the Great Awakening, 1625–1760* (New York: Oxford University Press, 1988); Alan Graebner, *Uncertain Saints: The Laity in the Lutheran Church-Missouri Synod, 1900–1970* (Westport, Conn.: Greenwood Press, 1975); and Kathleen Smith Kutolowski, "Identifying the Religious Affiliations of Nineteenth-Century Local Elites," *Historical Methods Newsletter* 9 (Winter 1975): 9–13.

15. County histories are listed in Clarence Stewart Peterson, comp., *Consolidated Bibliography of County Histories in Fifty States in 1961, Consolidated 1935–1961* (Baltimore: By the Author, 1961). An example of a church history that includes lengthy ministerial biographies is Adam Byron Condo, *History of the Indiana Conference of the Church of the United Brethren in Christ* (n.p., 1926). Analyzing the biographies in this volume shows that by the late nineteenth century the ministers were Scotch-Irish rather than German.

16. For example, Laurence R. Moore, *Religious Outsiders and the Making of Americans* (New York: Oxford University Press, 1986); Priscilla J. Brewer, "The Demographic Features of the Shaker Decline, 1787–1900," *Journal of Interdisciplinary History* 15 (Summer 1984): 183–197; Jon H. Butler, *The Huguenots in America: A Refugee People in New World Society* (Cambridge: Harvard University Press, 1983); Charles E. Jones, *Perfectionist Persuasion: The Holiness Movement and Methodism, 1867–1936* (Methuchen, N.J.: Scarecrow Press, 1974); and Doherty, *Hicksite Separation.* Probably the major exception is Jay P. Dolan, *The Immigrant Church: New York's Irish and German Catholics, 1815–1865* (Baltimore: Johns Hopkins University Press, 1975).

17. Ben Primer, *Protestants and American Business Methods* (Ann Arbor, Mich.: UMI Research Press, 1979); Philip R. VanderMeer, "Religion, Society, and Politics: A Classification of American Religious Groups," *Social Science*

History 5 (Spring 1981): 3–24; and Gary Burkart, "Patterns of Protestant Organization," in Ross P. Scherer, ed., *American Denominational Organization: A Sociological View* (Pasadena, Calif.: William Carey Library, 1980). See also Olivier Zunz, *The Changing Face of Inequality: Urbanization, Industrial Development, and Immigration in Detroit, 1880–1920* (Chicago: University of Chicago Press, 1982), which considers briefly the implications of costly ethnic religious institutions; and Margaret Susan Thompson, "To Serve the People of God: Nineteenth Century Sisters and the Creation of an American Religious Life," Cushwa Center for the Study of American Catholicism (University of Notre Dame), Working Paper Series 18, No. 2, 1987.

18. Harry S. Stout, *The New England Soul: Preaching and Religious Culture in Colonial New England* (New York: Oxford University Press, 1986); and Anne M. Boylan, *Sunday School: The Formation of an American Institution, 1790–1880* (New Haven: Yale University Press, 1988).

19. Philip R. VanderMeer, *The Hoosier Politician: Officeholding and Political Culture in Indiana, 1896–1920* (Urbana: University of Illinois Press, 1985); Paul Kleppner, *The Third Electoral System, 1853–1892: Parties, Voters, and Political Cultures* (Chapel Hill: University of North Carolina Press, 1979); William E. Gienapp, *The Origins of the Republican Party, 1852–1856* (New York: Oxford University Press, 1987); Paul Goodman, *Towards a Christian Republic: Antimasonry and the Great Transition in New England, 1826–1836* (New York: Oxford University Press, 1989); John L. Hammond, *The Politics of Benevolence: Revival Religion and American Voting Behavior* (Norwood, N.J.: Ablex Publishing Corporation, 1979); Robert Kelley, *The Cultural Pattern in American Politics* (New York: Knopf, 1979); John Gjerde, "Conflict and Community: A Case Study of the Immigrant Church in the United States," *Journal of Social History* 19 (Summer 1986): 681–692; Robert P. Swierenga, "Local-Cosmopolitan Theory and Immigrant Religion: The Social Bases of the Antebellum Dutch Reformed Schism," *Journal of Social History* 14 (Fall 1980): 113–135; Paul E. Johnson, *A Shopkeeper's Millennium: Society and Revivals in Rochester, New York, 1815–1837* (New York: Hill and Wang, 1978); and Doherty, "Social Bases for the Presbyterian Schism."

20. One very recent study that helps substantially to fill some of these gaps is Jon Butler, *Awash in a Sea of Faith: Christianizing the American Republic* (New York: Cambridge University Press, 1990).

2

HARRY S. STOUT and
CATHERINE A. BREKUS

Declension, Gender, and the "New Religious History"

For two generations after World War II, colonial American history was written as a history of ideas. Beginning with Perry Miller, historians "rescued" Puritanism from the domain of Church History, and approached it instead as an intellectual system that permeated an entire culture and informed a unique New England Way. Over time, that way declined. Puritan ideals were molded by the New World experience, and a new set of values emerged that could be readily identified as American. As *American* historians, rather than *church* historians, Miller and his students were less interested in charting religious patterns than in tracing the unfolding "meaning of America" as it moved from religious moorings to a new secular foundation in the American republic. By studying Puritanism, then, historians were also studying Americanization at its most formative level.[1]

From this "liberal" or "republican" point of view, political and social events invariably determined the key dates around which Puritan studies would be organized. For the most part, they would center around such issues as the Glorious Revolution, Salem witchcraft, or, most importantly, the American Revolution. For many historians, the Revolution marked the transformation from Puritan to Yankee, the historical moment when religious priorities gave way to politics and economics.

Besides dictating the chronological boundaries for Puritan studies, the republican point of view also determined the chief characters in the drama. While Puritan churches were inclusive, comprised of men, women, and children, literate and illiterate, rich and poor, the chief actors in the intellectual and political events were male (ministers, landowners, and rulers), and so they received top billing in the churches. Changes in their world or values were taken as a proxy for general religious (and political) change.

As social and political issues dictated the chronology and the central characters, so also did they dominate the script that invariably accompanied early American religious history. Throughout, the organizing question became: How did colonial people cease to be Old World, communalistic, and religious and become instead individualistic, secular, and recognizably American? With New England as a "laboratory" and males as the lead characters, historians could study change in process.

Clearly New Englanders were not the same people in 1790 that they had been in 1630, but exactly where and how did the change occur?

IN THIS CONTEXT, the central interpretive category (and narrative drama), as set forth in Miller's magisterial *New England Mind,* was "declension." From a religious perspective, this term implied what Herbert Schneider called a "loss of the sense of sin," and an estrangement from the settled, institutional church.[2] But this was not the meaning Miller and later American historians ultimately had in mind in employing the term. In fact, they largely ignored questions of sin, devotional piety, or religiosity. Miller's interests were those of an American historian, and in his usage the loss of religiosity became only an intermediary step towards Americanization. For American historians, then, "declension" came to mean "Americanization." Each represented the flip side of the other, meaning that variables and questions unrelated to Americanization and republicanism could be excluded from the analysis of declension. When historians discovered signs of Americanization, they at once discovered signs of declension or, conversely, when historians discovered evidence of declension in ministerial rhetoric they at once discovered signs of Americanization.[3]

With the lines between church history and American history firmly drawn, both professionally and methodologically, American historians used the traditional categories of church history to write a more socially and politically oriented American history in which the decline of religious purity signalled the advent of a new cultural form: the American individual. The outer shell of Puritan religion persisted in an active work ethic, a love of liberty, and a religious-like resistance to tyranny, but the inner soul had been transformed from otherworldly to this-worldly, from Puritan to Yankee.

With declension as the central interpretive category, the problem for American historians became dating the transformation. Given their script, declension *had* to take place before the Revolution and the creation of the republic, and it had to be all-inclusive, even as Americanization was all-inclusive. But exactly when and how did the religious universe begin to unravel and make way for a new secular American creation? Different methodologies and different evidence would produce widely different answers to this seemingly simple question.

For Miller, who concentrated his research in ministerial writings, decline set in with the native-born second generation, whose members ceased joining the church in large numbers and whose children (the third generation) could not be baptized. As colonial authorities relaxed baptism requirements with the Half-Way Covenant of 1662, the Puritans forsook purity in favor of power. For evidence, Miller relied chiefly on printed occasional sermons by Puritan ministers like John Wilson and Increase Mather whose jeremiads blasted the children for forsaking the faith of the founders and turning to an excessive concern with the things of this world.

Miller's most illustrious student, Edmund S. Morgan, retained the concept of declension, but disagreed on the timing, arguing that the Half-Way Covenant was, in fact, evidence of a "heightened scrupulosity" and *increased* piety.[4] Nevertheless, declension still framed Morgan's argument. Declension did occur, he insisted, but not until the early eighteenth century. By 1740, religion had become largely an affair of the heart, subject to periodic revivals, rather than a total worldview. It had lost its power to enlist the spirit of the age. The greatest intellectuals had shifted their interests from theology to statecraft.[5]

Later studies by T. H. Breen and David D. Hall reinforced Morgan's argument by pointing to a rising "sacerdotalism" in the seventeenth-century Puritan churches (Hall), and an "anglicization" of manners and government (Breen) in the late seventeenth and early eighteenth centuries.[6] The growing professionalization of the clergy and the increasing adoption of English morals and manners signaled the end of a once dominant religious civilization.

For the most part, these intellectual historians relied on legislative acts, church records, and sermons for their evidence. There were few attempts to examine church membership for evidence of the extent of decline in terms of actual numbers. Two notable exceptions were Robert Pope and Darrett Rutman. Both employed the rich sources of New England church membership lists to chart decline, although ironically, the two came to opposite conclusions. In his study *Winthrop's Boston,* Rutman examined the membership patterns at Boston's First Church throughout Winthrop's lifetime (to 1649). He noted a sharp drop-off in church membership in the 1640s that continued to Winthrop's death. For Rutman, then, declension began almost immediately after the Puritans first set foot on American soil.[7]

The problem with Rutman's analysis, as Robert Pope later pointed out, was its overly narrow chronological boundaries. Rutman's boundaries were fixed by political considerations, in his case the years of Governor Winthrop's life. Instead of studying Boston's First Church over a multigenerational period, Rutman concluded his analysis with

1649, assuming that the changes he observed were permanent and irreversible. Indeed, the changes *had* to be permanent or his entire depiction of decline would be called into question.

In Robert Pope's study of church membership patterns in Massachusetts and Connecticut throughout the seventeenth century, it immediately became clear that Rutman's declaration of declension was premature. In fact, there were second generation revivals in most New England churches that nearly rivaled the harvests of the founders. If declension did not begin with the second generation, neither did it coincide with the Half-Way Covenant. Instead, Pope discovered that despite ministerial pressure, most congregations refused to implement the Half-Way Covenant. Confirming Morgan's interpretation, Pope argued that New England Puritans were so religiously scrupulous that they rejected the Half-Way Covenant as fraudulent. The majority of churches did not relent until after 1675, when crises such as King Philip's War, the loss of the Massachusetts charter, and two great fires in Boston convinced the Puritans that God was angry with them for not heeding their ministers.[8] Thus, for Pope, declension was an eighteenth-century phenomenon.

Robert Pope's interest in local church records provided an advance preview of a new decade of early American scholarship that would be dominated by the New Social History. In 1970, major town studies appeared by John P. Demos, Philip J. Greven, Kenneth Lockridge, and Michael Zuckerman that promised to rewrite the colonial past from a new point of view, featuring new chronologies, new characters, and a new script.[9] More specifically, they promised to rewrite the story of Americanization "from the bottom up." Intellectual history, they argued, had distorted the past, not by its emphasis on Americanization (they too were *American* historians), but by an excessive reliance on elite sources that had no clear linkage to ordinary men and women. Only by recovering the social and cultural worlds of ordinary men and women would it be possible to discover the true roots and the meaning of Americanization. In the New Social History, common people became the creators of their own culture rather than merely ciphers.[10]

This new approach required a new methodology. How could the experience of ordinary men and women be recaptured? What kinds of sources could be recovered, and how could they be made to "speak" to the question of social change and Americanization? In the demography-based town studies of John Demos, Philip Greven, Kenneth Lockridge, and Michael Zukerman, vital statistics, tax lists, and land records displaced printed sermons as the controlling evidence. From these new sources and methodologies, they constructed studies where "community," "generation," "cohort," or wealth "decile" replaced "covenant," "jeremiad," "declension," "preparation" or "visible saint" as the central categories for understanding the meaning and significance of the early American experience. To be sure, most historians had little intrinsic interest in collecting this local data. But demography, economic analysis, and statistics would make possible what elite sources could not, namely a history that privileged the voices of common people.

Yet, ironically, despite the New Social History's use of these new sources and methodologies, they continued to follow the script that Miller had sculpted from elite sermons. Miller created a paradigm that continued to shape colonial scholarship, even among those who avoided his elite ministerial sources. Despite the very different agendas of intellectual and social historians, the two wound up looking at the same region—New England—and telling the same story—declension.

In looking at the overlap of intellectual and social history, the first parallel is location. Both groups of historians located their studies in colonial New England. They did so not because New England was typical or more important than other regions, but because the richness of its sources made sophisticated studies possible. New England remained as much a laboratory for social historians as it had been for intellectual historians. In both cases, historians focused on the region because of its abundance of records and its generally acknowledged influence on nineteenth-century American self-definitions.

A second overlap between the two approaches centered on their common objectives. Both groups of scholars perceived themselves chiefly as historians of America rather than historians of religion. Despite different bodies of evidence, both tended to organize their analyses around political and social events. And both scripted a story line of "rise and decline" in their attempts to recover the mental world of a total society. Intellectual historians assumed that theology and printed sermons articulated, in technical and artful terms, the preoccupations and concerns of ordinary people as well. Social historians assumed that their reconstruction of family, community, and material culture represented, in aggregate terms, the cultural values and preoccupations of the society. Both claimed to recover a lost world, and both located that recovery around a script tracing the rise and decline of corporate, communal Puritanism.

In intellectual studies from the "top down" and social histories from the "bottom up," the central problem was the same. For intellectual historians, declension was understood in intellectual terms as a loss of interest in theology and the "morphology of conversion," and a rising interest in Enlightenment thought and the science of government. For social historians, declension was understood as the loss of "community," or the transition from a traditional, face-to-face culture to one that was increasingly individual, mobile, and divided between elite and popular culture. Whether decline was described in terms of churches or communities, it served as a proxy for Americanization, and again, it *had* to be dated before the Revolution.

When all the data generated by all the community studies and the demographic reconstitutions of families was in, it still required explanation; it needed a story line to carry the analysis. At this point, intellectual historians became primary allies. Without recognizing how thoroughly Miller informed the plot—if not the substance—of early American history, these studies followed Miller's script, beginning with European, peasant communities where people shared common ideals and a sense of community, and ending with decline under the pressures of population growth, mobility, and democratization. This deterioration in community and the rise of individualism resulted in nothing less than Americanization. Like the characters in Miller's "Errand Into the Wilderness," the ordinary people of these community studies began as English men and women only to find themselves subtly altered by their experience in the new world. In Miller's words, "they had no other place to search but within themselves . . . they were left alone with America."[11]

Although historians in the 1970s may have produced a New Social History, they did not go far enough in recovering a *total* society—male and female. Instead, when all the data was in, they simply rewrote Perry Miller's drama of declension, enhanced by the aura of empirical data and everyday reality. In the end it was the same old story, dominated by the same—male—characters. The persistence of the declension paradigm is most clearly reflected in Kenneth Lockridge's study of Dedham, Massachusetts. In that study, Lockridge divided the history of Dedham into two fifty-year halves—the first marked by peace and consensus, the second by acquisitive, self-centered individualism. By 1736, a society of "one class, one interest, one mind" had disintegrated.[12] In its place was an increasingly stratified, American-like society of carping, but largely ineffective clergy, combative politicians, and greedy landowners.

In Philip J. Greven's analysis of Andover, the same pattern appeared over the course of four generations. As each generation came of age, the available common land shrunk until in the end all of Andover's land had been settled. In facing increased scarcity and declining expectations, a rising generation began to cast off reliance on the old Puritan corporate ways, and instead looked to their individual self-interest. For Greven, although the Great Awakening was substantively religious, it "really" represented the triumph of an increasingly youth-centered, more individualistic generation. Demographic forces, like the intellectual force of the Enlightenment in intellectual histories, established tensions that were ultimately resolved in the cataclysmic events surrounding the American Revolution.

In their study of the witchcraft hysteria at Salem, Paul Boyer and Stephen Nissenbaum traced a similar disintegration of a Puritan community trying to cope with the dislocations of economic change. Where Salem "Village" remained largely agricultural, communal, and Puritan, new commercial forces appeared in the more urban Salem "Town," creating unreconcilable tensions. Those tensions boiled over when Salem Village inhabitants began accusing their neighbors in Salem Town of witchcraft. The hysteria marked the coming-of-age of a new society.[13]

The narrative and analytical parallels between the old intellectual history and the New Social History are generally recognized. Less recognized is the extent to which both of these bodies of literature wove their narratives almost exclusively around male characters. True, Demos and Greven presented innovative insights into child rearing and motherhood in their town studies, but these did not inform their interpretive story line. For the most part, social histories no less than intellectual histories were male-centered. Both claimed to reconstruct cultures that were all-inclusive. But in fact, the organizing themes, events, and leading personalities were almost exclusively male. Whether ministers and elders in the churches, magistrates and judges in the legislature, selectmen in the town meetings, or landowners in the community, the leading actors were all men. Changes in their lives and preoccupations were made to stand for inclusive social and religious change. Only with the rise of women's studies in the mid-1970s would this paradigm begin to be challenged.[14]

Beyond their common attachment to declension paradigms that featured all-male casts, intellectual and social histories shared the further feature of orienting themselves around the American national republic and its formative events. Necessarily, religion per se was ignored. Methodologically, both intellectual and social historians tended to rush the process of change to get to the real story of Americanization that had engaged their interest in the first place. As a result, neither approach has produced what might be termed a New Religious History. That is, a history that applies the insights of intellectual and social history single-mindedly to religious phenomena, without regard to the limitations set by social or political events.

What happens if we approach the problem of declension from a religious vantage point? In this view, all the end dates are erased, and the ecclesiastical experiences of men and women are traced irrespective of the creation of the American republic. While the New Social History was adept at describing patterns and reconstructing the social structures of towns, it was not equipped to handle the central question of religious decline in the area where it mattered most—in the churches. Towns may have divided and subdivided but, as Michael Zuckerman pointed out in his study of several eighteenth-century Massachusetts towns, this may have been a means of preserving community (and religious concerns) rather than dissolving it.[15] Only recently have American historians addressed the question of when religion—the reigning cultural system of the age—declined, where, and for what groups of people.

Ironically, we are no closer to answering the pivotal question of decline in 1990 than we were in 1970 when "New" history began. This, despite the obsession with Protestant decline in post-World War II America. New social historians realized the importance of church membership lists, but their ulterior concerns prevented them from pursuing these records over a sufficiently long period of time. For the most part, the important aggregate data contained in church membership records was ignored or subordinated to vital statistics, tax lists, probate records, and gravestones. In any new religious history, devotional manuals, diaries, and aggregate church records of membership, discipline, and growth must also be considered important sources.

In the past five years there has been movement in the direction of what might be termed a New Religious History—a history that studies religion for its own sake and includes men, women, and children.[16] On the level of spirituality, pioneering studies by Charles Hambrick-Stowe and David D. Hall have confirmed a deep and pervasive piety among the New England rank and file that persisted into the eighteenth century. From the devotional experiences and literature of ordinary men and women, Hambrick-Stowe constructs an alternative model of Puritanism, less concerned with declension, intellect, and republicanism than with ongoing piety, spiritual interiority, and a powerful family-based piety in which mothers and fathers played a key role in perpetuating the faith.[17]

The persistence of this faith among laymen and laywomen has been the subject of recent innovative studies by David Hall. From his examination of diaries, lay confessions of faith, and almanacs, Hall reconstructs a popular piety in seventeenth-century New England that overlapped significantly with the religious worldview of elites. In colonial New England, there was no sharp disjunction between popular and elite culture such as that manifested in many European villages. Pastors no less than ordinary men and women invoked magic and enacted superstitious customs.[18] At the same time, both articulated in ongoing "morphology of conversion" in sophisticated, theological terms that would persist long after religion's supposed decline. From this evidence, Hall concludes that:

> It does us little good to divide up the intellectual world of seventeenth-century New England on the basis of social class, or even, for that matter, of literacy. Rather, we can move from the world of print, with its fluid boundaries and truths of long duration, to an understanding of intellectual history as itself having wider boundaries than many social historians seem willing to recognize.[19]

These wider boundaries, one might add, go beyond even social class and literacy, to include gender.

Besides popular literary sources, a New Religious History requires the sorts of aggregate data favored by social historians. And here long-term church membership lists are especially important. Several recent studies have pointed to church membership records as the clearest index to religious declension. The willingness of individuals to join a church does not, of course, provide a window into their inner piety, but it does represent the most reliable, empirical guide to religious convictions that we have. In New England, church membership was not automatic. At the very least, it required knowledge, regular church attendance, a profession of belief in the covenant, and a willingness to submit to church discipline. It also required active oversight of the ministry.

Church membership records were not ignored completely by the New Social History, though in general they were subordinated to vital statistics, tax lists, or property records. Historians of the Great Awakening looked specifically at membership patterns, but their focus was too narrowly defined to illuminate the central question of long-term, permanent transformations in church membership patterns.[20] One prominent exception to this oversight is Gerald Moran's 1974 Rutgers dissertation and his subsequent articles, which focused on membership lists from many Connecticut churches and drew on a much longer longitudinal perspective.[21]

Moran's findings were mixed and varied slightly from congregation to congregation. But in general he found no structural, irreversible decline in church membership in the colonial era. Rather, communities evidenced cyclical patterns of gains and losses in membership, suggesting less a straight-line declension than a generational phenomenon where membership rates were low as new unchurched generations came of age, and then rose with local revivals as these generations acquired property and began families of their own. The only exception to this life-cycle pattern, Moran found, was the Great Awakening, when large numbers of youth joined, upsetting the cyclical pattern for a generation.[22]

In the past decade, other studies have appeared confirming Moran's findings. Most recently, an essay by Stephen Grossbart in the *William and Mary Quarterly* examined conversion patterns in five Connecticut congregations throughout the eighteenth century.[23] Like Moran, Grossbart discovered that admissions rose and fell at periodic intervals. The major turning point seemed to be the Revolutionary War, when male membership dropped off precipitously. In all, Grossbart concludes, declension does not seem to be part of the picture for men and women through the Great Awakening.

The persistence of popular piety into the eighteenth century has been the theme of two important new books by Patricia Bonomi and Jon Butler. Both suggest patterns of continuity and increased religiosity throughout eighteenth-century America. Bonomi argues that religious tolerance allowed diverse religious sects to grow and flourish. Indeed, Butler suggests that "the eighteenth century may have left a far more indelible impression on the American religious tradition than did the seventeenth century."[24]

Clearly there is a need for more congregational studies, both of the colonial era and of later periods, that apply the techniques and insights of intellectual and social history to their own religious subject matter. With this need in mind, the University of Chicago has launched a large projected entitled "The Congregation in American Life." Funded by the Lilly Endowment, this study will ultimately comprise three volumes. The first volume will describe the histories of ten very difference congregations, ranging from the Mount Hebron Baptist Church of Leeds, Alabama, to the Greek Orthodox Congregation of the Annunciation Cathedral in Baltimore, Maryland, to Cincinnati's Rockdale Temple. The second and third volumes will discuss the ways congregations mediate between the public and private spheres of life, and the implications of congregational studies for religious studies in general. On the most general level, the purpose of the University of Chicago's project is to examine the way Americans have expressed themselves religiously through congregational organization.[25]

As part of this project, we are embarking on a long-term study of the First Congregational Church of New Haven, which recently celebrated its 350th anniversary. This longitudinal study of a New England church will differ from earlier demographic studies of New England towns in two regards. First, its focus will be religion and the church rather than the town and community. Our concern will be less with the workings of the American government, or the rise of trade, than with the ongoing life of one particular religious community. Secondly, and relatedly, the chronological focus will not be limited to the seventeenth century or pre-Revolutionary America, but will include the entire life experience of the congregation from its founding in 1639 through 1988. The American Revolution represents a premature end point for a New Religious History. The year 1776 works for social history, and it works for political history, but it does not work for religious history or, for that matter, women's history.

Any study as comprehensive as this requires long hours of data collection and analysis. In all, 7,379 members have joined the First Church over the centuries and have been included in the analysis. The technical problems of information storage and analysis for such a large body of information were forbidding. Where town studies involving several hundred families could rely on family reconstitution sheets and a hand tabulator, we quickly recognized the need for a computer, a code book, and a statistical program to handle the sheer volume of information. We have been rewarded by the ability to ask questions about the experience of this church which other, more narrow approaches wouldn't allow.[26]

Such a study is possible because of the First Church's meticulous record keeping. Over the long course of its history, each member has been registered in the church's records, along with additional information about that person's age, place of birth, marital status, and relatives in the church. A printed catalogue of members was prepared by Franklin B. Dexter in 1914.[27] For information on members since then, the First Church kindly allowed us access to current membership lists and records. We then entered the names of all 7,379 members in a computer. Along with names and dates of admission we entered data on twenty-two other variables, including the member's age, gender, year of birth, birthplace, marital status, race, and the number of his or her children who joined the church. We also collected information on whether the member was a Yale graduate or a church officer, whether he or she was excommunicated and for what offense, and whether the member had a parent, spouse, sibling, or child who had already joined the church or who joined the same year. Finally, we specified whether a church member was admitted by certificate from another church and where that church was located, and if the member chose to be dismissed, where he or she chose to go.[28]

By tabulating the frequency distributions for each variable, and then cross-tabulating each variable with every other variable, we have generated a massive amount of data about the history of First Church that spans three centuries. The computer has enabled us to determine how many members joined the church in each year of its history, and whether those members were male or female, white or black, single or married. Because of our interest in the changing familial basis of this church, we have also used the computer to record whether each individual had family members in the church at the time of joining. Did he or she have a spouse, parent, sibling, or child who was already a member of the church? How many people were the first in their nuclear families to join?

Among the central questions that can be illuminated by this study is the question of declension. In many ways, First Church of New Haven is a bellwether, mainstream church. At the time of its founding it was the most Puritan church in the most Puritan town. John Davenport had arrived in Massachusetts Bay in 1638 just in time to witness the trial of Anne Hutchinson, and he was determined that no such heresy would arise in his Puritan "new haven." The colony's laws were the strictest and most biblical in all of New England. Davenport instituted the law code that John Cotton had drawn up for Massachusetts, where it had been rejected because its harshness departed too much from the common law tradition. Later, in the 1660s, Davenport was one of the leaders in the campaign against the Half-Way Covenant.[29]

The analysis of data for the nineteenth and twentieth centuries is ongoing, but from our colonial data and other recent studies, two facts are becoming clear. First, seen from the vantage point of three centuries, colonial declension—as reflected in church membership—is a myth. Declension occurred, to be sure, but not in the colonial era. From Table 2.1, it is clear that membership rose and fell over the decades, but there was no permanent, irreversible slide in numbers. For the most part, moreover, the growth in membership kept pace with the growth in population. From 1639 to 1700, 556 members joined First Church. As the population more than doubled in the next century, so also did church membership. Through 1741, First Church enjoyed a religious monopoly in New Haven and maintained a growth rate comparable to general population expansion. After 1741, new meetinghouses appeared regularly, and First Church had to compete for its members. Collectively, in this period, New Haven churches maintained pace with the population, and within these churches First Church remained one of the largest, adding 997 members between 1700 and 1800.[30]

Besides looking at membership rates in the aggregate, it is important to distinguish membership by gender (Table 2.1). And here, a fascinating pattern emerges. From low points in the Revolutionary decades, membership rates recovered, but in overwhelmingly female numbers. For example, between 1800 and 1810, 76 percent of the 228 new members admitted were women. Although the trend towards feminization

TABLE 2.1.   Male and Female Church Admissions by Decade,
1639–1989

Decades	Percentage of male converts	Percentage of female converts	Total number
1639–49	64.5	35.5	189
1650–59	54.5	45.5	3
1660–69	16.3	83.7	43
1670–79	50.0	50.0	2
1680–89	35.2	64.8	142
1690–99	37.4	62.6	147
1700–09	35.2	64.8	88
1710–19	30.8	69.2	133
1720–29	37.1	62.9	124
1730–39	32.1	67.9	218
1740–49	39.0	61.0	77
1750–59	36.4	63.6	44
1760–69	34.9	65.1	86
1770–79	28.6	71.4	98
1780–89	31.9	68.1	69
1790–99	18.3	81.7	60
1800–09	23.7	76.3	228
1810–19	27.5	72.5	182
1820–29	31.2	68.8	346
1830–39	35.9	64.1	399
1840–49	30.9	69.1	337
1850–59	31.5	68.5	270
1860–69	26.1	73.9	234
1870–79	36.30	63.70	303

TABLE 2.1.   (continued)

Decades	Percentage of male converts	Percentage of female converts	Total number
1880–89	35.80	64.20	176
1890–99	40.85	59.15	164
1900–09	29.20	70.80	113
1910–19	38.82	61.18	832
1920–29	35.18	64.82	506
1930–39	36.16	63.84	307
1940–49	38.87	61.13	283
1950–59	39.56	60.44	503
1960–69	47.57	52.43	185
1970–79	34.10	65.90	393
1980–89	30.77	69.23	65

Total number of male converts—2,619 (35.49%)

Total number of female converts—4,760 (64.51%)

had begun as early as the second generation, it was partially reversed in the era of the Great Awakening. Women's dominance in the church did not become permanent until the Revolutionary era. Other historians have noted that men and women's conversion narratives were remarkably similar from the seventeenth century through the Great Awakening. However, after the Revolution, men and women increasingly spoke in different religious voices.[31] Their language, like their experience, was now distinct.

Declension, as measured by a permanent drop-off in membership and commitment, seems to have occurred in the Revolutionary generation, *but only for men.* During the Revolutionary period, the church was irreversibly "feminized" as men ceased joining the church but women continued to join in large numbers (see Table 2.1). Between 1790 and 1800 the percentage of new male members dropped to 18 percent, a low from which males would never entirely recover (although they made slight gains in the twentieth century). Significantly, the majority of men who did join the church were following their wives. Table 2.2 illustrates that while only 23 percent of men who joined between 1740 and 1750 had wives in the church, that percentage increased to 54 percent between 1770 and 1780 and continued to rise until 1800. In contrast, only 17 percent of new female members between 1740 and 1750 had husbands in the church, and that percentage never increased to more than 29 percent during the Revolutionary years. Apparently, women played an important role in encouraging their husbands to become members.

Our study corroborates the work of earlier scholars, such as Paul Johnson and Mary Ryan, who argued that women played a crucial role in perpetuating male membership. Although in *A Shopkeeper's Millennium* Johnson focuses almost exclusively on male converts, he does note briefly that "the organization of prayer meetings, the pattern of family visits, and bits of evidence from church records suggests that hundreds of conversions culminated when husbands prayed with their wives."[32] His impressions were more systematically confirmed by Mary Ryan, whose 1978 essay "A Women's Awakening" examines church membership records from four churches in Utica, New York. Ryan found that women not only comprised the majority of members, but that they helped convert their male relatives. Through organizations like the Female Missionary Society and the Maternal Association, Utica women became evangelists not only in their neighbors' homes, but in their own as well. The majority of male converts entered the churches after their wives, mothers, or sisters.[33]

New Haven and Utica were not the only places where women increasingly dominated the church rolls in the years after the Revolution. Women's predominance in New England's mainline churches has been demonstrated by many studies. Combining his own statistics with the work of other historians such as Gerald Moran and Cedric Cowing, Richard Shiels found that the percentage of female converts in Boston rose dramatically during the Revolutionary period. Between 1730 and 1769, women comprised 59 percent of all new members. Throughout these years, the percentage of women in the church remained fairly stable, neither increasing nor decreasing in any appreciable amount. But from 1770 to 1799, their percentage soared to 64 percent, and between 1800 and 1835 rose even further to 69 percent.[34] Further, the change in the percentage of women in the churches did not reflect a change in the sexual composition of the population at large. During the Revolutionary years, women remained about 50 percent of the population in both Connecticut and Massachusetts.[35] As both Shiels' statistics and our own

TABLE 2.2.   Church Admissions by Gender and Spouse, 1740–1799

	Spouse a member of the church	Spouse not a member of the church	Total n
1740–49			
Male converts	23.3	76.7	30
Female converts	17.0	83.0	47
Total n	15	62	77
1750–59			
Male converts	25.0	75.0	16
Female converts	17.9	82.1	28
Total n	9	35	44
1760–69			
Male converts	53.3	46.7	30
Female converts	28.6	71.4	56
Total n	32	54	86
1770–79			
Male converts	53.6	46.4	28
Female converts	27.1	72.9	70
Total n	34	64	98
1780–89			
Male converts	59.1	40.9	22
Female converts	23.4	76.6	47
Total n	24	45	69
1790–99			
Male converts	63.6	36.4	11
Female converts	8.2	91.8	49
Total n	11	49	60

illustrate, there was no declension for women during the colonial and Revolutionary periods.

As many women's historians have argued, men's experiences cannot always be regarded as normative. In Mary Maples Dunn's 1978 article "Saints and Sisters," she suggested that declension was really only the loss of *male* piety. This stands in sharp contrast to earlier views, which equated spiritual vitality with male involvement. Worse yet, many of these earlier views at least implicitly equated feminization with declension.[36] In his influential essay "Sex and Preaching in the Great Awakening," Cedric Cowing defended the importance of the Great Awakening by arguing that it profoundly affected men, and not just "weak groups, those presumed to have inferior nervous and intellectual equipment"— namely, women and adolescents.[37] In his view, the evangelical New Lights were "essential in revitalizing the male laity and restoring a measure of the historic congregationalism," while the early Baptists "tried to wed the Arminian faith to the Congregational polity and failed; their churches became static, other worldly and female-dominated."[38] Inadvertently, Robert Pope evidenced a similar male focus in attempting to confirm the myth of declension by showing how men continued to participate in the churches. Although women had been joining the church all along, Pope ignored this pattern and instead focused on an increase in *male* membership around 1675 to counter the myth of declension. In sum, whether the argument was for or against declension, males dominated the evidence. By implication, these historians followed the example of the colonial clergy and identified the vigor of the church with male participation.

Certainly, it is important to note that there was a decline in male piety during the Revolutionary era, else we simply reverse the gender-driven interpretations set forth in earlier history. But it is even more important to note that alongside this partial declension was an equally impressive resurgence and revival of religiosity among female members. The decline in male membership, and the shift in men's intellectual preoccupation from religion to politics was not indicative of a secular cultural transformation.

From Table 2.1 it appears that a generation of men had moved from being Puritans to being Yankees. They had left behind the communal ethic of their forefathers to celebrate the birth of a new individualism. In the post-Revolutionary climate of ideas, the individual was sovereign, and a new government emerged premised on self-interest rather than self-denial. Theologically, these changes were reflected in the growth of new religions, including evangelical Baptists and Methodists as well as Universalists and Unitarians, who turned away from Calvinism's emphasis on man's inability to help effect his own salvation. As political theorists stressed ordinary men's ability to govern themselves rationally, theologians from Charles Chauncy to Charles G. Finney denied that men were helpless before God. Even at First Church, a "New Haven Theology" emerged in the pulpit that ascribed an ever-increasing autonomy to human will.[39]

One possible reason for the decrease in men's church membership was their new faith in their ability to control their own destiny. A recent study of early nineteenth-century conversion narratives by Susan Juster suggests that men, unlike women, believed they could effect their own salvation by behaving morally.[40] While generalizations like this are always problematic and ignore innumerable exceptions, this does seem to fit the tenor of a new republican society, where the powers and responsibilities of ordinary men reached unprecedented heights. At the same time, female imagery increasingly dominated pulpit rhetoric. Margaret Masson has argued that as early as 1690, Puritan ministers used the typology of the female as a model for the regenerate. They described new converts as "brides" of Christ, who were expected to exemplify the feminine virtues of submission, devotion, and purity.[41] Recently, Ruth Bloch has illustrated this rhetorical feminization in the preaching of Jonathan Edwards, who frequently employed the metaphor of a mystical marriage.[42] This trend would continue into the Revolutionary era among itinerants like Henry Alline and Baptist exhorters, and would accelerate during the nineteenth century as women increasingly dominated church membership rolls.[43] Barbara Welter's path-breaking essay "The Feminization of American Religion," argues that as men drifted away from the church, ministers softened their sermons to fit the needs of their new female audience. They abandoned the idea of infant damnation, and in sermons and hymns they increasingly portrayed Christ in female terms as loving, submissive, and humble.[44] Although no scholar has demonstrated an intrinsic, causal connection between Calvinism and patriarchy or Arminianism and feminization, it is true that churches moved in increasingly Arminian directions even as women came to dominate the membership. In sum, while men stopped joining the churches, women found them more and more inviting.

Clearly, the political upheaval of the Revolution did not effect ordinary women as radically as it did ordinary men, and to the extent that it did, it actually *increased* their interest in religion and the workings of the institutional churches. As Linda Kerber has argued, the Revolution left women an ambivalent legacy. Legally, divorce became more possible in a few colonies, but the practice of coverture continued (despite its inconsistency with republican ideology). Under coverture, a married woman could not own property of her own unless special legal provisions had been made before her marriage. Socially, women gained greater access to education, but the special female curriculum was designed only to equip them to raise a virtuous citizenry. Finally, despite the politicization of their economic role during boycotts, most women continued to regard politics as outside of their sphere. Women did forge a revolutionary new role for themselves, the role of republican mother, which allowed them a greater voice in civic culture and would eventually be used to justify making the world their household.[45] However, the Revolution had a much more conservative impact on women than men. The self-made man depended on the existence of a republican wife and mother, who was willing to sacrifice herself for the good of her family and *her* church. If anything, women became *more* religious in the sense that the church depended on their efforts more than ever. If we look at religion from the pew, religiosity seems to have gained in intensity for many women who absorbed the language of popular sovereignty and self-rule, but who found the church the only outlet for their voices.

Economic changes reinforced the division between male and female worlds. In *The Bonds of Womanhood,* Nancy Cott has shown how the shift to a market economy between 1780 and 1835 diminished the importance of household manufacturing, and women's work was increasingly seen as being different from men's. Economic production now took place outside of the home. Men belonged to a competitive, capitalist world, while women were expected to offer a haven from the strains of economic and social transformation. Men were now pursuing goals that required them to be aggressive and independent, while women were increasingly urged to be submissive and dependent.[46] These changes were reflected in the literature of the period. While sentimental heroines like Charlotte Temple and Eliza Whitman learned the virtues of submission to authority, Ralph Waldo Emerson turned away from traditional Christianity to preach a creed of male self-reliance.

In short, the Revolution was a turning point for men's religiosity, but not for women's. Churches had ceased to be the center of New England communities even as they proliferated in numbers. New Haven alone had as many as eleven churches by 1829.[47] Both men and women searched for ways to order their world in a time of dramatic political and economic change, yet men had access to political and social organizations as well as religious ones. For them, political parties, small businesses, and the Masonic lodges were as important as churches and also excluded women.[48] In contrast, church membership and volunteer work—which was often religious in nature—were the only public roles sanctioned for women. As Nancy Cott has argued, religion provided women with both stability and a sympathetic community of other female converts.[49] Men found alternative ways to order their experience that were more in keeping with their new economic and political goals.

In conclusion, it is clear that a religious history of America has yet to be written on its own terms from the bottom up. More long-term, local studies are needed that do not impose a "declension" paradigm prematurely to satisfy external social, political, or intellectual interests. Such a history has as much to gain from the new field of women's history as it does from the older traditions of intellectual and social history. By combining insights and methods from all these disciplines, and applying them specifically to the American religious experience, it should be possible to present a "New" history that is at once "American History" and "Church History." Indeed, a New Religious History.

NOTES

1. Perry Miller, *The New England Mind: The Seventeenth Century* (Cambridge: Harvard University Press, 1939) and *The New England Mind: From Colony to Province* (Cambridge: Harvard University Press, 1953).

2. Herbert Schneider, *A History of American Philosophy,* 2d ed. (New York: Columbia University Press, 1963).

3. See Robert Middlekauff's essay "Perry Miller" in Robin Winks and Marcus Cunliffe, eds., *Pastmasters: Some Essays on American Historians* (New York: Harper & Row, 1969).

4. Edmund S. Morgan, *Visible Saints: The History of a Puritan Idea* (New York: New York University Press, 1963), 64–112.

5. Edmund S. Morgan, "The American Revolution Considered as an Intellectual Movement," in Arthur M. Schlesinger, Jr., and Morton White, eds., *Paths of American Thought* (Boston: Houghton Mifflin, 1963).

6. David D. Hall, *The Faithful Shepherd: A History of the New England Ministry in the Seventeenth Century* (Chapel Hill: University of North Carolina Press, 1972), and T. H. Breen, *The Character of the Good Ruler: A Study of Puritan Political Ideas in New England, 1630–1730* (New Haven: Yale University Press, 1970).

7. Darrett Rutman, *Winthrop's Boston; Portrait of a Puritan Town 1630–1649* (Chapel Hill: University of North Carolina Press, 1965).

8. Robert G. Pope, *The Half-Way Covenant: Church Membership in Puritan New England* (Princeton: Princeton University Press, 1969).

9. John Demos, *A Little Commonwealth: Family Life in Plymouth Colony* (New York: Oxford University Press, 1970); Philip J. Greven, *Four Generations: Population, Land, and Family in Colonial Andover, Massachusetts* (Ithaca: Cornell University Press, 1970); Kenneth Lockridge, *A New England Town: The*

First Hundred Years (New York: W. W. Norton, 1970); and Michael Zuckerman, *Peaceable Kingdoms: New England Towns in the Eighteenth Century* (New York: Knopf, 1970).

10. See Lawrence W. Levine, "The Unpredictable Past: Reflections on Recent American Historiography," *American Historical Review* 94 (June, 1989): 671–679, and Peter N. Stearns, "Social History and History: A Progress Report," *Journal of Social History* 19 (Winter, 1985): 319–334.

11. Perry Miller, "Errand into the Wilderness," reprinted in *Errand into the Wilderness* (Cambridge: Harvard University Press, 1956), 15.

12. Lockridge, *A New England Town,* 76.

13. Paul Boyer and Stephen Nissenbaum, *Salem Possessed: The Social Origins of Witchcraft* (Cambridge: Harvard University Press, 1974).

14. See especially Nancy F. Cott, *The Bonds of Womanhood: "Woman's Sphere" in New England, 1780–1835* (New Haven: Yale University Press, 1977), and Ann Douglas, *The Feminization of American Culture* (New York: Knopf, 1977).

15. Zuckerman, *Peaceable Kingdoms.*

16. See Barbara Welter, "The Feminization of American Religion," in Marty Hartman and Lois Banner, eds., *Clio's Consciousness Raised* (New York: Harper Torchbooks, 1973); Douglas, *The Feminization of American Culture;* Nancy F. Cott, *The Bonds of Womanhood: "Women's Sphere" in New England, 1780–1835;* and Mary Ryan, *Cradle of the Middle Class: The Family in Oneida County, New York, 1790–1865* (Cambridge: Cambridge University Press, 1981).

17. Charles E. Hambrick-Stowe, *The Practice of Piety: Puritan Devotional Disciplines in Seventeenth-Century New England* (Chapel Hill: University of North Carolina Press, 1982).

18. David D. Hall, *Worlds of Wonder, Days of Judgment: Popular Religious Belief in Early New England* (New York: Knopf, 1989).

19. David D. Hall, "The World of Print and Collective Mentality in Seventeenth-Century New England," in John Higham and Paul Conkin, eds., *New Directions in American Intellectual History* (Baltimore: Johns Hopkins University Press, 1979), 166–180, 177.

20. Connecticut and Massachusetts membership patterns during the Great Awakening are summarized in J. M. Bumsted and John E. Van de Wetering, *What Must I Do to be Saved? The Great Awakening in Colonial America* (Hinsdale, Ill.: Dryden Press, 1976), 128–133.

21. Gerald Francis Moran, "The Puritan Saint: Religious Experience, Church Membership, and Piety in Connecticut, 1636–1776" (Ph.D. diss., Rutgers University, 1974).

22. Gerald F. Moran and Maris A. Vinovskis, "The Puritan Family and Religion: A Critical Reappraisal," *William and Mary Quarterly* 39 (January 1982): 29–63.

23. Stephen R. Grossbart, "Seeking the Divine Favor: Conversion and Church Admission in Eastern Connecticut, 1711–1832," *William and Mary Quarterly* 46 (October 1989): 696–740.

24. Patricia Bonomi, *Under the Cope of Heaven: Religion, Society, and Politics*

in Colonial America (New York: Oxford University Press, 1986), and Jon Butler, *Awash in a Sea of Faith: Christianizing the American Republic* (Cambridge: Harvard University Press, 1990), 2. See also Patricia U. Bonomi and Peter R. Eisenstadt, "Church Adherence in the Eighteenth Century British American Colonies," *William and Mary Quarterly* 39 (April 1982): 245–46.

25. "The Congregational History Project," unpublished project description, Institute for the Advanced Study of Religion, University of Chicago. Vol. 1 of the series, *American Congregations,* is forthcoming from University of Chicago Press.

26. We used the Systat program for personal computers in conjunction with an IBM Personal System 2 Model 50. Systat is a basic statistics program that is ideal for studies such as this because of its relatively inexpensive cost and its excellent user manual.

27. Franklin Bowditch Dexter, *Historical Catalogue of the Members of the First Church of Christ in New Haven, Connecticut* (New Haven, n.p. 1914).

28. We are indebted to Deborah J. Stout for her assistance in entering the data into the computer and to Robert Boyd for teaching us to use Systat.

29. For Davenport's argument against the Half-Way Covenant, see his *Another Essay for Investigation of the Truth in Answer to Two Questions Concerning, I. The Subject of Baptism, II. The Consociation of Churches* (Cambridge: Printed by Samuel Green and Marmaduke Johnson 1663) and *A Reply to the Seven Propositions concluded by ye Synod sitting at Boston June ye tenth 1662 in answer to ye first question: vis:—who are the subjects of baptism.* (n.p., 1662) For a discussion of the founding of New Haven, see Isabel Macbeath Calder, *The New Haven Colony* (New Haven: Yale University Press, 1934).

30. On the religious history of New Haven in these years, see Oscar E. Maurer, *A Puritan Church And its Relation to Community, State, and Nation* (New Haven: Yale University Press, 1938).

31. For a discussion of seventeenth-century conversion narratives, see Patricia Caldwell, *The Puritan Conversion Narrative: The Beginnings of American Expression* (Cambridge; New York: Cambridge University Press, 1983). The first two chapters of Barbara Leslie Epstein's *The Politics of Domesticity: Women, Evangelism, and Temperance in Nineteenth Century America* (Middletown: Wesleyan University Press, 1981) discuss the similarities between male and female conversion accounts during the Great Awakening, and the differences that emerge during the Second Great Awakening. See also Susan Juster, " 'In a Different Voice': Male and Female Narratives of Religious Conversion in Post-Revolutionary America," *American Quarterly* 41 (March 1989): 34–62.

32. Paul E. Johnson, *A Shopkeeper's Millennium: Society and Revivals in Rochester, New York 1815–1837* (New York: Hill and Wang, 1978), 108.

33. Mary P. Ryan, "A Women's Awakening: Evangelical Religion and the Families of Utica, New York, 1800–1840," *American Quarterly* 30 (Winter 1978): 602–623.

34. Richard Shiels, "The Feminization of American Congregationalism, 1730–1835," *American Quarterly* 33 (Spring 1981): 48.

35. Ibid., 49.
36. Mary Maples Dunn, "Saints and Sisters: Congregational and Quaker Women in the Early Colonial Period," *American Quarterly* 30 (Winter 1978): 592.
37. Cedric B. Cowing, "Sex and Preaching in the Great Awakening," *American Quarterly* 20 (Fall 1968): 640.
38. Ibid., 644.
39. Sidney Mead, *Nathaniel William Taylor, 1786–1858, a Connecticut Liberal* (Chicago: University of Chicago Press, 1942).
40. Juster, " 'In a Different Voice'."
41. Margaret W. Masson, "The Typology of the Female as a Model for the Regenerate: Puritan Preaching, 1690–1730," *Signs* 2 (Winter 1976): 304–315. See also Amanda Porterfield, *Feminine Spirituality in America: From Sarah Edwards to Martha Graham* (Philadelphia: Temple University Press, 1980).
42. Ruth H. Bloch, "Women, Love, and Virtue in the Thought of Edwards and Franklin," unpublished paper, National Conference on Jonathan Edwards and Benjamin Franklin, Yale University, February, 1990.
43. On Alline and the use of sensual imagery, see George A. Rawlyk, *Ravished by the Spirit: Religious Revivals, Baptists, and Henry Alline* (Kingston: McGill-Queen's University Press, 1984). On female exhorters, see Catherine A. Brekus, "Female Preachers and Evangelical Religion in America, 1740–1840" (Ph.D. diss. in progress at Yale University).
44. Barbara Welter, "The Feminization of American Religion," in Hartman and Banner, eds., *Clio's Consciousness Raised*. See also Douglas, *The Feminization of American Culture*. For two provocative challenges to Douglas's view, see David S. Reynolds, "The Feminization Controversy: Sexual Stereotypes and the Paradoxes of Piety in Nineteenth Century America," *New England Quarterly* 53 (March 1980): 96–106, and Darrel M. Robertson, "The Feminization of American Religion: An Examination of Recent Interpretations of Women and Religion in Victorian America," *Christian Scholar's Review* 8 (1978): 238–246. An excellent overview of the literature on women and religion is Elizabeth B. Clark's "Women and Religion in America, 1780–1870," in John F. Wilson, ed., *Church and State in America: A Bibliographical Guide,* vol 1 (New York: Greenwood Press, 1986), 365–413.
45. Linda F. Kerber, *Women of the Republic: Intellect and Ideology in Revolutionary America* (Chapel Hill: University of North Carolina Press, 1980).
46. Cott, *The Bonds of Womanhood.*
47. Shiels, "The Feminization of American Congregationalism," 60.
48. On the rise of Masonic lodges and their exclusion of women, see Paul Goodman, *Towards a Christian America: Antimasonry and the Great Transition in New England, 1826–1836* (New York: Oxford, 1988), 80–102. For a discussion of men's political culture in the years after the Revolution, see Paula Baker, "The Domestication of Politics: Women and American Political Society, 1780–1920," *American Historical Review* 89 (June 1984): 620–647.
49. See Cott, *The Bonds of Womanhood,* Chap. 4, and also her "Young Women in the Second Great Awakening," *Feminist Studies,* 3 (Fall 1975): 15–29.

GERALD F. MORAN

3

"Sinners Are Turned into Saints in Numbers": Puritanism and Revivalism in Colonial Connecticut

One theme has dominated historians' thinking about the religious history of early American Puritanism: the notion of religious declension. The Puritans themselves used the language of declension to chronicle their history but only as a way of impressing upon the people the need for spiritual awakening. Their descendants took the term more literally, however. Advocates of the Great Awakening found in the concept of declension ammunition for their attack on the established church, arguing that only a Great Revival could save the church from the Great Declension that had befallen it since the days of the Puritan planters. Within several generations declension became one of the laws of "scientific revivalism" and a piece of the equipment used by nineteenth-century evangelicals to manufacture revivals. Thus, Charles Grandison Finney could argue in the 1830s that " 'A Revival of Religion' presupposes a declension," and "Almost all the religion in the world has been produced by revivals."[1] The theme of declension then found its way into the works of modern-day historians. By the 1930s, Perry Miller was using it to explain how New England colonies changed into provinces. While Miller hesitated to use the term literally, interpreting it as a species of jeremiad, his student, Edmund Morgan, showed no such inclination. In *The Puritan Family* Morgan argued that the New England church declined, and it declined because it became tribalistic and thus lost the support of the people. "Before the end of the century," Morgan says, "The Purtian system was tottering. . . . Though Increase Mather was still mumbling his phrases about the loins of Godly parents in 1721, it was long since clear, to anyone with eyes to see, that grace was not hereditary."[2]

Since the 1950s, however, the theme has been subjected to a barrage of criticism. Literary historians have criticized scholars such as Miller for focusing on the mind of the Puritans, at the expense of their spirit, while seminary historians have criticized them for their monolithic portrayal of New England doctrine.[3] In recent years social historians have joined the siege on declension. Like generations of historians before him, Morgan relied on literary evidence to study the Puritans, and thus incorporated into his studies the assumptions and biases of the group that produced the evidence, the New England clergy. Since the 1960s, social historians have argued that the regular life of New England parishes deserves as much attention as its clerical life, that Puritanism should be studied not only through the eyes of the men behind the pulpits but also through the eyes of the people in the pews, both men and women, children as well as adults. Their findings have even further weakened the interpretive power of declension.

Despite its shortcomings, the theme of declension remains in common usage today, because Puritan studies, notwithstanding the remarkable advances of recent years, has not cohered around a substitute. Rather, historians continue to debate how American Puritanism changed, or whether it changed at all. Consider several recent studies of New England religion. In a history of church and society along the Connecticut River valley, Paul Lucas argues that ecclesiastical discord, a standard symptom of declension, overshadowed New England Puritanism from the start, as ministers and laymen clashed continuously over doctrine and church practice and kept the conflict going for the remainder of the seventeenth century.[4] On the other hand, Christine Heryman tips the theme of declension on its head, arguing that at least in several New England towns the church rose, not declined. While religion languished for several decades after the settlement of the towns, by the middle of the eighteenth century the church had developed an active following within the communities.[5] Harry S. Stout, at the same time, argues that religion neither rose nor declined, but in terms of the substance of the ministry's sermons showed surprising continuity. "If there was 'decline' and resultant 'secularization' of Puritanism," he says, "it was not evident in the regular life of the church. The majority of inhabitants continued to go to church, and their ministers persisted in the subject matter of their sermons."[6]

For these and other historians, the history of the church and of church membership is central to an understanding of American Puritanism. Stout, for example, suggests that evidence on church membership is critically important for assessing the power of the sermon in the regular life of the religion. The authority of ministers, he indicates, was a function of the people's willingness to place their faith in them, to offer them the gift of evangelical obedience in return for the gift of church membership. If the people had not joined the church, the New England ministry would have lacked power, and their sermons, however changeless in content, would have lacked a receptive audience. In other words, if church membership had declined, so would have the power and resonance of the Word.

As David Hall has recently argued, "the crux of the matter" in the declension debate "is church membership,"[7] but surprisingly little effort has been made to explore this subject in a systematic way. While Puritan historians have realized the great potential of church records for some years, there is still no comprehensive history of church membership in New England.[8] This is an unfortunate oversight, for no other records shed as much light on the religious activities of as many people. To be sure, serious questions about the usefulness of such records can and have been raised, for they measure neither genuine religiosity nor church adherence.[9] But they do tell us how many people joined the church over time and what sorts of people they were, and in conjunction with other local records, where they came from, and what families they belonged to, among other personal information, and thus offer us a glimpse of parish life absent from other kinds of records. They offer us, in other words, a different perspective of American Puritanism and thus a different approach to such issues as that of declension. To the degree that they illuminate the relationship of religion to society, church records should also help us to complete the agenda of the new religious history of colonial New England, especially as it concerns the breadth of lay loyalty to the church and the influence of gender, kinship, and developmental rituals on the religious activities of the people.[10]

The church membership and vital records of one New England colony, Connecticut, for the period from the Great Migration to the Great Awakening form the basis of the present study. They point to a way of envisioning the Puritan movement in America that includes both declension and revival in its vocabulary and that focuses on the process of church revitalization. The history of church membership in Connecticut was cyclical in nature, and can be divided into four parts. First was the initial period of settlement, when the first churches were established and the first members admitted (from the 1630s to about 1650). Then came a period of protracted decline, during which few churches were founded and few members admitted (1650 to 1690). Next was a period of major ecclesiastical expansion and religious revival, when the church staged a dramatic recovery from declension and set in motion forces that would find fulfillment in the Great Awakening (1690–1745). During this period, and the preceding one, the relationship between religion and society changed profoundly, in a way that enabled the church to rebound from declension. Finally, after the Awakening had run its course, few churches were established and few members added to the church (1745 to 1776).[11]

THE COLONY OF CONNECTICUT, which came to include both the river valley towns and the towns along Long Island Sound, was born in a time of great religious excitement. In the early 1630s, just before the settlement of the colony, the inhabitants of eastern Massachusetts Bay, including the people preparing to emigrate to Connecticut, participated in a general awakening, one ignited by the preaching of the renowned English evangelist, John Cotton, who had arrived in Boston in 1633. As Roger Clap, an early settler of Dorchester, describes it:

> O how did men and women, young and old, pray for grace, beg for Christ, in those days. And it was not in vain. Many were converted, and others established in believing. Many joined unto several churches where they lived, confessing their faith publickly, and showing before all the assembly their experiences of the workings of God's spirit in their hearts to bring them to Christ.[12]

While the first towns of Connecticut, which were river-valley communities, were formed around nuclei of saints who had joined Bay Colony churches during the revival, the second set of towns established, which were Long Island Sound communities, were settled by people who had immigrated to New England after the Awakening. This meant that they had to start their churches from scratch, and to guide them through the process they drew upon the English Puritan practice of conventicling. Such was the case in New Haven. After founding the town in 1639, the settlers convened meetings for their mutual spiritual edification, which were held off and on for several months. By the summer of 1639 the conventicles had come forward with seven men, including the minister John Davenport, whose faith qualified them to be the nucleus of a church. Additional meetings were held to write a covenant and to determine the form and substance of the church, and from these meetings came the decision to gather the church around "visible saints," people capable of testifying in public to a true and lasting experience of religious conversion. In August 1639, the ceremony of the "first planting" of the church was held. After witnessing to their conversions and reciting the covenant before the community in the meeting house, the seven men united in Christian fellowship.[13]

The experience of conventicling and of first planting in New Haven and other Connecticut communities, along with the evangelism of the colony's preachers, sparked widespread interest in the church and another New England revival, albeit in a different corner of the region. Even tests of faith, which more and more churches adopted after the mid-1630s, failed to stem the flow of new communicants.[14] In fact, well into the 1640s admissions soared. Thus, in New Haven John Davenport brought forty-two people into the church over the four months following the gathering; over the next seven years, from 1640 through 1646, he admitted on average seventeen people per year, receiving as many as fifty new members in just one year, 1646. So widespread was this revival, that by the time Davenport had cut his evangelical swath through the community, people from nearly every family in town belonged to the church.[15]

The First Church of Milford, which was located just south of New Haven, also grew rapidly. In 1639, the year the church was founded, only three people became members, but soon the situation changed dramatically. In 1640 twenty-four men and women joined the church, and in 1641 another seven. By the end of 1644, church membership totalled eighty people, which amounted to 82 percent of the male inhabitants and 77 percent of their wives. Now 95 percent of the town's families had at least one spouse in communion, while 63 percent had both of them.[16]

The Connecticut awakening was not confined to New Haven and Milford. The First Church of Guilford grew rapidly after its founding, as did the First Church of Windsor. So too did the colony's most prestigious church—Thomas Hooker's Hartford First. Before his death in 1647, Hooker probably admitted most of the inhabitants of the town, if not all of them.[17] As the 1640s came to a close, the Connecticut church had an exceptionally strong popular base.

The 1650s introduced a darker era for the Connecticut church, and until the late 1680s and the 1690s the times were hard for most of the colony's evangelists. Over these years the pace of church growth slowed appreciably. In New Haven, for example, the declension of the church proved so disheartening to Davenport that he eventually fled the town. From 1649 to 1668, when the minister moved to Boston, the church averaged slightly under four admissions per year (as opposed to seventeen per year in 1639–1649). So slow was the pace of admissions, and so rapid the loss of members through death or dismissal, that popular representation in the church began deteriorating noticeably. In 1645 the ratio of communicants to families was one to one (110 members for 110 families), but by 1669 it had slipped to one to nearly two and a half (100 members for 230 families). After Davenport's departure the church continued to shrink in size while the town grew, and from 1668 until 1684, when New Haven hired a permanent minister, only thirteen people became communicants.[18]

Milford First Church followed a similar path of declension. From 1645 through 1656, when Peter Prudden, the town's first minister, died, new membership averaged slightly under three per year (as opposed to just over twelve per year for 1639–1644), and peaked at ten in 1654. After Prudden's death the church spent four years on finding a successor, but the installation of Roger Newton in 1660 had little initial impact on membership. Newton admitted only twenty-three people during the first nine years of his pastorate, a record of evangelism that fell far short of his predecessor's. At the same time, the church suffered a severe reduction in size when many church members immigrated to New Jersey. By the late 1660s, popular participation in the church had reached an all-time low, and now only 36 percent of the inhabitants were members.[19]

But Newton, unlike Davenport, persevered, and in 1669 his patience was rewarded when a revival hit the church. Forty-six people became members that year, more so than in any previous year. From 1670 until the minister's death in 1683, admissions per year remained above those in 1645–1664, though they declined gradually every five years. When Newton died, 47 percent of the townspeople belonged to the church.[20]

Milford's revival leaps from the pages of Connecticut's church records, for it was the only one of its kind at the time. Even the town's closest neighbors remained unaffected by it. Rather, admissions in the other churches with extant records failed to keep pace with population growth. By the 1670s and 1680s, towns such as New London, Stonington, and Woodbury had only one in seven men in the church.[21]

Just as the frequency of admissions decreased after 1650, so did the rate at which new churches were formed. While fourteen churches were gathered in 1636 to 1652, only nine were founded the next thirty years. Many of these new churches, in fact, were cut out of the old, as ecclesiastical discord rent a number of towns, even those once known for their harmony. Such a one was Hooker's Hartford, where expanding settlement on the other side of the river divided the inhabitants physically just as conflict over church practice divided them ecclesiastically. Hooker could keep them together, his successor, Samuel Stone, could not. Eventually the First Church subdivided into three churches and the town into several communities, one relocated in Massachusetts.[22] In some new towns, on the other hand, churches failed to appear because of doctrinal disputes among the people, such was the growing heterogeneity of the colony. A perfect case in point is New London. First settled in the early 1640s, the town failed to form a church until 1670, primarily because it had attracted settlers from different parts of New England with different views of church polity. Only after the town hired a minister who was capable of healing the divisions did it manage to gather a church.[23]

Who was to blame for the decline of the Connecticut church? The ministry? The laity? Certainly many of the new ministers lacked the charisma of their predecessors, and in its place preached jeremiads that, by virtue of their dreary repetitiveness, cause more, not less indifference among the people.[24] And certainly many of the laity lacked the faith that had empowered the fathers to chance crossing the ocean. But more impersonal forces lay behind the church's malaise. One such force was demography. As long as the Great Migration lasted, churches had access to a sizable pool of unchurched adults. But as the flow of migrants to New England stopped in the early 1640s, and as the pool dried up, churches had to rely on natural increases in population for future communicants, and this meant awaiting the maturation of the second generation.

A second force was the economy. The economic prosperity accompanying the Great Migration gave way after the 1640s to a protracted period of economic depression, characterized especially in the 1660s by crop failures and livestock epidemics.[25] In the competition for dwindling resources the church was often the loser. Finally, there was what one scholar has called "the problem of constructive Protestanism," arising inevitably within religious movements as they turn from protest and conflict to structure and thus fall prey to narrow legalism and constriction of that faith that had given birth to the cause.[26] As the declension rhetoric shows, the New England Puritans understood the problem of living in "secure habitations," and took steps to correct it, realizing, of course, that God's will would be done, whatever their effort to renew the spirit.

The major challenge was the conversion of the rising generation, and to meet it laws requiring family instruction were passed, schools were established, and covenant renewals introduced. The most important new measure was the Half-Way Covenant. As early as 1651, Peter Prudden advised the ministry to expand baptism to include the children of unchurched parents from church families, and in 1657 the Connecticut General Court endorsed the proposal.[27] While the initial response to the plan was not enthusiastic (many lay people and some ministers feared it would mean an end to the pure church), many churches did eventually adopt it, only to discover that it failed to do what it was intended to do, serve as a stepping-stone to full membership.[28] Despite the new measures, few members of the second generation were choosing to join the church, even as they began replacing the first generation in the adult population. Perhaps, as Morgan argues, the Puritan system was tottering and on the verge of collapse by the end of the century.

Just as the future of the church looked darkest, however, the situation started to improve. From 1690 to 1740 the Connecticut church grew stronger—it rose, to borrow a word from Christine Heyrman—and it garnered sufficient resources to fuel a great awakening in 1740–1745. To be sure, ecclesiastical discord continued in many parishes, and dissenting congregations, including the Anglicans and the Baptists, increased their following. But this should not distract us, as it has in the past, from the main story, which is the revitalization of the church. The process of religious renewal involved three major areas of parish life—new churches, the ministry, and church membership.

After slowing appreciably in the aftermath of the Great Migration, the rate at which new churches were established in Connecticut increased dramatically after 1690 (see Table 3.1). In no other period of Connecticut history, in fact, did the establishment expand as rapidly. The number of churches in the colony went from twenty-eight to 121, a more than fourfold increase. In one twenty-year interval, 1720–1740, nearly as many churches were founded as had been in the previous eighty-five years. While the expansion was fueled by rapid demographic

TABLE 3.1.   Growth of Church and Population in Connecticut, 1670–1770

Years	Churches	% Increase	Population*	% Increase
1670	19	26.8	15,799	40.1
1680	24	26.3	21,013	33.0
1690	28	16.7	27,464	30.7
1700	36	28.6	31,502	14.7
1710	46	27.8	38,339	21.7
1720	68	47.8	51,166	33.5
1730	99	45.6	68,169	33.2
1740	121	22.2	90,120	32.2
1750	154	27.3	112,921	25.3
1760	171	11.0	145,217	28.6
1770	188	9.9	181,583	25.0

NOTE: *Population data are based on Daniels, *The Connecticut Town*, p. 47, Table 1.

growth, the church actually grew faster than the population. Between 1690 and 1730 the ratio of churches to population went from one per 981 to one per 689, a 29 percent improvement. By the 1730s, there were more churches per capita in the colony than even before, or ever again. And the church was introduced into a number of areas of Connecticut that would feel the full effects of the Great Awakening.[29]

During the late seventeenth century the ministry for the most part had fallen on hard times.[30] Among the symptoms of decline was a shortage of qualified men with college degrees to preach the Gospel. By 1700, as many as 12 percent of ordained ministers were nongraduates, and towns at times could not find any preacher to minister to them at all.[31]

After 1700, the situation improved markedly, principally because of the founding of Yale College in 1703, which eventually enabled Connecticut to catch up with and then surpass the rapidly growing demand for ministers. In 1703–1740, the college produced 386 graduates, 46 percent of whom entered the ministry. By 1740 nongraduates accounted for only 3 percent of ordained ministers.[32] As the supply of qualified ministers caught up with the demand for them, fewer churches had difficulty filling vacant or vacated pulpits. As Table 3.2 shows, the percentage of pulpits remaining empty for more than a year decreased steadily over the period 1695 to 1740.[33] Church growth was thus accomplished with an increasingly well-trained ministry and with fewer disruptions in clerical services as well.

It was also accomplished with surprisingly little parish dissension. While chronic ecclesiastical discord in several churches has created the impression of generally deteriorating clerical authority, the actual proportion of preachers forced from the pulpit was quite low, despite the inexperience of many of them, especially in newly established parishes. To be sure, as the number of churches increased, so did the number of ministers dismissed by them, rising from one every decade in 1700–1720 to five, six, thirteen, and sixteen per decade in 1720–1760. Yet the rate of clerical dismissals stayed fairly steady throughout the period, never falling below five precent of all Connecticut parishes per decade.[34] The time and energy churches expended on examining candidates for clerical office apparently reaped the fruit of relative parish harmony.

Once installed, most clerical incumbents ordained in 1690–1740 preached from the same pulpit for life. As Table 3.3 shows, for most of the seventeenth century clergymen spent relatively little time in office before dying or departing for another town. But after the 1670s, their persistence in office improved significantly. After declining to a low of 6.6 years for preachers ordained in 1675–1679, average ministerial tenures in a parish increased rapidly over the next twenty-five years, peak-

TABLE 3.2.   Connecticut Pulpits
Vacant for More Than
One Year, 1650–1740

Years	Pulpits (%)
1650–1654	0.0
1655–1659	21.4
1660–1664	20.0
1665–1669	21.1
1670–1674	9.0
1675–1679	12.5
1680–1684	14.8
1685–1689	14.3
1690–1694	22.6
1695–1699	2.7
1700–1704	4.9
1705–1709	8.7
1710–1714	7.4
1715–1719	1.5
1720–1724	6.3
1725–1729	4.1
1730–1734	6.5
1735–1739	4.2

ing at 38.2 years for those installed in 1700–1704. Though the rates then decreased over the next thirty-five years, they stayed considerably higher than previous levels. The stability of the early eighteenth-century Connecticut ministry, which is generally overlooked in traditional accounts, shows up in a final statistic: ministers ordained in 1690–1740 lasted 27.8 mean years in office as opposed to only 15.6 mean years for those installed in 1636–1690.[35]

TABLE 3.3.   Clerical Tenure in Connecticut, 1640–1740

Years	Tenure (in mean years from ordination)	Number
1640–1644	11.6	8
1645–1649	14.0	3
1650–1654	17.7	3
1655–1659	7.7	3
1660–1664	13.6	14
1665–1669	16.8	11
1670–1674	20.8	5
1675–1679	6.6	5
1680–1684	19.0	8
1685–1689	25.2	6
1690–1694	21.8	16
1695–1699	26.6	16
1700–1704	38.2	5
1705–1709	34.0	10
1710–1714	27.7	16
1715–1719	31.4	14
1720–1724	25.0	21
1725–1729	23.3	27
1730–1734	32.1	23
1735–1739	29.2	25

As the establishment expanded, clerical standards rose, and careers stabilized, Connecticut ministers altered the substance and style of their sermons in the hope of raising their popular appeal and renewing popular interest in the church. One of the major proponents of the change was Solomon Stoddard, the minister of Northampton, Massachusetts, from 1672 to 1729. Frustrated by the ineffectiveness of the rhetoric of declension in producing conversions, Stoddard scrapped it for a fiery Gospel after 1710. His "new evangelicalism" found quick converts among ministers tied to him through neighboring clerical associations and through his extensive kin network.[36] Stoddardean evangelism was soon introduced to Yale, when the minister's grandson, Elisha Williams, became rector of the college in 1726. From then until he left office in 1739, Williams imparted his enthusiasm for experiential religion to his students, who entered the professional mainstream quickly, exceeding Harvard graduates within the newly ordained clerical population by the 1720s.[37] Williams's influence upon his students became evident during the Great Awakening, when the great majority of them (twenty-eight of forty-two, or 67 percent) ended up New Lights.[38] Another source of the new evangelism was Boston, where Cotton Mather, in the midst of mounting frustration over the failure of moral reformation, introduced a new, experimental piety, which found its way into Connecticut via such Boston-trained ministers as Eliphalet Adams of New London.[39] Altogether, the sermons of these ministers constituted a concerted campaign to revive religion throughout New England.[40] Even as the dispersal of the ministry onto the expanding frontier strained clerical networks, the campaign proved extremely effective, as local revivals erupted, then regional, and finally the Great Awakening.

Before becoming rector of Yale in 1726, Elisha Williams, like many of his youthful colleagues, started his career preaching to the people of a small, newly settled, frontier town, where opportunities for an ambitious preacher such as Williams seemed few. But Williams's pastorate at Newington, Connecticut, while short-lived, proved unexpectedly rewarding. By the time he left for Yale, he had achieved, it was said, great success as a preacher, exciting people to experience conversion and producing many new members for the church.[41]

The advent of revivalists such as Williams, combined with their rapid entry into the profession, contributed to another important development, the revitalization of church membership. Even before the new generation of preachers became established, admissions were on the rise, but thereafter the trend intensified. Decades before the Great Awakening, church membership had ceased to decline, and was growing rapidly by the time the Great Revival arrived.

In churches gathered before 1660, such as New Haven First and Milford First, church membership began to show marked improvement after the early 1680s, and until the late 1740s remained well above the numbers recorded during the mid-century decades (see Tables 3.4 and 3.5). Admissions increased steadily during the early eighteenth century,

TABLE 3.4.   Admissions in Milford First Church, 1639–1774

Years	Number	Years	Number
1639–1644	73	1710–1714	75
1645–1649	17	1715–1719	34
1650–1654	17	1720–1724	47
1655–1659	1	1725–1729	61
1660–1664	10	1730–1734	62
1665–1669	57	1735–1739	104
1670–1674	42	1740–1744	81
1675–1679	25	1745–1749	7
1680–1684	19	1750–1754	25
1685–1689	24	1755–1759	0
1690–1694	26	1760–1764	0
1695–1699	63	1765–1769	9
1700–1704	53	1770–1774	74
1705–1709	25		

peaking during the late 1730s. As communicants flowed into the two churches, adherence rates rose, increasing in New Haven, for example, from twenty average years per member in 1640–1670 to thirty average years in 1670–1740. Only in the aftermath of the Great Awakening did membership in both churches decline dramatically.[42]

Among churches founded at successive intervals after 1659, and before 1740, the pattern of admissions was, in general, the same (see Table 3.6). After 1710, new membership in these churches increased steadily every five years except for one period, 1730–1735, and in all cases was climbing steeply when the Awakening hit. After 1720, in fact, admissions moved in unison from one parish to the next, a phenomenon certainly reflective of the widening influence of the concerted campaign of the revivalists. It is clear that the Awakening marked the end, not the beginning, of broad popular participation in the Connecticut church;

TABLE 3.5.   Admissions in New Haven First Church, 1639–1774

Years	Number	Years	Number
1639–1644	94	1710–1714	66
1645–1649	88	1715–1719	67
1650–1654	12	1720–1724	60
1655–1659	21	1725–1729	64
1660–1664	36	1730–1734	49
1665–1669	7	1735–1739	170
1670–1674	0	1740–1744	58
1675–1679	2	1745–1749	21
1680–1684	9	1750–1754	21
1685–1689	133	1755–1759	23
1690–1694	73	1760–1764	51
1695–1699	74	1765–1769	34
1700–1704	46	1770–1774	63
1705–1709	43		

after it had ended, the ministry had little success reviving the religion among the people for the next twenty-five years.[43]

Aside from the influx of youthful revivalists into the population, the upsurge in church membership had sources unrelated, in part, to the actions of the ministry. One was demographic growth, which, by accelerating after 1700 (see Table 3.1), greatly enhanced the pool of people available for communion. Another was economic expansion, which improved the people's ability to subsidize ecclesiastical facilities, despite the increasing tax burden accompanying the proliferation of new churches.[44] A third involved the development of increasingly elaborate, informal networks of communication linking parent churches to their offspring, located usually in the subdivided areas of towns. As these secondary churches, connected often by family ties to primary churches, increased in number after 1690,[45] the potency of revivalism increased too, since groups

TABLE 3.6. Mean Admissions in Connecticut, by Date of Church Founding, 1639–1770*

	Churches Founded				
	1636–1659	1660–1709	1710–1719	1720–1729	1730–1739
Years	Number	Number	Number	Number	Number
1639–1644	83.5				
1645–1649	52.5				
1650–1654	14.5				
1655–1659	11.0				
1660–1664	23.0				
1665–1669	32.0	33.0			
1670–1674	21.0	12.7			
1675–1679	13.5	10.3			
1680–1684	14.0	9.5			
1685–1689	61.0	8.3			
1690–1694	45.0	31.0			
1695–1699	75.7	24.4			
1700–1704	36.0	30.2			
1705–1709	32.7	20.5			
1710–1714	67.7	23.5	22.7		
1715–1719	38.0	32.5	21.5		
1720–1724	44.7	33.1	24.3	28.3	
1725–1729	48.6	52.0	39.5	30.9	
1730–1734	46.3	37.5	26.2	25.0	17.2
1735–1739	102.0	58.9	45.4	37.5	32.0
1740–1744	58.7	89.2	52.0	69.2	44.5
1745–1749	11.0	10.2	10.4	18.7	12.4
1750–1754	17.7	11.0	7.4	16.9	10.1
1755–1759	12.0	12.5	17.0	11.2	13.5
1760–1764	22.0	19.6	14.0	10.2	15.9
1765–1769	18.0	18.2	11.3	16.1	15.8

NOTE: *The number of churches in each set is as follows: 1636–1659 (3); 1660–1709 (14); 1710–1719 (7); 1720–1729 (13); 1730–1739 (12).

could mobilize behind the movement through the "widening webs of interdependence and intercommunication."[46]

Finally, the rise of church membership was rooted in changes in the "natural" constituency of Connecticut churches, involving, initially, the family. While church membership had originally been widespread, uniting nearly all inhabitants of towns such as New Haven and Milford, it became increasingly confined to families related by blood to each other and to the first church members. This Puritan tribalism, as Edmund Morgan calls it, by distancing the church from the world, may have initially had a negative impact on church growth, contributing even further to declension. But over the long run it helped the church rebound from its malaise, and it did so in several ways. First, Puritan tribalism was not the destructive force of Morgan's *The Puritan Family,* but a highly constructive one, serving, through the unusually high birth rates characteristic of New England, as a constantly expanding source of new members with customarily high rates of adherence. Such was the case in Milford, for example, where only thirty-six kin groups accounted for 693 church members over a 130-year period, and for at least three out of every four communicants from one decade to the next.[47] Second, Puritan tribalism, by linking family rituals to those of the church, created new outlets for lay piety. Thus, people tended to join the church upon marriage or parenthood, or as spouses and siblings together, or in their capacity as eldest sons, carrying on the religious traditions of the line.[48] Finally, Puritan tribalism made the church attractive to people who might otherwise have remained away, promising to give core family members an identity in an increasingly heterogeneous society. For these people, Puritanism and the church had become "our religion" and "our church."[49]

One important source of Puritan tribalism was the core family, consisting of the planters of towns and their progeny, who tended to stay put in the same place across the generations, to intermarry, and to create socially dominant kin networks. They also managed to sustain, from one generation to the next, the faith of their forefathers and foremothers, joining the church far more frequently than newcomers. Their importance to religious renewal is clear in the case of Milford's nucleus of thirty-six church families, 83 percent of whom had settled the town before 1660 and 78 percent before 1650.[50] For these families, "our church" was another way of saying, "our town."

Another important source of Puritan tribalism was the ministry, which had little to do with its initiation, but much to do with its propagation, once its importance to the church had become clear, that is. As Cotton Mather observed in 1690, "the Continuation of churches is ordinarily to depend on the Addition of Members out of the Families already incorporated thereinto," and on the basis of this understanding, he and his fellow ministers sought to harness tribalism for the good of revivalism, even to the extent of advising sinners to get into "a good family," as servants or by marriage.[51] This also entailed cultivating the patronage of that "church within a church, leading men whom we privately consult before we offer anything to a public debate and vote."[52] By appealing directly to this special constituency, the ministry contributed significantly to the renewal of church membership.

But Puritan tribalism had a darker side, as the ministry knew only too well. Though it produced converts for the church, it limited the pool of them as well, confining it to local clans. Even in the midst of rising admissions, the limits of tribalism were apparent, as the majority of inhabitants remained, in most parishes, unchurched.[53] In towns where population turnover was increasing, the restrictions it imposed upon clerical evangelism were even clearer. Tribalism, at the same time, was nearly as exclusive as it was inclusive in practice, keeping people incompatible with the brethren, or they with them, away from the church. When Benjamin Wadsworth, in *Dialogue between a Minister and his Neighbour,* has the "neighbor" say, "I have some Difference & Controversy with some of my Neighbours, and know not how to sit down with them in so holy an Ordinance as the Lord's Supper is," he was clearly revealing the divisive properties of Puritan clanishness.[54] Many people never made it as far as Wadsworth's neighbor, however, being denied communion altogether by brethren jealously guarding access to the sacrament. As early as the 1640s, Thomas Hooker had complained of the "curious inquisitions and niceties" of the laity at admission, and in the 1660s John Woodbridge, the Killingworth, Connecticut, minister, criticized the fraternity for being "such a heavy stone at the ministers leggs that they cannot fly their own course."[55] By the early eighteenth century, such complaints had become more common. Thus, in 1725 Eliphalet Adams blasted the New London brethren for scrutinizing prospective communicants, and for the wrong reasons. "Particularly in Admission into & Excommunication out of the Church," he told them, you should work with your minister in "promoting of Order, Advancing the Interest of Christ's Kingdom and the giving an Efficacy to the Exercise of discipline, and by an unaccountable stiffness, affect to lay obstructions in the way of those who are approaching to the Lord's Table, after a due examination hath been made of their qualifications, and no just reason . . . can be alledged to hinder their admission (as some have done, whither to show their odd & Stubborn Humour, or else to try to what height their power and Privilege might be carried)."[56]

But Puritan tribalism, as Adams surely knew by 1725, was highly selective in its antagonism, affecting men much more than women, and separating families along the lines of gender, even as it brought them into the church. As Connecticut records show, no sooner had tribalism surfaced, than a second change occurred in the "natural" constituency of the church—the feminization of church membership. Like tribalism, the feminization of membership had an ambivalent effect on the church, raising its appeal though within a narrower constituency. As the timing of the two developments suggests, they were closely interrelated, as closely as women's lack of a public role was to their certain ineffectiveness as tribal antagonists.

As Table 3.7 shows, the crucial decade for the feminization of church membership was the 1660s, when the proportion of women admitted to communion increased sharply, reaching nearly 70 percent of total admis-

TABLE 3.7.   Percentage of Women Entering Connecticut Church, by Date of Church Founding, 1639–1770

Years	Churches Founded				
	1636–1659	1660–1679	1680–1699	1700–1709	1710–1719
1639–1649	42				
1650–1659	49				
1660–1669	67				
1670–1679	66	58			
1680–1689	61	59			
1690–1699	63	61			
1700–1709	64	52	65	59	
1710–1719	65	63	56	67	61
1720–1729	61	64	63	54	60
1730–1739	63	62	59	61	60
1740–1749	63	47	58	54	59
1750–1759	69	55	76	61	53
1760–1769	66	56	72	61	52

NOTE: All data are given in percentages.

sions. From 1670 to 1740 the proportion in separate sets of churches, while fluctuating, tended to hover around 60 percent, until the Great Awakening, that is. While the general appeal of the revival was not to men, as some historians have argued, it did lead to declining female preponderance at admission in two sorts of churches, those founded in 1660–1679 and in 1700–1709, producing actually in the former case more men than women for the church.[57] Except in this one instance, the Awakening did not stem the tide of feminization.

Like tribalism, the feminization of church membership was perceived as a mixed blessing by the ministry. Once they realized women's important contributions to the revitalization of their churches, they rewarded them with public recognition and praise, publishing numerous sermons on the sources and nature of their piety.[58] Yet they still held firm to the priority of male regeneration, and thus tended to view the conversion of women less as an end in itself than as the means to solving the nagging problem of declining male membership. As one preacher told an audience of women, the wife's "fidelity is no where more signalized, than in her sollicitude for the eternal salvation of her husband. . . . Thus every Paul may have Women that labour with him in the Gospel. Vast opportunities are those that a Woman has to bring over her Husband unto real and serious Godliness."[59] But such appeals backfired; by mobilizing women for the church, the ministry, whatever its real purpose, reinforced the trend toward feminization.

In the face of male resistance to conversion, the ministry turned to yet another group within the population, the young. For several generations conversion had been considered an experience of adulthood, confined to people who had reached the "years of discretion" and could "discern the Lord's body."[60] But the revivalists of the early eighteenth century scrapped tradition and undertook a campaign to convert the young. The youth of New England were now viewed as a vehicle of church growth, not, as in former times, as an obstacle to it. Eliphalet Adams was typical of the ministers of the period in his optimistic assessment of youthful religiosity. A "chosen Generation" would begin "as a tender Plant & a Root out of a dry ground," he imagined in 1734, and "in the stead of a stiffnecked, rebellious People" there would "rise up in time to come, a more obsequious, willing & religious Race, that shall make it their business to please, serve and honour God."[61]

The clerical campaign for the souls of the young elicited a widening response, as increasing numbers of teens and unmarried people entered the church. With the advent of the Great Awakening, as many as 50 percent of new members in some parishes were under the age of twenty, and as many as 75 percent in some places were single.[62] Many of the youthful converts were also male, and thus a prize catch in the eyes of ministers. While mining for youth, the clergy struck a rich vein, for well over 50 percent of Connecticut's white population was under the age of twenty.[63] Their reward was the greatest revival in the colony's history.

As was the case with Puritan tribes and women, the religious mobilization of Connecticut's youth and the related rise in church membership brings to light an undiscovered quality about the Puritan system: its remarkable resilience and capacity for self renewal. While external forces affected the system, including European pietism, its recovery from declension was accomplished pretty much on its own. In the face of growing social diversity, the "natural" constituency of the church was continuously repartitioned, in a way that heightened its appeal to various groups within the expanding population. While this process of differentiation had negative effects upon the religion, producing a certain amount of intolerance of outsiders, it also enabled the church to adjust to rapid social change. Had the system been staid and unbending, there would have been no live orthodoxy for George Whitefield to tap upon his arrival in New England in 1740, and thus no Great Awakening.

There was an ironic side to the system, however, and this was in greatest evidence during the Great Awakening. When initiating the mission to the young, ministers set out to do what they had always done, alter the church's social appeal to advance its general appeal. But this time the outcome was totally unexpected, and explosive as well. The youth converting during the Awakening proved to be neither "a more obsequious" nor a more "willing" people than their forebears, as Adams hoped they would. Instead, in the heat of the revival the young lost patience with the formalism of their elders and ministers, accusing them increasingly of spiritual deadness. In their quest for spiritual truth, the young discovered the pure, covenanted church of their Puritan ancestors, using the insight to justify separatist movements and separatist churches.[64] At the same time, the church, now acutely and painfully aware of the rebelliousness of regenerate youth, reunited around the tried and true practice of Puritan tribalism. The result was a generation of popular apathy toward the church.

How the religion then went about reviving itself in the period following the American Revolution is an issue beyond the purview of this essay. Suffice it to say that recent practitioners of the new religious history, in their studies of the social sources of the Second Great Awakening, have uncovered patterns of church growth that echo those from our own era, suggesting that the New England way of religious renewal was its most enduring legacy to American evangelism, even amidst the lengthening influence of scientific revivalism.

NOTES

1. William G. McLoughlin, ed., *Lectures on Revivals of Religion by Charles Grandison Finney* (Cambridge: Harvard University Press, 1960), 9.

2. Edmund S. Morgan, *The Puritan Family: Religion and Domestic Relations in Seventeenth-Century New England,* rev. ed. (New York: Harper & Row, 1966), 185.

3. David D. Hall, "On Common Ground: The Coherence of American Puritan Studies," *William and Mary Quarterly* 44 (April 1987), 193–229.

4. Paul Lucas, *Valley of Discord: Church and Society Along the Connecticut River Valley, 1636–1725* (Hanover, N.H.: University Press of New England, 1976).

5. Christine Leigh Heryman, *Commerce and Culture: The Maritime Communities of Colonial Massachusetts, 1690–1750* (New York: W. W. Norton, 1984).

6. Harry S. Stout, *The New England Soul: Preaching and Religious Culture in Colonial New England* (New York: Oxford University Press, 1986), 6.

7. Hall, "On Common Ground," 223.

8. Among the most comprehensive studies of church membership in colonial society are Patricia U. Bonomi and Peter Eisenstadt, "Church Adherence in the Eighteenth-Century British Colonies," *William and Mary Quarterly* 39 (April 1982), 245–286; Patricia U. Bonomi, *Under the Cope of Heaven: Religion, Society, and Politics in Colonial America* (New York: Oxford University Press, 1986); and Gerald F. Moran, "The Puritan Saint: Religious Experience, Church Membership, and Piety in Connecticut, 1636–1776" (Ph.D. diss., Rutgers University, 1974).

9. For an analysis of these arguments, see Robert Currie, Alan Gilbert, and Lee Horsley, *Churches and Church Goers: Patterns of Church Growth in the British Isles Since 1700* (Oxford, England: Clarendon Press, 1977), 14–20.

10. For the agenda of the new religious history relative to colonial America, see John Butler, "The Future of American Religious History: Prospectus, Agenda, Transatlantic *Problematique,*" *William and Mary Quarterly* 42 (April 1985), 167–183.

11. I have consulted the following church records, almost all of which are in manuscript or on microfilm at the Connecticut State Library, Hartford: New London, Stonington, North Stonington, Preston, Suffield, Norwich, Bozrah, Colchester First and Second, Groton, Woodstock, Voluntown, Wethersfield, New Milford, Middletown, West Hartford, Old Lyme, Hartford, Branford, Windham, Woodbury, Franklin, Canterbury, East Haddam, New Canaan, Brooklyn, Fairfield, Westfield, Cromwell, Mansfield, Trumbull, Redding, Lebanon, Milford, Portland, Somers, Griswold, Scotland, Putnam, New Hartford, Bloomfield, Bethlehem, Columbia, Cheshire, and Stratford. See, also, Franklin B. Dexter, *Historical Catalogue of the Members of the First Church of Christ in New Haven, Connecticut (Center Church) A.D. 1639–1914* (New Haven, Conn: published by the author, 1–12.

12. *Memoirs of Captain Roger Clap* (Boston, 1807), 7.

13. Charles J. Hoadley, ed., *Records of the Colony and Plantation of New Haven, From 1638–1649* (Hartford: Case, Tiffany and Co., 1857), 15–16.

14. Edmund S. Morgan has argued that "probably, a large number of the first church members became so before the new admission system was completely set up." But church membership records suggest otherwise. Morgan, *Visible Saints: The History of a Puritan Idea* (New York: New York University Press, 1963), 137.

15. Dexter, *Historical Catalogue of First Church New Haven,* 1–12.

16. Milford First Congregational Church Records, I, 2.

17. George Leon Walker, *History of the First Church in Hartford, 1633–1883* (Hartford, Conn., 1884); Linda Auwers Bissell, "From One Generation to Another: Mobility in Seventeenth-Century Windsor, Connecticut," *William and Mary Quarterly* 31 (January 1974), 79–110; and Lucas, *Valley of Discord,* 33. See also the table in Darrett B. Rutman, "God's Bridge Falling Down: 'Another Approach' to New England Puritanism Assayed," *William and Mary Quarterly* 19 (July 1962), 409, fn.3.

18. Dexter, *Historical Catalogue of First Church New Haven,* 9–19.

19. Milford First Congregational Church Records, I, 3–8.

20. Milford First Congregational Church Records, I, 8–20; "The List allowed for 1686," Milford, Conn., Register of Deeds, 1714–1718, vol. 5, 78–79, microfilm copy. See also Gerald F. Moran, "Religious Renewal, Puritan Tribalism, and the Family in Seventeenth-Century Milford, Connecticut," *William and Mary Quarterly* 36 (April 1979), 245–246.

21. New London First Congregational Church Records, I, 5–7; Woodbury First Congregational Church Records, 1: 10–16; William Cothren, *History of Ancient Woodbury, Connecticut . . . ,* 3 vols. (Waterbury, Conn.: Bronson Brothers, 1854–1879), 1: 816–817; and Stonington First Congregational Church and Ecclesiastical Society Records, 3: 1–8. The data on parish ratables come from *The Public Records of the Colony of Connecticut,* 15 vols., vols. 1–3, ed. J. H. Trumbull; vols. 4–15 ed. C. J. Hoadley, (Hartford: Press of Case, Lockwood, and Brainard, 1850–1890), 2: 290; 3: 66–67; 4: 33.

22. "Controversy in the Church in Hartford, 1655–59," Connecticut Historical Society *Collections,* 2 (Hartford, 1870), 53–125; Lucas, *Valley of Discord,* 43–50; 63–64; and Robert G. Pope, *The Half-Way Covenant: Church Membership In Puritan New England* (Princeton, N.J.: Princeton University Press, 1969), 82–87.

23. Frances M. Caulkins, *History of New London, Connecticut* 2d ed. (New London, Conn.: Published by the author, 1860), 111–117; 131–145; and Lucas, *Valley of Discord,* 52–53; 61–62; 129–131.

24. David D. Hall, *Worlds of Wonder, Days of Judgment: Popular Religious Belief in Early New England* (N.Y.: Knopf, 1989), 139–140.

25. Jackson Turner Main, *Society and Economy in Colonial Connecticut* (Princeton, N.J.: Princeton University Press, 1985), 97–98; Lucas, *Valley of Discord,* 10.

26. H. Richard Niebuhr, *The Kingdom of God in America* (New York: Harper & Row, 1937), esp. ch. 1.

27. Pope, *Half-Way Covenant,* chs. 1–3; Williston Walker, *The Creeds and Platforms of Congregationalism* 2d ed. (Boston: Pilgrim Press, 1969), 308–309.

28. Lucas, *Valley of Discord,* 133–134.

29. Information on church foundings comes from The General Association of Connecticut, *Contributions to the Ecclesiastical History of Connecticut* . . . (New Haven, Conn.: William L. Kingsley, 1861).

30. See David D. Hall, *The Faithful Shepherd: A History of the New England Ministry in the Seventeenth Century* (Chapel Hill: University of North Carolina Press, 1969), esp. ch. 8.

31. James W. Schmotter, "The Irony of Clerical Professionalism: New England's Congregational Ministers and the Great Awakening," *American Quarterly* 31 (Summer 1979), 157.

32. Schmotter, "Irony of Clerical Professionalism," 157.

33. Information on Connecticut clergymen comes from Frederick Lewis Weis, *The Colonial Clergy and the Colonial Churches of New England* (Baltimore, Md.: Genealogical Publishing Co., 1977).

34. At five-year intervals in 1700–1740, the rate of clerical dismissals as a percentage of existing pulpits was as follows: 0.0, 2.5, 0.0, 1.2, 5.2, 2.5, 4.3, and 1.0.

35. Weis, *Colonial Clergy.*

36. Lucas, *Valley of Discord,* chs. 8–9; Kevin M. Sweeney, "River Gods in the Making: The Williamses of Western, Massachusetts," in Peter Benes, ed., *The Bay and the River* (Boston: Boston University Press, 1982), 101–116.

37. Richard Warch, *School of the Prophets: Yale College, 1701–1740* (New Haven, Conn: Yale University Press, 1973), 304–305.

38. Warch, *School of the Prophets,* 272–273.

39. Robert Middlekauff, *The Mathers: Three Generations of Puritan Intellectuals, 1596–1728* (New York: Oxford University Press, 1971), 306.

40. Michael J. Crawford, "The Invention of the American Revival: The Beginnings of Anglo-American Religious Revivalism, 1690–1750" (Ph.D. diss., Boston University, 1978), 40.

41. Warch, *School of the Prophets,* 131–134.

42. Dexter, *Historical Catalogue of First Church New Haven,* 20–87; Milford First Congregational Church Records, 1: 10–42.

43. See note 11.

44. Main, *Society and Economy in Colonial Connecticut,* esp. ch. 10.

45. In 1630–1660 all new churches were established in new towns, were coterminous with them, and were thus primary in nature. The situation changed after 1660, when the secondary church, formed from a schism, a peaceful separation, or settlement in outlying areas of preexisting parishes, became predominant. See *Contributions to the Ecclesiastical History of Connecticut, passim,* and also the church records listed in note 11 and the numerous local histories found in the Connecticut State Library.

46. Stout, *The New England Soul,* 188.

47. Milford First Congregational Church Records, I, 2–42; Barbour Collection

of Connecticut Records, Births-Marriages-Deaths, Connecticut State Library; James Savage, *A Genealogical Dictionary of the First Settlers of New England . . .* 4 vols. (Boston: Little, Brown, 1860); and the numerous genealogies contained in the Connecticut State Library. For the names of the early settlers of Milford with the dates of their arrival, see Federal Writers Project, *History of Milford, Connecticut, 1639–1939* (Bridgeport, Conn.: Press of Braunworth & Co., 1939), 7–8.

48. For a detailed study of the familial circumstances accompanying admission to Connecticut churches, see Moran, "The Puritan Saint," esp. chs. 5, 8–10. For Massachusetts, see in particular Mary MacManus Ramsbottom, "Religious Society and the Family in Charlestown, Massachusetts, 1630 to 1740" (Ph.D. diss., Yale University, 1987).

49. Currie et al., *Churches and Church Goers,* discuss how some groups acquire from a particular religion an identity in a heterogeneous society, where identity is otherwise problematic. See especially ch. 3, "Churches and Their Constituencies."

50. See note 47.

51. Morgan, *The Puritan Family,* 181.

52. Benjamin Colman, quoted in J. William T. Youngs, Jr., *God's Messenger: Religious Leadership in Colonial New England, 1700–1750* (Baltimore, Md.: Johns Hopkins University Press, 1976), 95.

53. In Milford, for example, the ratio of male members to townsmen, after reaching a low of 36 percent in the late 1660s, climbed to 46 percent in the 1690s, a level at which it remained well into the eighteenth century. As is clear, despite the improvement in the church's outreach, however, a majority of inhabitants remained unchurched, a situation that obtained in other parishes as well. In 1731 in Woodbury, for example, 44 percent of the taxables belonged to the church; in 1729 in Pomfret fifty males in a society of one hundred families were church members; and in 1729 in Killingly eighty men in a village of 180 families were communicants. More inclusive churches were Windham, where in 1729, 127 males were church members in a town of 150 families, and Groton, where in 1727, 124 people were communicants in a town of 200 families. Moran, "Religious Renewal, Puritan Tribalism, and the Family in Milford," 245–246; Woodbury First Congregational Church Records, 1: 10–70; Woodbury Town List for the Year 1731, Woodbury Town Hall; Groton First Congregational Church Admissions and Baptisms, 3–5; "Extracts of Letters," Connecticut Historical Society *Collections,* 3 (Hartford, Conn.: 1892), 291–298; and Franklin B. Dexter, *Extracts from the Itineraries and Other Miscellanies of Ezra Stiles . . . With a Selection from his Correspondence* (New Haven, Conn.: 1916), 295; 297–298.

54. Benjamin Wadsworth, *Dialogue between a Minister and his Neighbour* (Boston, 1724), quoted in Hall, *Worlds of Wonder, Days of Judgment,* 159.

55. Thomas Hooker, *A Survey of the Summe of Church-Discipline* (London, 1648), pt. 3, 5; John Woodbridge, Jr., to Richard Baxter, 31 March 1671, "Correspondence of John Woodbridge, Jr. and Richard Baxter," *New England Quarterly* 10 (September 1937), 574.

56. Eliphalet Adams, *The Works of Ministers, Rightly to Divide the Truth* (New London, 1725), 33.

57. Cedric Cowing, "Sex and Preaching in the Great Awakening," *American Quarterly* 20 (1968), 624–644.

58. Lonna M. Malmsheimer, "Daughters of Zion: New England Roots of American Feminism," *New England Quarterly* 50 (September 1977); Margaret Masson, "The Typology of the Female as a Model for the Regenerate: Puritan Preaching, 1690–1730," *Signs: Journal of Women in Culture and Society* 2 (1976); Laurel Thatcher Ulrich, "Vertuous Women Found: New England Ministerial Literature, 1668–1735," *American Quarterly* 28 (Spring 1976), 20–40; and Ulrich, *Good Wives: Image and Reality in the Lives of Women in Northern New England, 1650–1750* (New York: Knopf, 1982).

59. Cotton Mather, *Ornaments for the Daughters of Zion, or the Character and Happiness of a Vertuous Woman* (Cambridge, Mass., 1692), 96.

60. Hall, *The Faithful Shepherd,* 62.

61. Eliphalet Adams, *A Discourse Shewing New London* (New London, 1734), 31.

62. In nine Connecticut churches, for example, the percentage of males admitted under the age of twenty went from four in 1710–1719 to eight, nine, and twenty-seven respectively for the next decades in 1720–1749, while the percentage of females added under the age of twenty increased from nine in 1710–1719 to twenty-one, twenty-six, and forty-seven respectively for the next three decades in 1720–1749. These calculations are based on the church, town, and vital records of Milford, New London, Canterbury, Stonington, North Stonington, Woodbury, Suffield, Preston, and Stonington East.

63. *The Public Records of the Colony of Connecticut,* 14, 485–491.

64. C. C. Goen, *Revivalism and Separatism in New England, 1740–1800* (New Haven, Conn.: Yale University Press, 1962).

4

Enthusiastic Piety—

From Scots-Irish Revivals

to the Great Awakening

For students of American religious history, the Great Awakening has been a chronological watershed dividing the colonial and revolutionary periods. Just as seventeenth-century scholarship has been preoccupied with the developments of distinct colonies or regions, historians have seen post-1740 British North America as a single unit: provincial America. To the Great Awakening has been attributed the massive upheavals and changes of the eighteenth century, not only within church organizations but in the very infrastructure of society and culture. Yet despite the immense historical importance attributed to the Great Awakening, no one has produced a comprehensive, synthetic work that attempts to pull together all the facets of this phenomenon into a united, coherent interpretation. Instead, a canonical view has been formulated piecemeal. This mainstream interpretation has been little more than a set of assumptions, almost cliches, displayed and challenged as continued research produces results inconsistent with the canon.[1]

This canon begins with a definition: What was the Great Awakening, when did it occur, and where? The general understanding has been that the Great Awakening was a brief, intense period of religious revival that "swept through the American colonies between 1739 and 1742," but recent authors have shown that this definition does not work.[2] Several colonial regions, for example Germantown, Pennsylvania, and South Carolina, remained untouched by revival throughout the eighteenth century.[3] Moreover, the chronological boundaries are far too narrow. Jonathan Edwards's revival at Northampton began in 1734, John Tennent awakened Freehold, New Jersey, in 1729, and Solomon Stoddard had enjoyed "harvests of souls" in western Massachusetts as early as the 1680s.[4] And, as Rhys Isaac has pointed out, the revival did not even come to Virginia until the late 1750s and 1760s.[5] Still, historians should not reject "Great Awakening" as a descriptive label. They must merely recognize that this was not an event but an eighteenth-century movement. Many revivals, not one, sprang up in various regions such as New England, Pennsylvania, and the Chesapeake, and the narrowest chronological boundaries would probably be 1725 to 1765.

The standard interpretation also explores the effects of the Great Awakening upon colonial society. The revival has been seen as an innovative force, transforming cities and countryside, uniting disparate peoples in preparation for the American Revolution. In his *Religion and the American Mind,* Alan Heimert argued that the Awakening's evangelical/Calvinist theology was a primary influence upon revolutionary and, later, Jacksonian ideology.[6] Nathan Hatch, however, claimed that the most important religious aspects of this political ideology were those beliefs shared by both Old and New Lights, and Gary Nash could argue a connection between politics and religious upheaval only for Boston.[7] From a different perspective, both Harry Stout and Rhys Isaac have argued that the Awakening provided new sets of symbols and methods of communication by which the revolutionary ideology was spread throughout New England and Virginia.[8] Given the problems of evaluating the Awakening's effect upon society, perhaps a different approach is needed. I suspect that the developments of the eighteenth century first produced widespread religious revivalism and then a political revolution.

In examining the causes of the Awakening, the canon offers two possibilities. Perry Miller's model has been adopted, with minor alterations, by nearly all intellectual historians. Enamored of the brilliance of Jonathan Edwards, Miller and his followers examined the theology of Edwards as a reworking of seventeenth-century Calvinism to meet the intellectual challenges, especially scientific discoveries, of the eighteenth century. This is particularly apt since Edwards was also the identified leader of the Awakening in New England and produced the best theological apologia for revival.[9] One obvious flaw is that Edwards did not preach outside the bounds of New England. This model also implies that lay persons understood science and theology, perceived a conflict between them, and therefore embraced a new, synthetic ideology: a level of sophistication probably beyond the average lay person. Furthermore, this model implies a shared ideology among all the revival participants, and it is demonstrable that the participants did not share a theology. Unless one is willing to remove Virginia, North Carolina, and many of the middle-colony communities from the scope of the Great Awakening, scholars are left with an ideologically diverse revival whose participants accepted a spectrum of theologies, from conservative Calvinism to Methodist Arminianism.

An alternative explanation views the Great Awakening as the convergence of disaffected lower classes against the elite. Although this hypothesis has produced some remarkable and fascinating historical scholarship, it too has been unsatisfactory. In an early exposition of this thesis in denominational terms, Martin Lodge posited anticlericalism as a primary force driving the community toward Awakening in the middle colonies.[10] Unfortunately, Lodge's argument depends upon the colonial environment's providing new challenges to which immigrants responded. He hardly considers the possibility that clerical-lay tensions may have had deep roots in the Old World, and he neglects the fact that the religious environment in the middle colonies was like the one left behind by the large numbers of immigrants from Ireland.

However, linked to in-depth, regional investigation, the results of this social research have been contradictory. James Walsh and Gerald Moran both found that class conflict had very little impact upon the revival in two Connecticut towns, while Harry Stout and Peter Onuf demonstrated a central role for social factors in the same region.[11] Rhys Isaac discovered in the Great Awakening an organizing principle for lower-class protest in Virginia.[12] And Gary Nash found evidence in his examination of colonial cities to support this conclusion for Boston and question its applicability to New York and Philadelphia.[13] A more important problem with this hypothesis is that the Great Awakening was, first and foremost, a religious movement. Any explanation must account for that element. When Gilbert Tennent quoted Paul's letter to the Ephesians, "Awake thou that sleepest, and arise from the dead," he was not warning the lower classes of their oppression; he was calling all persons to awaken to their sinful state, and realize the grace offered by Jesus Christ.[14]

In the past decade, some historians have rediscovered the religious aspects of the Awakening, bringing new light to known clergy, like James Davenport and Gilbert Tennent, and pointing up the importance of unknown men, such as Andrew Croswell.[15] These studies offer insights about clergymen, but they do not address the behavior of the masses swept away by eighteenth-century enthusiasm. Too often historians consider religion only in terms of churches and clergy. The traditional, denominational model constructs an analysis of institutional and clerical behavior from institutional and ministerial records and calls this religion, forgetting the vast lay membership of the church as well as those outside the church. Within this model, any approach to the laity, even an exploration of the impact of religion on society and culture, must assume simplistic, illogical connections between the institutional church and its lay adherents: if the preacher is Calvinist, all his hearers must be Calvinists.

Besides equating church with religion, these investigations have been restricted by the availability of institutional and clerical documents and the relative absence of any other sort of records. Historians outside the denominational track who are interested in popular behavior also confront this dearth of evidence. When documents do exist, historians explore them in detail, but a few autobiographical accounts cannot explain popular behavior.[16] In search for breadth, social historians have collected quantifiable data on the population. Yet, despite the excellence of the data, measurable behavior is often too far from religion to be useful.

Minimizing the religious heart of the Awakening takes the revival out of its historical context. Any description not focused upon participants' spiritual experience would have rendered the Great Awakening unrecognizable to those participants. A better approach explores the religious system through its four distinct, interdependent components: shared beliefs, common rituals, institutional manifestations, and participants. The first component includes both the theology self-consciously developed and debated by the intellectual elite and a popular belief system gleaned by the uneducated laity from that original theology expressed in sermons, catechisms, and creeds. Rituals are symbolic behavior patterns established and reinforced by the community. They include both community events and private behaviors that most community members act out individually. For example, private prayer would not necessarily be a common ritual, but Puritan devotional exercises as structured in seventeenth-century New England would be, since individuals followed privately a behavioral formula laid out in the prescriptive literature. The institutional component includes the churches—their policies, organizations, record keeping, and procedures for maintaining the institution. Finally, the participants, both the leaders and their followers, must be placed within the social context.

Intellectual historians have focused upon the theology of the Great Awakening. Although some scholars have proclaimed a monolithic ideology, their combined efforts disprove this argument: orthodox Calvinism and Methodist Arminianism are ideological opposites. Nonetheless, adherents to both systems participated in the Awakening, indicating that ideology was a secondary characteristic of the movement. Social historians have discovered the similar discrepancies in studying people. In some regions economic or social status was critical; in others it hardly seemed to matter. But if the Awakening cannot be described across the colonies as a social protest within a religious structure, neither can it be seen as an institutional phenomenon. Some churches, such as the Baptist church, wholeheartedly supported it; some groups, such as the Quakers, absolutely rejected the revival; and others, notably Congregationalists and Presbyterians, sported both advocates and detractors.

What remains as the defining characteristic of the Great Awakening is ritual; and, indeed, whenever scholars discuss the Awakening, their investigative environment is, generally, the ritual behavior. "Flamboyant and highly emotional preaching made its first widespread appearance . . . and under its impact there was a great increase in the number and intensity of bodily effects of conversion—fainting, weeping, shrieking, etc."[17] This coincides nicely with eighteenth-century perceptions of this movement. Contemporary divines were so awed by the extent and intensity of the "great and general awakening" that for several months they published a periodical entitled *Christian History,* comprising reports on the great works of religion throughout the colonies and the British Isles.[18] The eighteenth-century writers explained such phenomenon as simply the work of the Holy Spirit. Twentieth-century scholars still begin with descriptions of this frenetic behavior, though they then discover its cause through a relationship to some other factor, be it class protest or philosophy. Yet whatever the explanation, all observers and historians agree that revival participants everywhere swooned, shouted, panted, and convulsed. They indulged in ritualized spontaneity, traditional creativity, structured outbursts; they behaved in patterns so easily recognized and compared that contemporary observers and scholars alike have since proclaimed "A Great Awakening."

Reconsidering the Great Awakening with an emphasis upon rituals establishes a different series of questions. An anthropological construct of a religious system is a useful starting point for exploring the Great Awakening. It significantly broadens the field of inquiry by connecting, through analyses of ritual structures, aspects of eighteenth-century culture that have appeared only tangentially connected—for example, elite philosophy and popular behavior. Furthermore, this model is historically appropriate since it places the revival into its original context and provides a code through which the historical evidence can be sorted and analyzed.[19]

To understand the seventeenth and eighteenth centuries, I propose a framework that incorporates both substantive and anthropological elements. Briefly stated, a religious system is a conceptual system concerned with God, humanity, and the supernatural and natural worlds. These ideas are discussed in a consciously constructed language and theology so that they attain the stature of reality in the mind of the believer. These beliefs are expressed and acted out through symbolic, communal language and behavior patterns or rituals that bring emotional satisfaction to the participants.

In constructing this definition I have appropriated Clifford Geertz's well-known emphasis upon the symbolic quality of the system and his discussion of religion as fulfilling a specific function.[20] Including a substantive dimension is an historical accommodation to the ideological reality of the seventeenth and eighteenth centuries. Nevertheless, a definition of religion that incorporates only belief systems about a deity need not restrict investigation, for example by excluding scientific beliefs; but it does establish the way in which both sacred and scientific truths are incorporated within the conceptual schema. Since these beliefs are expressed in behavioral as well as linguistic symbols, the study of religion must include an analysis of its symbol systems. Through these symbols, religion shows how the believer does and should perceive the world.[21] A public witnessing to conversion, for example, certainly revealed the path of sin and salvation experienced by the individual believer, but it also laid out in blueprint fashion expectations for the unconverted.

The purpose of religion—emotional satisfaction or, in eighteenth-century terms, spiritual fulfillment—might be explained as answering the ultimate question of human existence. As Geertz explains, "the Problem of Meaning . . . is a matter of affirming, or at least recognizing, the inescapability of ignorance, pain, and injustice on the human plane while denying that these irrationalities are characteristic of the world as a whole."[22] Religion helps account for the dilemmas of human experience by arranging those contradictions within a cosmic order. For example, the religion of seventeenth-century Scotland, as discussed later, developed certain rituals that helped people cope with a level of political chaos that might otherwise have destroyed their identities and communities.

Therefore, an anthropological approach offers several advantages in understanding the Great Awakening. It involves placing ideas to one side in order to trace the origin of these rituals as behavior patterns and to decode the symbolic structure of the ritual. Participants and their society are thus examined in relation to this symbolic behavior, and community identity as revealed in ritual can be explored in terms of institutional religion. Ideological issues can then be addressed in light of their role in the symbolic network as well as in terms of the quality and content of contemporary philosophy.

This essay traces the history of those symbol systems or rituals that characterized the Great Awakening in the middle colonies, rituals that will be identified as revivalism. Thus, it seems appropriate to establish some key features of revivalist rituals. The first is size, or number of participants; revivalist meetings were not necessarily large on an absolute scale, but they were characteristically larger than regular weekly or monthly services. Many revivals had thousands attending, but considering the wide geographic dispersion of the residents of eighteenth-century rural America, an attendance of several hundred at a gathering must be considered quite large. A second feature was the duration of such meetings. Religious services during this period lasted, at most, three to four hours; a revival meeting might easily last three to four days and could extend to weeks. The most remarkable feature was the intense emotional response, often manifested in bizarre physical symptoms, to preachers and pastors who by rhetoric and style deliberately provoked such response. The purpose of the ritual was to free participants from guilt, shame, and sin, enabling them to identify with a community that was loving, good, and protected by God—in the revivalists' own language, to experience conversion. Participation in the ritual allowed participants to attain or retain membership in the desired community, while the community itself was elevated to a holier status.

Exploring the source of revivalism first requires identifying the revivalists. Colonial Presbyterian records, with their rich social data and amazingly detailed accounts of internal battles, may provide great stories of the struggle for holiness, but the scant information on the revivalists themselves reveals very little. However, one salient factor does stand out: the numerical predominance of Scots-Irish congregants among those Presbyterians. In addition, most pre-Whitefield revivals in the middle colonies occurred in Scots-Irish congregations. These two factors indicate that a transatlantic framework would provide the best analytical model. Recently, historians have come to realize that cultural developments in the colonies often resulted from the transference of Old World structures and values to new geographic and social environments. Traditional religious historians, such as Leonard Trinterud, have long suggested a German impact upon Gilbert Tennent and other New Light clergy in the middle colonies, but this early emphasis was generally clerical.[23] Recently, John Frantz and Elizabeth Fisher have traced the cultural migration of religious patterns among German settlers in the middle colonies.[24] And in the Presbyterian arena, Elizabeth Nybakken has demonstrated the clerical/institutional connections between the colonial and Scottish and Irish Presbyterian churches, while Ned Landsman has discussed the Scottish character of the revival in Freehold, New Jersey.[25] The success of these scholars and the reality of Scots-Irish predominance among middle colony Presbyterians point up the possibilities of a transatlantic study. Perhaps the cultural roots of revivalism should be sought in seventeenth-century Ireland and Scotland.

In fact, the revivalist rituals so popular in mid-eighteenth-century America can be traced back to the religious enthusiasm of the Six-Mile-Water Revival, a seven-year revival that broke out among the original Scottish settlers of Ulster.[26] This revival began in 1625 with the preaching of a crazy man, James Glendinning (at least everyone said he was crazy, and he did light out for Asia searching for the seven somethings), who preached hellfire and brimstone sermons. He was soon followed by other Scottish ministers in Ulster. People were severely affected by these sermons, responding not only with screaming, panting, and crying, but with the physical contortions and convulsions that have come to be associated with revivalism. This response was interpreted as the terror and panic of persons who had realized the horrible punishment awaiting them in hell. Later, the truly saved would discover the joys found in an assurance of salvation. In words reminiscent of George Whitefield's 1740 revival, Andrew Stewart, in 1625, said,

> I have seen them myself stricken, and swoon with the Word—yea, a dozen in one day carried out of doors as dead, so marvellous was the power of God smiting their hearts for sin, condemning and killing; and some of those were none of the weaker sex or spirit, but indeed some of the boldest spirits . . . the stubborn—who sinned and gloried in it, because they feared not man—are now patterns of sobriety, fearing to sin because they fear God; and this spread through the country to admiration, so that, in a manner, as many as came to hear the word of God, went away slain with the words of his mouth.[27]

At the same time in western Scotland there was such excitement at Stewarton that the phrase "Stewarton Sickness" was coined. This revivalism was a bona fide Scots-Irish phenomenon, existing simultaneously in northern Ireland and western Scotland in the early seventeenth century.[28]

The obvious similarities between this early, seventeenth-century revivalism and the enthusiasm experienced during the Great Awakening introduces the possibility of cultural transference. If, following upon the 1625 revival, Scots-Irish religiosity was characterized by these intense, emotional rituals, then the appearance of revivalism among colonial Scots-Irish Presbyterians would become a predictable, comprehensible phenomenon. In fact, the continuation of this pattern can be followed through the seventeenth century in light of the importance of religious form and the tremendous significance of its connection with political questions. During these years, Great Britain was enmeshed in severe political turmoil that deeply involved the common people, Scottish and Irish, Protestant and Catholic. The English persecuted the Presbyterian Scots in Scotland and Ireland at different times, for different reasons, so that many families moved back and forth from Ulster to west Scotland, depending upon the severity of regional persecution. The established Church of Scotland changed structure every twenty years or so from Episcopalian to Presbyterian and back again. In the middle of it all Cromwell entered, turned church and government upside down, and congregants and ministers turned one against another as they fought to determine and dominate the character of the Scottish religious community. In the midst of this chaos, partly because of it, the religious pattern continued.

Field conventicles in Scotland began in the 1650s during Cromwell's rule, when large numbers of Presbyterians were persecuted for supporting Charles II. They continued and grew to giant size following the restoration of the latter to the throne in 1660, for Charles II broke his covenant with the Scots, made the Church of Scotland Episcopalian (again), and persecuted nonconforming Presbyterians.[29] As many as two thousand people would gather together in open fields while a Presbyterian minister harangued them. Sometimes conventicles lasted several days; they generally lasted all night at least. They drew highly emotional, violent responses from the participants. People loved them, sometimes saving up baptisms or marriages for the conventicle preachers. There were also conventicles in Ireland, brought by the angry young ministers persecuted in Scotland. Because Presbyterians were only unofficially tolerated in northern Ireland, and because the conventicles aroused the angry attention of the government and brought punishment, the clergy in Ireland rejected conventicles and tried to suppress them. The laity, however, clamored for more and rejected their own pastors as cowards.[30] Emerging in response to English efforts to curtail Scottish religion, these conventicles were obviously celebrations of Scottish national identity against the English as much as they were spiritual revivals. However, over time the religious character was strengthened rather than weakened by the political overtones. Being Scottish meant being Presbyterian, and being Presbyterian meant being Scottish, and Presbyterianism included revivalism.

While the conventicles generally disappeared with the accession of William III in 1689 and the establishment of the Presbyterian Church of Scotland, there continued another ritual connecting the early revivals with the Great Awakening—the elongated communion service.[31] These were exceedingly popular during the years of the Six-Mile-Water Revival and continued through the seventeenth century. One great 1630 revival has come down as the "Communion at Shotts."[32] Communion services lasted anywhere from three days to a full week. They began with a fast day, either Wednesday or Thursday, and ran from Friday evening until Monday, sometimes Tuesday afternoon. Often an additional fast day would be celebrated the following Thursday. Moreover, the Sundays before and after the service were set aside as special beginning and ending points. These services attracted tremendous attendance from the surrounding countryside, many of whom would stay Saturday through Monday, and stay awake all night. A service would require at least three and as many as eleven ministers. There was also that exciting, emotional response. These services were held continuously from 1625 to 1760 at least. In western Scotland, communions were a central part of the 1742 revivals following Whitefield's visit.

Both the conventicles and the ritual communion services demonstrate the continuation of a religious pattern from the north of Ireland of 1625 onward more than a hundred years, but not because of the superficial similarity of noise, fainting, and convulsions. The conventicles, communions, and other rituals exhibited a common ritual structure, a structure that has long been recognized by religious historians: the conversion experience. These celebrations were congregational conversion experiences, the renewal and purification of the community.

Most historians are familiar with the Augustinian conversion as it was experienced by the Puritans. The standard conversion experience includes realization of sin, death, and the coming eternal punishment; repentance; acceptance of grace and reconciliation with God; ecstasy at union with God; realization of the peace of the new life combined with doubts, relapses, and reassurances.[33] Among New England Puritans, this experience was a personal journey for each individual. All who had experienced conversion were labeled visible saints and could join the church; all others were excluded as sinners. By the very nature of their membership, New England churches retained their purity.

Presbyterians also believed that individuals could experience salvation and union with God, but they rejected the polity of visible sainthood. Any attempt to determine a person's state of grace they found presumptuous of divine authority.[34] Presbyterian church membership, therefore, was only marginally restricted; although a few flagrant sinners were denied entrance, most people within the congregation's geographic boundaries were granted the responsibilities and privileges of membership. Presbyterians knew that all congregations must include many who were damned, but the church recognized no earthly means of excluding the unsaved. For Presbyterians, therefore, the community conversion experience served the necessary function of purifying a community that by nature included sinners as well as saints.

Communion services began with a fast day emphasizing the unworthiness of the congregation. Each individual was to examine his or her conscience. Throughout the week preceding the communion, the elders had visited all congregants, testing their understanding and examining their holiness. Those who were cleansed and prepared received a concrete sign of approval, a token admitting them to communion. As the real work of conversion began, sermons focused upon sin, death, and eternal punishment. Friday evening and Saturday the community repented. On that Saturday the elders held a special session meeting to bring all sinners publicly before the congregation and convince them of their sins. Sinners who repented would make public confession that same afternoon and receive the community's absolution. Any who refused were ostracized and denied admission to the sacrament. Thus, many people came before the congregational court who otherwise might not have bothered, for they wanted to be included in the service, in the community. The community was thence pure and reconciled to God.

On Sunday occurred the distribution of communion, which could easily last ten to twelve hours. During that time ministers would preach on the joys of Christ's atonement and the glory shining upon the elect, the children of God. Sermons were either gentle and loving, or rhapsodic and ecstatic. Congregants on Monday and Tuesday experienced the final conversion steps, a combination of sermons of thanksgiving for the new peace with exhortations to remain firm and not fall away from God's grace.

Conventicles provided a similar ritual purification of the community, although this conversion was not merely spiritual. Many community sins could be best described as betraying Scottish culture and identity, a judgment aimed not merely at individual congregations or even presbyteries, but at the entire Scottish nation. After 1660, the Scots could actually see impure elements within their nation—the English and their ways, both political and religious. Efforts that might easily be characterized as political took on a deep religious significance, and the political and the religious causes were united, with each side gaining greater strength and legitimacy from this union.

The conversion structure of the conventicle is well-displayed in Michael Bruce's 1672 sermon *The Rattling of the Dry Bones*.[35] A gifted young conventicler, Bruce preached a rhetorical masterpiece that demonstrated the full intent and method of such preachers. The sermon's text recounted the tale of Ezekiel commanded by the spirit of God to stand before a vale filled with dry bones and prophesy to the bones. "So I prophesied as I was commanded: and as I prophesied, there was a noise, and behold a shaking, and the bones came together, bone to his bone. And when I beheld, lo, the sinews and flesh came up upon them, and the skin covered them above: but theere was no breath in them." The prophet then addressed the four winds, and the breath of God entered the new men so that they "stood upon their feet, an exceeding great army."[36] This text incorporated glorious images and auditory constructions, "bone to his bone," sinews and flesh, breath and shaking. It provided a self-justification: Michael Bruce, prophet to the Scottish people, his actions commanded by God. The valley of dry bones was an excellent biblical type for the church, for the bones were the bones of individual persons. Bruce even selected texts from the middle of the narrative reflecting his conviction that the work of reformation was still in progress.

In his sermon, Bruce railed at individual sinners while he pointed up the dead condition of the Scottish church. "What sense have ye of your own sad and dolefull Condition? and of the Sad Case and Condition of the Kirk of GOD, and of the sin that hath brought Sad Judgments on you both? . . . Is there any *noise* or *shaking* among your Dry Bones?"[37] Thus he rendered the sins of individuals, condemned by all, equivalent to the current state of the church and used the emotional energy aroused in the cause of each to support the other. Sinners converted for the good of Scotland, and they fought for the Church of Scotland to benefit their own souls.

This culture, with its rituals of congregational conversion and political purification, was brought to the New World and immediately had an impact. The Scots-Irish arrived in large numbers in the late 1720s, and in 1730 the first revival broke out in John Tennent's congregation in New Jersey.[38] Revivals continued in the middle colonies throughout the 1730s. However, in the winter of 1739 and 1740, George Whitefield's preaching tour really set everything off, and the Great Awakening began in earnest.

George Whitefield, a twenty-four-year-old follower of John Wesley, came to the British colonies preaching repentance and salvation. Everywhere he went he attracted audiences of thousands; his hearers wept, screamed, and fainted at his words. People who came to heckle stayed to be converted. He preached out of doors—most churches would not admit him, and indeed his audiences were too large to be enclosed in a building.[39] His voice could be heard a half-mile away as he called people to God.[40] He would stay only a few days in any location, for he felt himself called to a career of itinerant preaching. Because he appealed to the unchurched as well as to active religionists, because he could disturb the hostile and the complacent as well as the virtuous and the anxious, George Whitefield was important to the Awakening. Yet, how successful, ultimately, could he have been without the support of the resident congregations? The region had already experienced sporadic revivals; they were primed for more. And long after Whitefield had left an area, the pastors carried on the work of conversions. In fact, regions without this predisposition toward revivalism experienced no major religious transformation. Whitefield came; he conquered; he moved on; and the excitement disappeared. It cannot be coincidence that the Awakening explodes in Virginia in the 1750s, long after Whitefield's tour, but coterminous with the Scots-Irish immigration and the arrival of revivalist preachers, Presbyterian and later Baptist.

Rituals observed in seventeenth-century Ireland and Scotland are easily recognized in the eighteenth-century middle colonies. In 1739, a Boston printer published *Sermons on Sacramental Occasions,* a collection of communion sermons by Gilbert Tennent, William Tennent, and Samuel Blair.[41] The construction and identification of these ten sermons by date and use indicate clear continuation of the communion service. The headings describe a service of at least three days, with at least three ministers present. Moreover, the content and structure of the sermons themselves closely resemble those of similar works by Irish ministers.

The first two sermons were delivered consecutively before the communion. In the opening sermon, Gilbert Tennent invited all hearers to participate; he emphasized both the benefits attending the sacrament and the sin of staying away. Refusal to join showed "rebellion" and "ingratitude," "unkindness to God and barbarous Cruelty to our Own Souls." For the sake of the community, all but the openly sinful must take part. "Therefore let every honest experienc'd Persone, come to the Table of the Lord; in Obedience to his Command, that they may profess his Name before Man and Angels, and renew their Covenant with him here, in order to enjoy him hereafter."[42] The second preparatory sermon began the journey through the conversion experience. Here, Gilbert Tennent described his listeners' sense of sinfulness, self-knowledge of their inability to change, and the discovery of Christ. The truly converted would labor after Christ, close with him, and work to preserve their enjoyment of grace. He ended with the warning that "such as have not experienced the foresaid Characters of a True Claim to the Riches of Christ, wou'd not venture to come to the Lord's holy Table, in their present Condition, least they eat and drink judgment to themselves."[43] Although this appears to contradict the first sermon, the two together cover alternate aspects of the same process. All good Christians must join the congregational communion; any who lacked holiness were debarred as bringing defilement.

On this same occasion, Samuel Blair preached one of the Sunday sermons during the distribution of the bread and wine. He explored the scheme of Christ's atonement, the great love that brought salvation to sinners. More a meditation upon Christian mysteries than an exhortation, the Sunday sermons hoped to give participants further, prayerful stimulation toward a union with Christ, rather than to push forward a course of action.[44] Finally, there were the Monday-after Thanksgiving pieces, well represented by William Tennent's sermon. Gone were all references to original sin, suffering, the need for repentance; gone too were the images, metaphors, and ecstatic celebration of salvation. Instead, Tennent reminded participants that it was "the Duty of all those that have received the Lord Jesus to walk in him." He exhorted his listeners to follow the commandments deliberately and constantly; he warned against backsliding. Now that conversion was complete, there was little to do except keep people steadfast.[45]

In recounting the revival of his congregation at Faggs Manor, Samuel Blair noted that many experienced their ecstasies at the communion table, including one woman who spoke of "unspeakable Ravishments of her Soul at a Communion Table."[46] As late as 1764, Samuel Buell described a Lord's Supper held in East Hampton that included a time of trial so that individuals could prepare for receiving the sacrament. Not only had ninety-eight persons joined the church beforehand, but twenty-four congregants experienced conversion during the trial days of the service itself.[47] While many historians have emphasized the itineracy of Whitefield or the preaching of Gilbert Tennent, both laity and clergy retained the centrality of sacramental rituals in their community experience. In and through these rituals, the Great Awakening flourished.

Why this phenomenon should gel at this particular time is best explained by comparing the colonial revival with the Scottish and Irish experience. After the establishment of the Presbyterian church as the national Church of Scotland in 1690, conventicles lost their political overtones. Many ministers saw no reason to continue the revivals. With the advent of enlightenment philosophy, clergy became less interested in the life of the community than in the life of the individual. Moreover, coming out of the enlightenment, they translated inward, personal growth as intellectual development. The laity continued to want and participate in revivals; yet because the leading Irish and Scottish clergy were not supportive, revivalism became peripheral, involving far greater proportions of lay persons than clergy. Clerics, no longer fighting the political establishment, were not concerned with the maintenance of a pure community. Since they could see no other justification for revival meetings, and, in fact, found them rather ridiculous, the clergy wanted the meetings stopped. The laity clearly disagreed and the services must have continued, as shown by the numerous complaints and resolutions attempting to curtail "disorderly" meetings.[48]

In the colonies the Scots-Irish clergy faced an entirely different situation. They met and worked with old New Englanders (serving English Presbyterian churches in New York and New Jersey) who espoused a theology and piety that focused upon individual conversion. Revivals not only converted communities, they also served to lead individuals through the conversion experience. Like the European clergy, the American clergy focused upon the individual. However, by emphasizing experiential piety instead of intellectual achievement, they discovered a rational justification for revivalism. This was just as well, since it was evident to Presbyterian ministers on both sides of the question that the laity wanted revival. It might also be added that in return for their theology, the New Englanders discovered a method of hastening and punching up the conversion experience for their own congregations.

The clergy in Scotland and Ireland turned to individual reform. This was opposed by the laity, who were exceedingly conservative and who joined, en masse, splinter groups that still emphasized community rituals. One group, the Seceders, even invoked the old Scottish identity agenda of the late seventeenth century.[49] In the colonies the intellectual elite discovered a new theology that emphasized the individual quest, rendering revivalism a means for achieving individual conversion. In this, clergy and laity agreed, which was important since the laity were committed to revivalism.

The power of the laity to have its way should not be underestimated. The records of the Presbyterian church in Ireland and the middle colonies are filled with examples of congregations demanding that their ministers abide by their decision, sometimes forcing uncooperative ministers out. In both communities, ministers' salaries were paid by voluntary contribution, and congregations learned quickly that the power of the purse provided solid control.[50] A congregation unhappy with its pastor would often refuse to pay his salary. The minister would then complain to the presbytery; the congregation would apologize but defend itself, claiming poverty. This might continue for several years, until the congregation owed the pastor three or four years salary. The minister would finally ask to be dismissed, and the presbytery would grant it, reminding the congregation that they still owed him his salary. The congregation would then ask for another preacher and be told to pay the first. They would pay, perhaps, ten pounds as a sign of good faith, and a substitute pastor would be sent out every three months or so. A year later the congregation would ask to hear a candidate; the presbytery would instruct them to pay the previous minister. They would pay another ten pounds and get the candidate. Usually, they could ordain a second minister to their pastorate having paid about 25 percent of what they owed the first. If they were patient and cunning, a congregation could get what they wanted.[51]

The laity were also masters of the disciplinary structure. In Ireland, in the 1720s, charges of heresy were brought against several ministers because they would not subscribe to the Westminster Confession. These

These nonsubscribers claimed that this type of subscription offended the principle of liberty of conscience. There was no evidence that they actually held heretical beliefs, and year after year the nonsubscribing ministers were acquitted. Church leaders tried to quiet and reassure the dissenting voices; but at every assembly meeting the laity raised the issue. In 1726, several ministers were thrown out of the Irish Presbyterian establishment. Many critics claimed that this was entirely the work of the laity.[52]

In Pennsylvania, William Orr offended his congregation at Nottingham by preaching unorthodox theology, and the laity brought charges against him and forced him out of the church.[53] Or consider the case of Thomas Creaghead, pastor of a congregation in Pesqua, Pennsylvania.[54] He committed a grave sin. One Sunday he refused to give his wife communion. Within the structure of the communion service, all matters of sin should be cleared up the Saturday before. Mrs. Creaghead had been given a token, clear evidence of her worthiness, yet her husband refused her as a sinner. When challenged after the service, he claimed that she was indeed a sinner: her sin had been committed the night before, it was a matter between the two of them, and he could not in good conscience give her communion. (In later accounts, she explained that she had acted out of anger; her stepson's family was visiting without her consent and she didn't like the family and they were a bother and so forth. No one noted the exact nature of her sin.)

The congregation was scandalized. Creaghead had made a mockery of the Lord's Supper. How dare he presume to sit in judgment of anyone, much less use this service to act out his own anger! He had ruined the entire occasion. He had opened the community to the scorn of its neighbors. He had polluted the community, and he had brought this gross pollution into the most sacred of times and acts, the sacrament. He had tempted God to vengeance. Creaghead was brought before the presbytery on these charges, and during these hearings his family problems were worked out. He admitted his error, gave full repentance, and paid a hefty penance of suspension. When he was restored to the ministry, the congregation warned the presbytery that it would not allow him in the pulpit. Without a challenge, the presbytery dismissed him from the congregation. While it was without a pastor the presbytery sent Creaghead as substitute; the congregation refused to allow him into the pulpit for even one day. There was no discussion. No recriminations. He was gone.

This was power. This was an authority that the laity claimed and fought for. During the years of the Great Awakening, congregations used whatever power they could muster or manipulate to bring pastors to support revival or, alternatively, to bring them to account. In 1740, the congregation at the Forks of Brandywine brought formal charges against pastor Samuel Black, including seeking after his stipend, complaints of fatigue during pastoral visiting, little regard to the promotion of family and personal piety, intemperance, lying, and sowing sedition. The accusations of immoral conduct, particularly intemperance to which Black confessed, appeared well-founded.

A second look, however, reveals that the true dissatisfaction lay in Black's antagonism toward the revival. The people had recently enjoyed the uninvited preaching of revivalist David Alexander. Black "lied" when he first condemned field preaching, then praised it, then expressed renewed distrust. He "sowed sedition" when he censured congregants who supported the revivalists. In fact, the last two charges were summarized as "his seeming to oppose the work of God appearing in ye land." The presbytery exonerated Black and condemned the "malice" with which the laity had brought the charges.[55] And while the congregation did not succeed in removing Samuel Black from the pastorate, they did, a few years after, secede completely from Donegal and join a pro-revival presbytery.

When the revivals first began and the journeys of itinerants provided the laity with a choice, the people had no problem choosing and making their choices known. Wherever revivalist preachers went, they stirred people up against their own pastors. The Presbyterian church split into two synods in 1744, to reunite only fourteen years later. However, during that fourteen years, the full strength of lay power was realized. When the church split, congregations were served by twenty-six Old Light (antirevivalist) ministers and twenty-eight New Light (pro-revivalist) ministers; the church reunited with twenty Old Light ministers and seventy-two New Light ministers. Of course, the New Light Synod of New York could train native-born ministers in its new College of New Jersey, and this ability to supply ministers could have accounted for its popularity. Yet in those localities where an Old Light cleric was installed, New Light congregations often split off, requesting independently supply from a New Light presbytery.[56]

In the Old Light Philadelphia Presbytery the congregations of Hopewell/Maidenhead, Cohanzy, Neshaminy, and Great Valley split. The New Light Presbytery of New Brunswick was stretched to its limit as one church after another asked to join. In 1740, the congregations from Tinnacum, Newtown, and Tredyffrin asked to be dismissed from Philadelphia and joined to New Brunswick, a request that was granted.[57] Four congregations in New Castle placed themselves under the care of New Brunswick, while five communities—New Castle, Drawyers, Red Clay,

Elk River, and Pencader—divided. And in Donegal, almost every congregation either withdrew from the presbytery or experienced a separation.

As early as 1740, the congregation at Nottinham asked to be removed from the jurisdiction of Donegal.[58] The following year, Adam Boyd reported that most of his congregation had left him for the sake of the New Brunswick preachers.[59] In 1743, William Bertram reported that his congregation at Londonderry had split. Several members had brought a complaint against Bertram and his elders for admitting John Ireland as an elder, for Ireland had often criticized, insulted, and harassed people attending the revivals.[60] And poor John Thomson, the most stalwart, vocal opponent of the revival, proved unable to collect his salary for three years until, in 1744, he was granted a release from Chestnut Hill.[61]

Many have laid the revivals at the feet of preachers like George Whitefield, but Whitefield's successes were fleeting unless supported by a New Light pastor. In the middle colonies at least, while ministers were committed to leading their people to salvation, the people were committed to revival, rewarding those clerics who shared or simply accepted that commitment. From 1739 onward, the opponents of the Awakening had complained about the enthusiasm and excesses of the revivalists, but their primary complaints were directed against the laity. Gilbert Tennent's *Danger of an Unconverted Ministry* had called upon the laity to reject those ministers who had not experienced conversion. The rejected clergy shouted their indignation at the laity, who had no right to pass judgment on clergy, as well as at Gilbert Tennent and other ministers who encouraged the laity.[62] Both clerical parties recognized the laity as a major force, but the New Light ministers considered the laity as a valid force. While the Old Lights tried vainly to assert some pastoral authority, the revivalists used their abilities to build a power base.

Perhaps the most exciting transformation was the change in the rituals themselves and their effects upon the participants. Although the overall structure remained the same, the focus of the revival moved from community purification to individual conversion. As long as the godliness of the community remained at the center of the experience, popular energy and activity were devoted outward to community. This reinforced a cultural tradition that solidified interpersonal networks and further strengthened group identity. In the seventeenth century this was explicitly recognized as a goal. As this tradition crossed the Atlantic, it enabled the Scots-Irish to maintain their cultural integrity: this time in the face of a pluralistic environment. The Freehold congregation, for example, had experienced serious competition between old residents, originally hailing from New England, and the new arrivals. Through revival the Scots and Scots-Irish were able to gather the old New Englanders into a Scots-Irish culture.[63]

However, even as the revivals reinforced cultural integrity, a new meaning was laid over the experience. Revival participants still experienced ritualized conversion, but the goal had moved from community purification to individual salvation. With this raising up of the individual believer, revival participants experienced confirmation of an already healthy respect for their own power. Although Irish congregations had already demonstrated an amazing facility in the use of their power as a group, the Great Awakening further enhanced this power by reinforcing the individual's spiritual journey. Not only were lay persons powerful as a group; individually each could claim a personal relationship with God and thus a clear right to make religious decisions.

Since religious leaders in eighteenth-century Scotland and Ireland had no longer felt that the community was threatened by a hostile, encroaching government and culture, they moved away from rituals that they found unnecessary. They believed, in fact, that by intensifying group structures these rituals worked against the personal development so dear to the enlightened clergy. But in pursuing their goals these clergymen found themselves in opposition to their own people. Continuation of the revivals became a question of power, since in their efforts to stop them ministers were attempting to force lay persons to reject popular rituals. By failing to stop these revivals, the Scottish clergy increased institutional power but weakened pastoral authority.

In the middle colonies, those ministers who would not support the Awakening lost the support of many among their pastorate, while the New Light ministers increased their own influence and authority. Yet in treating those celebrations not as community conversions, but as roads to individual salvation, the New Light pastors forfeited their own indispensability. Godly preachers did play a necessary role in religious process, but it was the believer, with his or her direct, personal relationship with God, who claimed the right to make that decision. As Gilbert Tennent discovered, though too late, persons in control of their own salvation could wrest control of church and society.[64] Thus, in the continuation of those rituals, the Great Awakening represented in its truest sense neither the abilities of the clergy nor even the success of clerical-lay cooperation, but the ultimate power of the laity.

NOTES

1. This historical discussion previously appeared in a somewhat different form in the Introduction to my *Triumph of the Laity: Scots-Irish Piety and the Great Awakening* (New York: Oxford University Press, 1988), 1–10. Here the essay

has been expanded to incorporate recent research and to explain further the anthropological approach taken.

2. Alan Heimert and Perry Miller, eds., *The Great Awakening* (Indianapolis: Bobbs-Merrill, 1967), xiii. See also Richard L. Bushman, ed., *The Great Awakening: Documents on the Revival of Religion 1740–1745* (New York: W. W. Norton, 1970); and Sidney Ahlstrom, "The Century of Awakening and Revolution," in his *A Religious History of the American People* (New Haven: Yale University Press, 1972), 261–284. An excellent essay summarizing and challenging recent historiography is Jon Butler's "Enthusiasm Described and Decried: The Great Awakening as Interpretive Fiction," *Journal of American History* 69 (September 1982): 305–325.

3. Stephanie Grauman Wolf, *Urban Village: Population, Community, Family Structure in Germantown, Pennsylvania, 1683–1800* (Princeton: Princeton University Press, 1976); Jon Butler, *Power, Authority, and the Origins of American Denominational Order* (Philadelphia: American Philosophical Society, 1978); and William Howland Kenney, "Alexander Garden and George Whitefield: The Significance of Revivalism in South Carolina, 1738–1741," *South Carolina Historical Magazine* 71 (1970): 1–16.

4. Edwin Scott Gaustad, *The Great Awakening in New England* (New York: Harper & Row, 1957); Patricia Tracy, *Jonathan Edwards, Pastor: Religion and Society in Eighteenth-Century Northampton* (New York: Hill and Wang, 1980); and Ned Landsman, "Revivalism and Nativism in the Middle Colonies: The Great Awakening and the Scots Community in East New Jersey," *American Quarterly* 34 (Summer 1982): 149–164. For Solomon Stoddard's impact on western Massachusetts, see Tracy, *Jonathan Edwards, Pastor,* 13–70. Other research on Stoddard has focused upon his influence on Edwards, particularly his conversion model. See, for example, Philip F. Gura, "Sowing for the Harvest: William Williams and the Great Awakening," *Journal of Presbyterian History* 56 (1978): 326–341; and David Laurence, "Jonathan Edwards, Solomon Stoddard, and the Preparationist Model of Conversion," *Harvard Theological Review* 72 (October 1979): 267–283.

5. Rhys Isaac, *The Transformation of Virginia, 1740–1790* (Chapel Hill: University of North Carolina Press, 1982).

6. Alan Heimert, *Religion and the American Mind from the Great Awakening to the Revolution* (Cambridge: Harvard University Press, 1966). See also Cedric B. Cowing, *Great Awakening and the American Revolution: Colonial Thought in the Eighteenth Century* (Chicago: University of Chicago Press, 1971); William G. McLoughlin, "The Role of Religion in the Revolution: Liberty of Conscience and Cultural Cohesion in the New Nation," in Stephen G. Kurtz and James H. Hutson, eds., *Essays on the American Revolution* (New York: W. W. Norton, 1973), 197–255; McLoughlin, " 'Enthusiasm for Liberty': The Great Awakening as the Key to the Revolution," *Proceedings of the American Antiquarian Society* 87 (1977): 69–85; and Mark Noll, "Ebenezer Devotion: Religion and Society in Revolutionary Connecticut," *Church History* 45 (September 1976): 293–307.

7. Nathan O. Hatch, *The Sacred Cause of Liberty: Republican Thought and Millennium in Revolutionary New England* (New Haven: Yale University Press,

1977); and Gary B. Nash, *The Urban Crucible: Social Change, Political Consciousness, and the Origins of the American Revolution* (Cambridge: Harvard University Press, 1979).

8. Harry S. Stout, "Religion, Communication, and the Ideological Origins of the American Revolution," *William and Mary Quarterly* 34 (October 1977): 519–541; and Rhys Isaac, "Dramatizing the Ideology of Revolution: Popular Mobilization in Virginia, 1774 to 1776," *William and Mary Quarterly* 33 (July 1976): 357–385.

9. Perry Miller, *Jonathan Edwards* (1949; New York: Meridian Books, 1959); Miller, "Jonathan Edwards and the Great Awakening," in his *Errand into the Wilderness* (New York: Harper & Row, 1959), 153–166; Heimert, *Religion and the American Mind;* and Tracy, *Jonathan Edwards, Pastor.*

10. Martin E. Lodge, "The Great Awakening in the Middle Colonies" (Ph.D. diss., University of California, Berkeley, 1964). James Schmotter has applied this argument to New England's clergy in "The Irony of Clerical Professionalism: New England's Congregational Ministers and the Great Awakening," *American Quarterly* 31 (Summer 1979): 148–168.

11. James Walsh, "The Great Awakening in the First Congregational Church of Woodbury, Connecticut," *William and Mary Quarterly* 28 (October 1971): 543–562; Gerald F. Moran, "Conditions of Religious Conversion in the First Society of Norwich, Connecticut, 1718–1755," *Journal of Social History* 5 (Spring 1972): 331–343; Harry S. Stout and Peter Onuf, "James Davenport and the Great Awakening in New London," *Journal of American History* 70 (December 1983): 556–578; and Onuf, "New Lights in New London: A Group Portrait of Separatists," *William and Mary Quarterly* 37 (October 1980): 627–643.

12. Isaac, *Transformation of Virginia.*

13. Nash, *Urban Crucible.*

14. Ephesians 5:14, King James Version. This verse was used by Gilbert Tennent in his *A Solemn Warning to the Secure World from the God of Terrible Majesty* (Boston: S. Kneeland and T. Green for D. Henchman, 1735).

15. Richard Warch, "The Shepherd's Tent: Education and Enthusiasm in the Great Awakening," *American Quarterly* 30 (Summer 1978): 177–198; Milton J. Coalter, *Gilbert Tennent, Son of Thunder: A Case Study of Continental Pietism's Impact on the First Great Awakening in the Middle Colonies* (Westport, Conn.: Greenwood Press, 1986); David C. Harlan, "The Travail of Religious Moderation: Jonathan Dickinson and the Great Awakening," *Journal of Presbyterian History* 61 (1983): 411–426; and Leigh Eric Schmidt, " 'A Second and Glorious Reformation': The New Light Extremism of Andrew Croswell," *William and Mary Quarterly* 43 (April 1986): 214–244. Patricia Tracy's biography of Edwards also fits this model since she focuses upon his pastoral career. Moreover, because she sees the pastorate as a relationship, she can also explore lay activity in Northampton. So too, in their essay "James Davenport and the Great Awakening," Stout and Onuf first explore Davenport's career and then use the book burning as a means through which to examine the laity.

16. For examples of conversion narratives, see Kenneth P. Minkema, "A Great Awakening Conversion: The Relation of Samuel Becker," *William and Mary*

Quarterly 44 (January 1987): 121–126; and Michael J. Crawford, "The Spiritual Travels of Nathan Cole," *William and Mary Quarterly* 33 (January 1976): 89–126.

17. Ahlstrom, "Century of Awakening," 286–287.

18. Thomas Prince, ed., *The Christian History* (Boston: S. Kneeland and T. Green, 1744–45).

19. Isaac's work cannot be categorized with most social history, for it does not share the quantitative method. Although Isaac does not focus upon religion in his analysis of Virginia society and culture, he is concerned with symbol systems, including religion. His methodology, derived from Clifford Geertz, is the best model available for the historian borrowing from anthropology. Other essays using a ritual model in exploring popular behavior include Stout and Onuf, "James Davenport and the Great Awakening" and Gregory H. Nobles, "In the Wake of the Awakening: The Politics of Purity in Granville, 1754–1776," *Historical Journal of Western Massachusetts* 8 (1980): 48–62.

20. Clifford Geertz, "Religion as a Cultural System," in Michael Banton, ed., *Anthropological Approaches to the Study of Religion* (Edinburgh: Tavistock Publications, 1966), 1–46.

21. Ibid., 5.

22. Ibid., 24.

23. Leonard J. Trinterud, *The Forming of an American Tradition* (Philadelphia: Westminister Press, 1949). See also Coalter, *Gilbert Tennent, Son of Thunder.*

24. John B. Frantz, "The Awakening of Religion among German Settlers in the Middle Colonies," *William and Mary Quarterly* 33 (April 1976): 266–288; and Elizabeth B. Fisher, " 'Prophesies and Revelations': German Cabbalists in Early Pennsylvania," *Pennsylvania Magazine of History and Biography* 109 (July 1985): 299–333.

25. Elizabeth I. Nybakken, "New Light on the Old Side: Irish Influences on Colonial Presbyterianism," *Journal of American History* 68 (March 1982): 813–832; and Landsman, "Revivalism and Nativism in the Middle Colonies."

26. For first hand accounts of the revival, see: Robert Blair, *The Life of Mr. Robert Blair,* Thomas M'Crie, ed. (Edinburgh: The Wodrow Society, 1848); John Livingstone, *A Brief Relation of the Life of Mr. John Livingston,* Thomas Houston, ed. (Edinburgh: John Johnston, 1848); and Andrew Stewart, "History of the Church of Ireland," in Patrick Adair, *A True Narrative . . . of the Presbyterian Church in Ireland (1623–1670)*, with introduction and notes by W. D. Killen (Belfast: C. Aitchison, 1866).

27. Stewart, "History of the Church of Ireland," 317.

28. Blair, *Life of Blair,* 19.

29. Excellent records of individual conventicles can be found in the presbytery records of Paisley, Auchterarder, and Lanark. Another good source is the correspondence of James Sharp, Bishop of St. Andrews and Alexander Burnet, Bishop of Glasgow and later of St. Andrews with the Duke of Lauderdale, located at National Library of Scotland. All Scottish church records are located at the Scottish Record Office.

30. For accounts of conventicles in Ireland, see the records of the Laggan Meet-

ing. All Irish church records are part of the collections of the Presbyterian Historical Society, Belfast, stored at Union Theological College, Belfast.

31. Early communion services are described in Blair, *Life of Blair,* 71; Livingstone, *Brief Historical Relation,* 78–80; Stewart, "History of the Church of Ireland," 320–321; Carluke (Scotland) Session Records, 1645.

32. Robert Wodrow, *A short account of the life of . . . D. Dickson* Edinburgh, 1764) as cited in George Grubb, *An Ecclesiastical History of Scotland* (Edinburgh: Edmonston and Douglas, 1861), 2: 339–340.

33. An excellent outline of the Puritan conversion experience can be found in Edmund S. Morgan, *Visible Saints, The History of a Puritan Idea* (Ithaca: Cornell University Press, 1963), 67–70.

34. For a fine discussion of the distinctions between Presbyterians and Independents see A. H. Drysdale, *History of the Presbyterians in England* (London: Publication Committee of the Presbyterian Church in England, 1889). Although he is concerned with English groups, the same characteristics apply to Scottish and Irish Presbyterians. The primary difference between Scottish and English Presbyterians involves allegiance to a hierarchy. The Scots had established a clear, pyramid structure of congregation, presbytery, synod, and national assembly, while the English were less formally organized.

35. Michael Bruce, *The Rattling of the Dry Bones, preached at Carluke May 1672* ([1672]).

36. Ezekiel 37:7–8, 37:10, King James Version.

37. Bruce, *Rattling of the Dry Bones,* 5.

38. John Tennent, *The Nature of Regeneration Opened,* printed following Gilbert Tennent's *Solemn Warning to the Secure World* (Boston: S. Kneeland and T. Green for D. Henchman, 1735). For a description of this revival see Landsman, "Revivalism and Nativism in the Middle Colonies."

39. George Whitefield, journal entries for 30 October–2 December 1739 and 13 April–14 May 1740, printed in *Journals* [1738–1747] (Edinburgh: Banner of Truth Trust, 1960), 338–364, 405–427.

40. Benjamin Franklin, *Benjamin Franklin's Autobiography,* J. A. Leo LeMay and P. M. Zall, eds. (New York: W. W. Norton, 1986), 87–88.

41. *Sermons on Sacramental Occasions by Divers Ministers* (Boston: J. Draper for D. Henchman, 1739).

42. Gilbert Tennent, Sermon One, *Sacramental Occasions,* 21, 22.

43. Gilbert Tennent, Sermon Two, *Sacramental Occasions,* 52–57, citation 57. See also Gilbert Tennent, Sermon Five.

44. Samuel Blair, Sermon Three, *Sacramental Occasions.*

45. William Tennent, Sermon Four, *Sacramental Occasions,* 108.

46. Samuel Blair, *A Short and Faithful Narrative of the late Remarkable Revival of Religion* (Philadelphia: William Bradford, [1744]), 27.

47. Samuel Buell, *A Faithful Narrative of the Remarkable Revival of Religion in the Congregation of East-hampton, Long Island* (New York: Samuel Brown, 1766).

48. Attempts to curtail emotional communion services are noted in the records

of the Synod of Ayr and Glasgow, and those of the General Synod of Ulster, 1690–1720.

49. For the factors that led several ministers to secede from the Church of Scotland, see the Associate Presbytery's *Act, Declaration, and Testimony for the Doctrine, Worship, Discipline, and Government of the Church of Scotland* (Edinburgh: Thomas Lumisden and John Robertson, 1737). For the chronicle of their success, see the Minutes of the Associate Presbytery, 1732–1745.

50. Although the British crown had, since the reign of Charles II, authorized a *Regium Donum,* or king's gift, to be distributed among Presbyterian ministers, this gift never amounted to more than 1,200 pounds, to be divided among all Presbyterian ministers in Ireland. So Irish clergy's dependence upon its laity was quite real.

51. Various Irish cases of pastor-congregation debates over salary can be found in the records of the General Synod of Ulster, the Presbyteries of Strabane, Belfast, Laggan, and Templepatrick. Colonial equivalents are noted in the records of the Synod of Philadelphia, Synod of New York, and the colonial Presbyteries of Donegal, Philadelphia, New Brunswick, and New Castle.

52. More than sixty pamphlets were published during this seven-year controversy. The best, or perhaps more characteristic, of these publications would include, on the side of the nonsubscribers, [James Kirkpatrick], *A Vindication of the Presbyterian Ministers in the North of Ireland* (Belfast: James Blow, 1721), and, on the side of their opponents, C. Masterton, *Christian Liberty founded in Gospel Truth* (Belfast: Robert Gardner, 1725). The details of this controversy are recorded in the Records of the General Synod of Ulster, 1720–1727, and in a pamphlet published by those thrown out of the community, *Narrative of the Proceedings of Seven General Synods . . . in which they issued a synodical Breach* (Belfast: James Blow, 1727).

53. Records of the Donegal Presbytery, 2 April 1734–13 October 1736. All colonial church records are located at the Presbyterian Historical Society, Philadelphia.

54. Records of the Donegal Presbytery, 26 May–5 October 1737.

55. Records of the Donegal Presbytery, November–December 1740.

56. Richard Webster, *A History of the Presbyterian Church in America, From its Origin Until the Year 1760* (Philadelphia: Joseph M. Wilson, 1857), 175–176. Webster lists several congregational separations gleaned from presbytery and synod minutes, some of which records are now lost.

57. Guy S. Klett, *Minutes of the Presbyterian Church in America 1705–1789* (Philadelphia: Presbyterian Historical Society, 1976), 172; and Presbytery of Philadelphia Minutes, 1740–1741.

58. *Minutes of the Presbyterian Church in America,* 171.

59. Records of the Donegal Presbytery, 11 August 1741.

60. Records of the Donegal Presbytery, 21 June 1743.

61. Records of the Donegal Presbytery, 18 June 1740, 9 April 1741, 1 August 1744; and *Minutes of the Presbyterian Church in America,* 173.

62. Gilbert Tennent, *The Danger of an Unconverted Ministry* (Philadelphia: Benjamin Franklin, 1740).

63. Landsman, "Revivalism and Nativism in the Middle Colonies."

64. By the end of the 1740s, Gilbert Tennent began to have misgivings about the popular enthusiasm. The Moravian disruption, the embarrassing activities of James Davenport, and the refusal of New Light congregations to abide by synodical decisions all influenced his attitude. See, for example, his *The Danger of Spiritual Pride represented* (Philadelphia: William Bradford, [1745]) and his *The Necessity of studying to be quiet, and doing our own Business* (Philadelphia: William Bradford, 1744).

5

The Spirit in the Flesh:

Religion and Regional

Economic Development

Religious and economic change have been closely intertwined in North American history. The nation's foremost period of economic expansion between 1790 and 1860, for example, accompanied the Second Great Awakening and the ascent of a powerful theology called evangelicalism.[1] Promising that men and women, with the help of God, could control their own destinies, this new Protestant belief complemented emerging ideas about increased productivity, technological advances, and material success. At the same time, economic expansion brought millions of foreign laborers into the United States, introducing Roman Catholicism and Judaism into the religious mainstream of the new nation. Full-scale industrialization of the late nineteenth century and the postindustrialism of the next century further coincided with critical periods of religious ferment.[2]

Despite this continuous interplay, the study of the relationship between religion and economic development in the United States has been sporadic and circumscribed. In Europe prominent scholars such as Max Weber focused directly on the interaction of religious beliefs and the origins of capitalism, but in this country, the connection has not been thoroughly examined. A handful of American historians have studied some socioeconomic aspects of religion, especially on the frontier, but even Frederick Jackson Turner left the subject of religion to others.[3]

Blaming historians for their sins of omission is convenient, but historical circumstances have sharply curtailed the investigation of American religion and economic development as well. In the first place, the other-worldly qualities of religion make worldly perspectives actually unwelcome. Because religious beliefs, behaviors, and institutions are based on faith, secular views seem to contradict the spiritual essence of religion. Perhaps anticipating critics invoking supernatural evidence, historians have shied away from exploring material influences on religion.

Developing a socioeconomic analysis of religion is also difficult because of the staggering variety of religions in the United States. Sectarian passion and American individualism make religion an unusually personal decision. The compelling Puritan symbol of "God's New Israel" alone inspired a myriad of religious movements. In addition, Native American pantheists, Spanish and French Catholics, and the thoroughly Protestant, but variously Anglican, Quaker, Mennonite, and Moravian colonists contributed unprecedented religious heterogeneity to the incipient nation. The military and political victories of their Protestant descendants guaranteed the success of privatized religion in the United States. Religious diversity, zeal, and upheaval were already two centuries old when economic development exploded across the new nation after 1790. By the Civil War, hundreds of denominations claimed 54,009 distinct congregations.[4]

Finally, the isolation of religious history from mainstream historical pursuits has inhibited a sustained social analysis of religion in the United States. Seminaries, where most religious history is still written, have a stake in fostering the history of their own religious traditions from the point of view of believers rarely conscious of cultural or social influences on their faith.[5] This division of labor has encouraged all historians to narrow the study of religion to specific actors, organizations, theologies, and rituals or to generalize religious experience based on national, usually mainstream, patterns. Happily, seminary studies of minority religions, lay beliefs and actions, and religious symbolism are replacing denominational histories and biographies of famous men. But they do not yet probe the intersection of religion and economy.

These traditional restrictions initially limited the impact of social history on the study of religion. Most early social historians chose to explore secular institutions with little regard to issues of religion. Quite by accident, however, they uncovered evidence of religion's remarkable influence on the developing United States. For example, political historians discovered that opposing political parties often espoused conflicting religious worldviews in the nineteenth century. Labor historians identified the new industrial work ethic of the period in terms of evangelical principles. And historians of women demonstrated that the most important ideological foundation of "separate spheres" was evangelicalism.[6]

Perspectives implicit in the social-history approach increasingly have illuminated the relationship of religious and economic change in the United States. In the pursuit of a history of ordinary people, social historians borrowed interactive views of human behavior from other social sciences. Using a model designed by anthropologist Anthony F.C. Wallace, William McLoughlin demonstrated that religious upheavals, or awakenings, regularly occurred in the United States during periods of intense social change.[7] Other social historians have characterized the direction of this change as modernization, showing that religion, along with class, race, ethnicity, and gender, has been a primary factor in creating and reflecting a modern, industrial nation.[8]

Three classic social history studies provide clues about the influence of an accelerating economy on American religion in the early nineteenth century. Whitney Cross, in *The Burned-Over District* (1950), demonstrated that revivalism was most successful in counties along the bustling Erie Canal where individuals could reasonably believe they controlled their own destiny. Ten years later, Lee Benson, in *The Concept of Jacksonian Democracy* (1961), wrote that evangelicalism strongly influenced republican ideas in the same region of western New York. Finally, British historian, E. P. Thompson, in *The Making of the English Working Class* (1965), speculated that evangelical Methodism incorporated work disciplines necessary for emerging capitalism in England.[9]

Over a decade later, a detailed study of one community tracked the rise of evangelicalism directly to the doorstep of economic development. Paul Johnson demonstrated that the impulse for evangelical religion in Rochester, New York, came from small businessmen. In this commercializing town, the frontline troops in the battle to increase productivity were the first Christian soldiers motivated by the famous revivalist, Charles Finney.[10] Other historians subsequently disagreed over the specifics, but acknowledged the contribution of economic development in the religious reorientation of the Second Great Awakening. For example, Mary Ryan illustrated that the actual conversions in Utica, another Burned-Over District town, originated not with the shopkeepers themselves, but with the wives of this new middle class. In other communities, large numbers of new industrial laborers were attracted by the evangelical promise of God's help in all things.[11]

Religion in the early nation is currently receiving unprecedented attention. In nearly every case, researchers have grown impatient with the limitations of community studies. A single location simply is not sufficiently varied for a thorough study of religion. Larger geographical units, ranging from the nation as a whole to specified regions, have replaced individual communities as the focus of religious study. Two major studies of antebellum American religion by Jon Butler and Nathan Hatch have returned economic development between 1790 and 1860 to the periphery of the national religious landscape.[12] Both accounts attribute religious change in the nation to political forces and past religious traditions, dismissing the possibility of significant socioeconomic influences. Although such panoramic views of the United States are impressive, they necessarily substitute general discussions of religion for an analysis of specific developmental factors in religious change.

Without local and regional excavation, interaction between religion and economic development is impossible to specify at the national level.

More often, social historians of religion have turned to regional studies, exploring a middle ground between a single location and the entire nation. They do so because a region contains an area compact enough to have a common history and comparable sources, while varied enough to represent a wide range of social contexts. Regions that have been the focus of recent studies of religion and society include post-Revolutionary Vermont; the antebellum Upper Ohio Valley; Texas at the time of statehood; the Great Plains and Mountain West during the Gilded Age; and several Northern regions in postbellum America.[13]

The remainder of this essay explores the advantages of a regional investigation into religion and early economic development. The following case study of religion in one region, the Upper Ohio Valley, reveals common religious responses to particular demographic and social structures on the frontier and to subsequent economic transformations between 1770 and 1860. The final section of the essay suggests how such a regional study can function as a crucial building block for a comprehensive analysis of religion and the transformation of the United States from a preindustrial to modern society.

IN THE CENTURY before the Civil War, the first colonial settlements of the new nation converted the Upper Ohio Valley from a wilderness territory into a region of productive farms, small- and large-scale industry, and growing cities. Western New York and Pennsylvania, the state of Ohio, and the Virginia and Kentucky counties bordering on the Ohio River encompassed the infamous Burned-Over District and religious, ethnic, political, and economic similarities and differences. This region drew pioneers from all of the original colonies and European countries providing immigrants to the United States. By 1860, the 180 counties carved out of this back country reflected nearly a complete range of socioeconomic and religious conditions present in the country.

Economic development was rapid in this emerging region, but uneven and sporadic. Three frontier periods changed the face of the Upper Ohio Valley. The first began prior to 1790 with early settlements around Pittsburgh, in central New York, and on opposite sides of the Ohio River. A town called Losantiville, founded to ferry settlers across the river, quickly gave rise to Cincinnati. Dominating commerce in the region within thirty years, this town became the sixth largest city and third leading manufacturing center in the United States by 1850.[14] The second frontier period began with the acceleration of trans-Appalachian migration in the 1790s. New migrants populated earlier locations, with Ohio gaining enough residents for statehood by 1803. After 1825, the Erie Canal begin to stimulate commercial development around the new regional centers of Buffalo and Cleveland. In some areas of the region, however, Frederick Jackson Turner's frontier definition applied until the 1840s. Before this third wave, Turner, quoting William Dean Howells, spoke of "primeval forests" and stumps "as thick as harvest stubble" in the Western Reserve Territory in northeastern Ohio and of Native Americans living side by side with American colonists in the northwest quadrant.[15]

Nineteenth-century historical records provide systematic accounts of economic and religious growth in this region. Beginning in 1790, the U.S. census published socioeconomic descriptions of each county in the nation during every decennial year. As counties moved from preindustrial self-sufficiency into economic development, the census recorded dramatically changing levels of population, farming, manufacturing, and urbanization.[16]

The most complete information about religion comes from accounts of congregations and other religious institutions in the region. Although only one of several dimensions of religiosity, the congregation is the primary outlet for personal religious beliefs in the United States. These local meetings of like-minded believers are usually organized into denominations that preserve information on affiliated congregations. In addition, secular reports from several sources are available to corroborate denominational records for the region. For example, the U.S. Census aggregated the number, seating capacity, and value of congregations by denomination in 1850 and 1860, and ubiquitous nineteenth-century county histories reported on nearly every congregation organized in a county prior to publication.[17]

The distribution of religious congregations illuminates the relationship between economic development and religious change in the early nineteenth-century Upper Ohio Valley in two ways. Economic and religious factors reported by the census provide the socioeconomic context of religion for the 180 regional counties in the decade prior to the Civil War. And an in-depth look at twenty-six counties (selected for geographic location, frontier period, and economic status) illustrates the evolving relationship between religion and the economy in varied settings from 1770 to 1860.[18]

Although each county exhibited a unique blend of religious and economic influences, common religious patterns emerged within the ante-

bellum Upper Ohio Valley. Predictable religious growth and development corresponded closely to general characteristics of a modernizing
society, including population growth and migration into a locality; the
optimistic community building of an expanding town; and the spatial
and social organization of commercial farming versus industrial development. These basic characteristics of economic development had at least
as much impact on the religious configuration of a county as charismatic
personalities or particular denominational strategies.

Focusing on regional patterns is not meant to minimize the role of
ordinary men and women who labored mightily to bring religion to the
new West. Yet personal dramas of pioneer families, the itinerant ministers
who served them, and the emerging leaders of the burgeoning religious
bureaucracies often have inhibited an analysis of collective actions. Individual religious decisions, no matter how personal, gave rise to common
patterns. In the antebellum West, secular influences interacted with denominational strategies and individual piety to produce complex patterns
of religious variation.

The relationship between population growth and religious development provides one of the clearest designs to emerge from the Upper Ohio
Valley between 1770 and 1860. Frontier conditions promoted rather than
inhibited the establishment of religious communities in this region. After
the first decade of settlement, the number of congregations began to
multiply at a greater rate than population. This rate quickly reproduced
the per capita number of congregations the settlers had left at home, and
by 1860, the amount of religious organization was greater in the Upper
Ohio Valley than in the older sections of the country.

Congregational organization began with settlement. (see Table 5.1)
Based on evidence from the twenty-six sample counties, the rate of new
congregational growth began slowly during the first decade, accelerated
rapidly during the second through fifth decades of a county's existence,
and then dropped off sharply. On the average, the first decade of a
county accounted for only 4.3 percent of the 1860 congregations, with no
more than one congregation usually founded by a single denomination.
The percentage of congregations rose quickly in the next few decades, so
that after fifty years, the collective counties had more than two-thirds of
all the congregations they would have by 1860.

This congregational configuration related to population growth in
some interesting ways. Congregations were founded at the rate of about
one per 1,000 people on the Upper Ohio Valley frontiers. (see Table 5.2)
With the sample counties averaging 500 square miles, congregations
began appearing when the population concentration was approximately
two people per square mile, exactly the point at which frontier society is

TABLE 5.1.   The Founding of Congregations by Settlement Decade in the Upper Ohio Valley, 1770–1860.

Settlement decade	Number	Percent	Cumulative Percent
Within first 10 years	71	4.3	4.3
Within second 10 years	168	10.2	14.5
Within third 10 years	274	16.7	31.2
Within fourth 10 years	278	16.9	48.1
Within fifth 10 years	312	19.0	67.1
Within sixth 10 years	261	15.9	83.0
Within seventh 10 years	197	12.0	95.0
Within eighth 10 years	57	3.5	98.5
Within ninth 10 years	16	1.0	99.5
Within tenth 10 years	11	0.7	100.2
Total	1,645	100.2	100.2
Missing dates of congregations	370		
Grand Total (n=26 counties)	2,015		

SOURCE: County histories for twenty-six counties in the Upper Ohio Valley.

TABLE 5.2.   Congregations per Capita in the Upper Ohio Valley, 1780–1860.

	1780	1790	1800	1810	1820	1830	1840	1850	1860
Congs per 1000 population (n=26 counties)	1.0	0.9	1.0	1.4	1.7	1.9	2.1	2.1	1.9
Frontier 1 (n=9)	1.0	0.9	1.0	1.2	1.4	1.5	1.8	1.7	1.6
Frontier 2 (n=12)			1.3	2.1	2.2	2.5	2.4	2.4	2.3
Frontier 3 (n=5)					1.3	2.6	3.3	3.1	2.4

SOURCE: U.S. Census and county histories for twenty-six counties in Upper Ohio Valley.

said to begin.[19] Regardless of whether a traveling Methodist preacher appeared or a camp meeting was held, about two hundred families was a critical mass for the creation of a congregation. This initial religious density remained basically the same for each of the different frontier periods. As early as 1780 in the southwestern Pennsylvania area, the ratio of congregations to population was 1-to-1,000 people. The second and third wave of initial frontier settlement in the sample counties, coming in 1800 and then again in 1820, saw that ratio increase only slightly to 1.3.

After the first decade, religious organization outstripped population growth. (see Table 5.3) Prior to 1800, congregational foundings and population increases were proportional. Both multiplied at a rate of about 200 percent per decade in the twenty-six sample counties. Between 1800 and 1810, congregations grew nearly twice as fast as people, at a 136 percent rate of increase compared to 72 percent. The congregational rate dropped slightly during the next few decades, but congregational foundings continued to occur at one-and-a-half times the rate of population increases until 1840. After that, both population and new

TABLE 5.3.   Comparative Congregational and Population Growth Rates in the Upper Ohio Valley, 1780–1860.

	Population	Increase (percent)	Congregations (number)	Increase (percent)
1780	11,000		11	
1790	34,345	212	32	191
1800	96,689	182	99	209
1810	166,582	72	234	136
1820	262,856	58	447	91
1830	381,452	45	722	62
1840	526,353	38	1,123	56
1850	701,629	33	1,463	30
1860	865,448	23	1,670*	14

SOURCE: U.S. Census and county histories for twenty-six counties in Upper Ohio Valley.

N = 26 counties

*Missing dates of founding for 345 congregations

congregational growth slowed. Each gained about 30 percent during the 1840s decade and 20 percent in the final antebellum decade.[20]

This is a surprising finding, because nineteenth-century participants constantly complained that their trans-Appalachian journey left behind religious organization. Quite the contrary occurred. The frontier infrastructure quickly supported the same number of congregations per person as did the nation. With congregational foundings sharply outstripping population growth from 1800 to 1840, more per capita religious institutions existed in the new West than in more settled areas by 1850. In that year, the nation had a ratio of 1.6 congregations to 1,000 population, with the Burned-Over District counties mirroring this figure exactly and the twenty-six counties managing an even higher 2.1 ratio.[21]

The misleading perspective of settlers is understandable. In a population explosion of such magnitude, congregational expansion took a long time to notice. If a family was without access to religious services, religion was indeed not keeping up with western migration. To John Carter, a Methodist shopkeeper without a Methodist congregation in the 750-person village of Cincinnati in 1803, the fact that the average number of congregations was growing faster than the population was irrelevant.[22] And lamenting the failure of organized religion to keep up with the population growth made good strategic sense. Reverend Lyman Beecher of Cincinnati's prestigious Second Presbyterian Church wisely did not dwell on regional successes when he made an 1835 fund-raising trip to his former East Coast stomping ground, presenting the famous "A Plea for the West" speech.[23]

The knowledge that even one soul was denied spiritual guidance in the West spurred the founding of congregations at a record rate. Some historians have missed this point because they have paid more attention to what the migrants were saying than to what they were doing. In fact, newcomers from every religious tradition quickly submitted themselves to religious discipline in all parts of the region.

Population, although an excellent indicator of the total number of congregations, did not predict the specific religious makeup of an Upper Ohio Valley county. Nativity and previous religious affiliation of county migrants were the most important factors in determining the religious variety in newly settled areas. Requiring congregations that met the theological, ritual, and often kinship standards of home, settlers organized churches because none yet existed or because the ones they discovered were unfamiliar or unacceptable. Streams of migrants transferred the religious faith of their homeland to their new frontier homes.[24]

The effect of migration on religious diversity was most noticeable within the first decade of settlement. In the case of the original founders of Cincinnati, "as soon as the little band of Presbyterians had been somewhat reinforced and was ready for organization, an informal society was constituted and began to worship."[25] This occurred in 1790, only two years after the first settlers arrived. Even so, the first congregation in Hamilton County was the First Baptist Church of Columbia, organized a year earlier in an area east of the city along the river where six of the twenty-five original settlers were Baptists.[26]

Migrants from the same religious persuasion, but different homelands, also contributed to religious diversity. For example, within one decade of settlement, four separate Baptist churches—a Regular Baptist, an Anti-Mission Baptist, a German Baptist, and a non-specific Baptist Church—were operating in Clermont County, Cincinnati's neighbor to the east. The Regular Baptists had come from Virginia, while the Stonelick German Baptist Church made their ethnic claim in the title of their congregation. The remainder of the Baptists were from New Jersey and Pennsylvania, where the controversy over whether Baptist associations ought to sponsor western missions divided those who supported new denominational initiatives from those Anti-Mission believers who said that individual members and churches should take responsibility for spreading the Gospel.[27]

The link between nativity and religion actually inhibited the ability of denominations to compete in areas dominated by other religious traditions. No matter what innovative strategies were utilized, the ethnic cast of a county could present formidable barriers to religious recruiters. The diaries of Methodist circuit riders recorded as many places where they were not allowed to preach or where they were not welcome because of other religious predilections as places where food, shelter, and encouragement were plentiful. Reverend John Kobler, an early Methodist rider in southwestern Ohio, described his first visit to the outskirts of Cincinnati in 1798 this way: "I found settlements very sparse indeed, only now and then a solitary family. About four o'clock in the afternoon I came to an old garrison called Fort Washington, situated on the bank of the big river, which bore very much the appearance of a declining, time-stricken, God-forsaken place . . . here I wished very much to preach, but could find no opening or reception of any kind whatever."[28]

Nor were Methodists any more successful inside the village of Cincinnati. Reverend Kobler's colleague, Reverend James B. Finley, put it this way: "Those who were in any way interested on the subject of religion would not, in consequence of belonging to the Presbyterian or Baptist Churches—both of which were strongly Calvinistic—be likely to invite a Methodist preacher to come into their midst, especially in those early times."[29] Even though Methodist circuit riders held religious services in the area, none of the seven churches founded in Hamilton county within the first ten years of settlement after 1788 was Methodist.

But, where residents were from the same denomination and home-land, congregations multiplied. Barely thirty miles east of Cincinnati in Clermont County, migration from the states of Virginia and Maryland provided a nurturing environment for the Methodist Episcopal Church. Circuit-riding Methodists could count on home-style hospitality here, because the American denomination was born in Maryland after the Revolution. As a result, six congregations were organized within ten years of white settlement.

The dominant influence of nativity on religious organization dimin-ished as a settled population pushed frontier conditions westward. By mid-century, place of birth was only one of several factors influencing congregational formation in the Upper Ohio Valley. Even so, a closer look at all Ohio counties demonstrates the continued influence of ethnic-ity on religious variety in 1850. Regression analysis illustrates the statisti-cal influence of nativity on selected religious groups.[30] (see Table 5.4)

In an average 1850 Ohio county, the strength of particular religious groups still depended heavily on where the county population origi-nated.[31] Methodist congregations were the most plentiful in counties with large numbers of residents born in the South and in Germany. Baptists came from both northern and southern states, but were weak in counties with a high number of foreign-born. Not surprisingly, Roman Catholicism was strongest in counties with many foreign-born Irish and Germans, while the Episcopal church still drew people born in England. Members of only one major religious group in Ohio cannot be traced to specific eastern seaboard states or foreign countries. The new, thor-oughly evangelical Disciples of Christ group was strongest in counties with a large population born in western states, including Mississippi, Kentucky, and Tennessee.

Migration streams initially imprinted religion on a county and contin-ued to influence religious patterns throughout the antebellum period. But ethnic background did not get congregations organized, churches built, or ministers hired. The speedy creation of religious institutions resulted from community development priorities and remarkably similar religious strategies developed by different religious groups.

GATHERING THE transplanted population together for worship and moral development was the purpose of frontier religion. Whether the faith was sectarian or liturgical, the religious priority in newly settled

TABLE 5.4.   Religion and Ethnicity in Ohio Counties, 1850

	Methodist		Baptist		Disciples		Catholic		Episcopal	
	beta	(F)	beta	(F)	beta	(F)	beta	(F)	beta	(F)
North	.06	(.3)	.39	(10.5)*	.09	(.6)	−.21	(3.5)	.21	(3.4)
South	.63	(48.4)*	.35	(12.2)*	.14	(2.2)	−.07	(.5)	.03	(.2)
West	.12	(2.1)	.27	(9.1)*	.71	(63.9)*	.19	(5.3)*	−.07	(.6)
Britain	.21	(3.7)	.22	(3.5)	−.12	(1.1)	.30	(7.4)*	.57	(24.9)*
Germany	.21	(5.7)*	.13	(1.9)	−.11	(1.4)	.52	(34.9)*	.04	(.3)

SOURCE: Wilhelm, *Ohio: 1850* and the U.S. Census. SPSS Regression of five ethnic categories (determined by SPSS Factor Analysis) on the number of seats for each religious denomination. North included all those county residents born in Connecticut, Massachusetts, New Hampshire, Rhode Island, Vermont, New York, Maine; South includes Delaware, Maryland, Virginia, North Carolina; West from Louisiana, Illinois, Missouri, Indiana, Mississippi, Kentucky, Alabama, Tennessee. Britain and Germany include immigrants from those respective countries. The beta weight, or standardized regression coefficient, measures the influence of each ethnic factor, apart from all other ethnic factors, on the number of denominational seats in an average county. The closer the beta is to 1.0, the stronger the relationship between the particular nativity and religious group.

n=72 counties, df (1,67)

*Significant at .05 level or below

areas was building congregations around the imported religious beliefs of migrants. Historians, unfortunately, have focused on the flamboyant and sometimes odd religious practices on the frontier, emphasizing camp meetings, sectarian fractiousness, and itinerant preachers. The origins of congregations in the twenty-six counties during the first two decades of settlement show that neither revivals, sectarian splintering, nor circuit riders played a primary role in religious organization.[32]

Most early congregations were not founded in the context of a revival. (see Table 5.5) Only one congregation originated in a revival during the first decade and only two, both Shaker communities, during the second decade of county existence. In subsequent decades, more congregations did originate in revivals. Of the thirty-six congregations founded by revivals in the twenty-six counties, thirty-three (91.6 percent) were organized after the first twenty years of settlement. Although these totals do not include all revivals occurring during this period, they suggest that revivalism was neither distinctive to frontier circumstances nor critically important for the future religious development in a county.[33]

Furthermore, religious controversies leading to congregational divisions were less likely to occur in frontier areas than elsewhere. In fact, developed counties featured more sectarian splintering than did frontier ones. Religious divisions accounted for nearly 25 percent (317) of all congregational foundings in the twenty-six counties from 1780 to 1860 (1301), but they accounted for only 6 percent (twelve out of 196 foundings) during the first two decades. In only two cases did a theological controversy cause a congregation to divide. Most early divisions came about because one group within the original congregation wanted a more convenient location.

Itinerants, or ministers without a regular parish who traveled preaching circuits, accounted for a larger portion of frontier congregations than camp meetings or schisms. But even this method did not predominate during the settlement stage in the twenty-six counties. A regular minister in the vicinity organized more congregations than did itinerants during the first ten years of settlement. More important were future members who constituted themselves a congregation in the absence of clergy. The use of itinerants increased during the second ten years of settlement but so did the frequency of organizing a congregation without professional help. Members were responsible for thirty-three foundings and itinerants for thirty-one congregations within twenty years of settlement.

Religion, then, was part of a generalized community building in the new West. Individual spiritual needs were expressed in a collective vision of civilization that included a particular religious life. Each new frontier

TABLE 5.5.   Congregational Organizational Motives in the Upper
               Ohio Valley, 1770–1860

	All decades		First decade		Second decade	
	#	%	#	%	#	%
Individual	68	5.2	3	4.8	8	6.0
Future members	174	13.4	11	17.7	33	24.6
Revival	36	2.8	1	1.6	2	1.5
Minister in vicinity	64	4.9	13	21.0	14	10.4
Itinerant minister	249	19.1	9	14.5	31	23.1
Local minister	234	18.0	6	9.7	21	15.7
Denom. sent minister	34	2.6	2	3.2	1	x
Agent or stated supply	7	x	1	1.6	—	—
Missionary	78	6.0	11	17.7	12	9.0
Ethnic split	18	1.4	—	—	—	—
Slavery split	11	x	1	1.6	—	—
Location split	164	12.6	2	3.2	7	5.2
Religious split	124	9.5	—	—	2	1.5
Merger	2	x	—	—	—	—
Union	30	2.3	2	3.2	3	2.2
School organization	3	x	—	—	—	—
For slaves	2	x	—	—	—	—
Other	3	x	—	—	—	—
Total	1,301	100.0	62	100.0	134	100.0
Missing cases	714		9		34	
All cases (N = 26 counties)	2,015		71		168	

SOURCE: County histories for twenty-six counties in the Upper Ohio Valley.
NOTE: x indicates less than 1%.

required religion to pay homage to the past and to lay paths to the future. An early western Pennsylvania historian put it this way: "Men from all nations meet together around a common altar, and declare in the very commencement of their labor, their religious principles."[34]

The promise of economic advancement lured millions of settlers across the Appalachian Mountains by mid-century. One railroad advertisement hyperbolized: "Stranger! Stop one moment to contemplate the progress and grandeur of this Western Empire."[35] Their optimism infected every social institution, including religion. But the realities of economic circumstances also influenced these geographical and economic pioneers. Both local boosterism and specific economic contexts contributed to the complex religious configuration of the Upper Ohio Valley.

Whatever else they were, religious organizations were cards in the hands of local entrepreneurs. Early nineteenth-century boosters, partisans who attempted to accelerate economic development by boasting about local advantages, often pointed to the number and variety of churches as signs of progress in a fledgling community. Their claims were so widespread that the Northwest Ordinance was informally reinterpreted to mandate land set aside for churches as well as schools. Whereas the 1787 congressional ordinance said that no persons were to be "molested" for religious beliefs or mode of worship, developers regularly donated land and materials to congregations in order to encourage the construction of churches.[36]

Every congregation did not have the desire, need, or opportunity to turn boosterism into God's will, but many in the twenty-six counties were quick to take advantage of such incentives. Where information is available, about one-quarter had substantial financial help from people outside the congregation in building their first church (eighty-five of 396 congregations). This proportion jumped to 40 percent (sixteen of forty-two) when the first two settlement decades were considered. Neither the type of denomination or location in the county affected the pattern. The original surveyors of Pittsburgh, for example, reserved three large lots for the first Protestant congregations organized at the Point. A few miles south, along the Monongahela River, the first developers of McKeesport granted four lots for "the use of a place of worship and a seminary of learning." Land speculators continued to invest in churches throughout the nineteenth century. When Wilkinsburg and Edgewood became railroad suburbs of Pittsburgh in the 1860s, the largest landowner, Squire Kelley, donated church lots to Protestant congregations while selling off large chunks of his estate to land developers.[37]

In some cases, the benefactors were of the same religious persuasion.

St. Augustine's, the first Catholic church in Napoleon, Ohio, was financed by and named for a local Catholic businessman in 1856. Augustus Pilliod, "together with such aid as could be obtained from other Catholics and some generous outsiders," built a "modest" frame church.[38] Furthermore, all of the Methodist churches in Henry County, Ohio, had their lots donated, usually by the host of the local Methodist class.

Often the congregational contributors were not even from the same religion. Also in Napoleon, the first Presbyterian Church had its lot donated by an important lawyer and real estate developer, Justin H. Tyler, who "in matters pertaining to the church, and to the erection of church edifices generally throughout the entire county, has contributed liberally of his means, without regard to denomination." And in the case of the first Methodist church in the village of Defiance, Henry County's neighbor to the west, a "devout Catholic" German immigrant and important merchant "assisted in its erection."[39]

Whether booster assumptions about churches were correct is questionable. Evidence is scant that the presence of churches brought in more settlers than would otherwise have come. Instead, congregations followed population. The persistent population and congregational correlation observed earlier demonstrates that a critical mass of population accounted for congregational organization in the twenty-six counties. Outside financial aid did not create congregations as much as it allowed infant congregations to build churches sooner than if they had had to rely solely on their own resources.

Specific economic contexts, as well as economic pretensions, influenced the religious array of the Upper Ohio Valley. The number of church seats provides the best measure of religious concentration in 180 counties, although a limited amount of membership information available from the twenty-six sample counties confirmed these conclusions.[40] People in commercial farming areas created the largest number of religious institutions, while the fewest religious facilities existed in early frontier areas. Regression analysis based on economic and religious information from the census demonstrates these associations for the region as a whole in 1850 and 1860.[41] (see Table 5.6.)

Religious organization in commercial farming areas exceeded that in other locations of the Upper Ohio Valley in 1850 and 1860. In other words, the higher the commercial value of farms, the more congregations existed in an average county in the region. Although population size had the strongest affect on the total number of religious seats, the value of farms was positively related to religion in both years. In contrast, neither manufacturing nor urbanization had a systematic influence on the number of religious facilities in either year. The absence of any

TABLE 5.6.   Religion and Economic Factors in the Upper Ohio Valley, 1850 and 1860

	Total seats		Evangelical		Liturgical	
	beta	(F)	beta	(F)	beta	(F)
1850						
Total population	.83	(77.6)*	.64	(22.9)*	.79	(26.1)*
Value farms	.22	(10.3)*	.36	(13.5)*	−.11	(7.9)
Value manufacturing	−.02	(.1)	.15	(1.9)	−.32	(6.2)*
Largest town	−.10	(2.0)	−.40	(13.8)*	.43	(12.9)*
n=152 counties, df (1,148)						
1860						
Total population	.69	(55.0)*	.34	(5.5)*	.67	(28.2)*
Value farms	.26	(25.6)*	.56	(45.9)*	−.12	(3.1)
Value manufacturing	.00	(.0)	−.11	(.8)	.30	(7.3)*
Largest town	.03	(.2)	.10	(.8)	.04	(.2)
n=178 counties, df (1,174)						

SOURCE: U.S. Census. SPSS Regression of economic variables on the total number of congregational seats reported in 1850 and 1860 for Evangelical and Liturgical categories. Evangelical includes those in Methodist, Baptist, Disciples, Union, Congregational, Quaker, and Free denominations. Liturgical includes those in Roman Catholic, Lutheran, Episcopal, German Reformed, Dutch Reformed and Jewish denominations. Total Seats includes all denominations present in region. Only counties with full information available were included in 1850 and 1860. The beta weight measures the influence of each economic factor, apart from other economic factors, on the number of congregational seats in each category. The closer the beta is to 1.0, the stronger the relationship between the specific economic and religious variables.

*Significant at .05 level or below

signs of economic progress, including population advances, resulted in the fewest religious institutions.

Economic variables were related to the type, as well as quantity, of religion in the region. In the middle of the nineteenth century, evangelicalism was especially associated with commercial farming. Taken together, evangelical denominations (Methodists, Baptists, Disciples of Christ, Congregationalists, Quakers, and Union churches) were strongest in terms of church seats in counties with the highest amounts of commercial farming. Population was also related to evangelical seats in 1860, but the influence of farming was greater. On the other hand, the presence of urban areas and manufacturing activity was statistically insignificant on the number of evangelical seats in a county. Evangelical denominations were most successful in well-populated, wealthy commercial farming environments without a large town or city.

Non-evangelical religious groups flourished in different economic environments. In both 1850 and 1860, population had a much stronger relationship to the collective presence of liturgical groups (Roman Catholics, Episcopalians, Lutherans, German and Dutch Reformed, and Jews) than did any other economic factor. And if the county boasted a significant town or city, liturgical groups were even more successful. In 1850, the size of the largest town was the second most predictive economic factor after population for Catholics and members of other liturgical groups. In 1860, a large population and the presence of manufacturing, instead of urban development, enhanced liturgical strength.[42]

The extant membership figures for congregations in the sample counties in the year 1860 support this pattern of religious concentration. In that year, counties exhibiting high commercial farming values averaged around 18 members per 100 population in religious congregations, while self-sufficient counties had only about ten members and counties with rising manufacturing totals had only about thirteen members per one hundred people. These figures also show that evangelical groups were strongest in commerical agriculture counties, with liturgical denominations most successful in industrializing counties.[43]

Historians would hardly be surprised that the Roman Catholic church thrived in urban areas with large numbers of immigrants. Nor that Methodist and Baptist churches were strongest in the agricultural hinterland of the West. What historians of religion have missed, however, is the dynamic pattern of religious variation caused by these socioeconomic features. Taken together, population, migration, community building, and economic base created Upper Ohio Valley environments in which individual clergy and lay people acted predictably. This did not mean that individuals had no control over religion or that denominational innovation went unrewarded, but only that religious people in similar circumstances made similar choices between 1770 and 1860 in the nation's heartland.

AS RELIGIOUS HISTORY comes out of the denominational shadows and on to center stage of social history, regional studies can contribute to a full-scale synthesis of religion and economic development. Even though no single case replicates the regional norm and no region is an American microcosm, regional analyses of religious and economic change transform individual communities into a collection of religious patterns or unusual occurrences. The findings in one region then direct research into religion and economic development elsewhere. Taken together, regional studies offer an analytic framework for a comprehensive analysis of American religion and economic development.

The remainder of this essay illustrates how a study of the socioeconomic context of religious activity in a region like the Upper Ohio Valley informs the story of religion everywhere. From the smallest hamlet to the nation as a whole, this regional portrait stands as a valuable building block in religious history. In particular, such a regional study illuminates the typicality or uniqueness of individual counties within the region; provides a conceptual basis for exploring individual religious actors, events, congregations, and denominations in the region and elsewhere; offers a comparative framework for religious variation in other regions and time periods; and suggests some systematic approaches to hypothesized relationships between modernization and religion, including the thorny issue of secularization.

At the most local level, the Upper Ohio Valley study is especially satisfying because it helps to explain apparently idiosyncratic occurrences in the region. Washington County, Pennsylvania, immediately southwest of Pittsburgh, is a telling example of how wide-angled regional views explicate information about each constituent county, even one not particularly well-known nor important to the nation. On the surface, Washington County looks quite atypical, but in fact, predictable regional trends substantially qualify this county's differences. Placed within a regional context, Washington County is no longer simply a quaint setting of unusual religious features.

Washington, for example, had an elaborate religious structure by mid-century, including an unusually large number of churches. This would be puzzling, except for the regional finding that well-populated, commercial farming counties had more religious organization than average counties. In fact Washington ranked first in per capita value of farms ($447.34) and third in total population (46,805) among the twenty-six sample counties by 1860. This wealthy agricultural environment sustained 172 congregations between 1772 to 1860, well over three congregations for every 1,000 people in 1860.[44] Only Clermont County, also a successful farming area, had a higher ratio of churches to population.

The religious variety of Washington represented both the nativity and commerical values of county residents. Before the defeat of the local Delaware and Shawnee nations, the Bane family joined other Baptist land squatters from Virginia in 1772 to organize one of the first congregations west of the Alleghenies, North Ten Mile Baptist Church.[45] During the next eighty-eight years, eighteen additional Baptist churches were founded, often taking the names of the region's other plentiful streams, including Chartiers, Pike, Pigeon, Mingo, Peters, Raccoon, and Buffalo.

Despite the initial Baptist advantage, sustained Scots-Irish migration gave southwestern Pennsylvania one of the strongest Presbyterian orientations in the nation. In 1774, Presbyterians near Chartiers Creek petitioned the Associate Synod to elect church elders. Less than a year later, Reverend John McMillan began his illustrious career as a Presbyterian pastor, missionary, itinerant minister, educator, and theologian in Washington County.[46] Migrants from northern Ireland and eastern Pennsylvania streamed into western Pennsylvania after 1790, organizing eighty-six congregations of various Presbyterian persuasions by 1860, including those in the Associate, Associate Reformed, U.S.A. Old School and New School, Cumberland, Reformed, and Covenant Reformed Presbyterian denominations. This locale continues to the present to have more per capita Presbyterian churches, varieties, and prominent members than elsewhere in the nation.

The strength of the strongly Calvinistic Regular Baptists and most of the Presbyterians predicts that Washington County would resist nineteenth-century evangelicalism. But contravening factors, including a large commercial farming environment and active proselytizing, produced unexpected evangelical strength in the county. In all, 72 percent of congregations founded before 1860 in Washington were evangelical in outlook. This figure is slightly below other settled farming counties but much above industrial or rapidly urbanizing centers.

Methodism was surprisingly robust in Washington County. Despite the scant attention given to the Methodists by the three major county histories, as opposed to their lavish coverage of Presbyterians and Baptists, the followers of the Wesley brothers were the second largest in the country after the Presbyterians by 1860. In addition, Washington was also a Cumberland Presbyterian stronghold. Excluded from the main

Presbysterian denomination after participating in the Kentucky frontier revivals early in the century, these evangelicals organized nine congregations in the county by 1860.[47]

As elsewhere, successful evangelizing engendered vicious public conflicts. For example, Thomas Campbell and his son, Alexander, arrived from northern Ireland as orthodox Scots-Irish Presbyterians. But by 1809, they had forsaken their Calvinism, moved into a local Baptist fellowship until excluded for evangelical heresies, and finally founded the Christian Church, later known as the Disciples of Christ. In the process, the Campbellites intensified divisions within the Baptists, causing the Redstone Association to shatter and reorganize around evangelical practices. Triggered by these convulsions, the county also spawned some of the most flamboyant cults in the nation. An angel revealed to the original Halyconites and Rhodianites that hell did not exist and that a vegetarian diet would assure their bodily transfer into heaven at death. Washington County was also the original residence of Solomon Spaulding, the man who claimed that he was the author of a fictional manuscript later appropriated as revealed truth by Joseph Smith for the Book of Mormon.[48]

In addition to interpretations of single counties, a regional study also allows for more confident analyses of congregation building, the changing role of religious minorities, and the creation of denominational organizations. Congregational formation is at the heart of modern American religion, because the congregation is the most intimate religious setting about which historians have access to information. Each congregation demonstrates a particular cycle of origin, development, division, and demise. Promising earlier studies of the social bases of church membership have not been duplicated, in part because scholars were uneasy about generalizing from a single case.[49] The Upper Ohio Valley offers a systematic account of why people came together, who attended regularly, when they built churches or sponsored missionaries, what social characteristics they shared, which families were unhappy and left the congregation, and under what conditions a church disbanded.

This kind of congregational analysis provides a particularly instructive view of the changing role of "outsiders" in American religion. Historians have conceded the importance of religion to communities of ethnic, racial, and gender groups, but only recently have they detailed the evolving relationship between congregational organization and the socioeconomic position of social groups. In Cortland County, New York, as well as elsewhere, the minutes from local congregations demonstrate that women, in addition to becoming revival converts in greater numbers, initially contributed more financial and organizing resources to evangelical congregations than did their husbands or brothers. And in Pittsburgh, issues of cultural accommodation, including temperance, English-language services, and Masonry, contributed to evangelical inroads and barriers in the industrializing city's immigrant communities at mid-century.[50]

A regional perspective also can illuminate the institutional evolution of national denominations. Some social historians have argued that traditional history has provided enough information about religious organization.[51] In fact, both approaches have taken for granted the nineteenth-century transformation of the major denominations into bureaucratic corporations.[52] The Upper Ohio Valley provides excellent evidence of the costs and benefits of the new organizing strategies that emphasized marketing, rationalization, specialization, and standardization. It was the imperative of vast new settlements in the new West that promoted interdenominational cooperation, ministers who served more than one congregation, and the addition of a new layer of regional bureaucracy between 1790 and 1860. At the same time, however, these innovations alienated some of their own members who then joined less bureaucratic, more sectarian movements.

But a comparison of religious change in several developmental contexts throughout the United States is necessary for a comprehensive view of religion and economic development. Commercialism, manufacturing, and industrialization followed the frontier, repeating the process of transformation from a preindustrial "wilderness" to an ultimately postindustrial society. Religious studies can isolate related religious patterns in locations at various stages of economic development. If the points of comparison are the same for each region—individual religious actors, congregations, denominations, religious symbols, or distinctive religious orientations—what emerges are general conclusions about religion in a national context.

The Upper Ohio Valley offers valuable comparisons with areas explored in other regional studies of religion. In terms of congregational formation, several studies demonstrate that the population component of economic development correlates closely with the number of congregations in an area during its initial developmental period. In the disparate frontier locations of Texas in the 1850s and Vermont in the 1790s, the congregation-to-population ratio was nearly the same as in the Upper Ohio Valley during each successive settlement period. Apparently, the critical mass of population necessary to support congregations in newly settled, "western" areas was about 1,000 people for every church. As each location experienced its greatest economic advances during the next fifty years, the congregation-to-population ratio in Texas grew to nearly four congregations per 1,000 people, about the same as in Washington county during its peak economic performance in 1850.[53]

Although the basic demographics of religious development in the United States are remarkably similar, other religious patterns accompanying regional economic development depend more on historical circumstances. New varieties of religion and the development of a dominant religious culture are two good examples. Evangelicalism swept aside more traditional religious orientations in the Upper Ohio Valley, while no such cleansing religious wind swept across the trans-Mississippi West of Texas, the Great Plains, the Northwest, and California. The Roman Catholic influence of the Spanish missions in Texas and California, the intractability of Utah Mormons, and the continued presence and cultural strength of Native Americans prevented the wholesale imposition of dominant Protestantism on the Far West.[54]

Regional comparisons across time and space finally bring the historical study of religion and economic development to a question of popular interest: What is the overall impact of religious change on the nation? From the pulpit, the kitchen table, and the lecture hall, people ask how a modern society, organized according to the principles of economic development, has influenced American religion. Religion looks different now than it did in Puritan New England and or on the Spanish borderlands, but what does this mean? Has economic development led to religious decline, marking the transformation of a religious America into a secular one? Or has religion been fundamentally impervious to socioeconomic changes, retaining an original American essence?

The regional studies of today do not directly confront these issues of secularization. Even if they did, no uniform evaluation of American religious change would appear. But current regional studies do provide a conceptual context for dialogue that extends beyond the thoughts and words of contemporary religious actors. In the Upper Ohio Valley, for example, religion was booming in the optimistic climate of economic development before the Civil War. New congregations and churches, the variety of religious alternatives, and conversions and church members mulitplied. At the same time, participants were lamenting denominational unresponsiveness, the decadent qualities of other religions, and the barbarity of their surroundings. For this society, secularization seemed to represent the worst fears, not the actual experiences, of people caught in rapid social change.

Scholars have floundered over questions of secularization because the terms of the discussion have not been carefully defined. In particular, historians have avoided the issue, allowing sociologists of religion to stake out the territory, because traditional historical approaches did not foster an analysis of the evolution of American religion. Regional social history studies of religion and economic development, however, help to fulfill the goals of identifying long-term changes affecting ordinary people. A precise examination of where religion fits in particular developing locations is the only way to untangle the complex relationship between religion and modernization.

NOTES

I would like to thank my former colleagues, Susan Smulyan and Philip Van-derMeer, whose thoughtful comments on many drafts immeasurably improved the quality of this essay.

1. For a comprehensive account of the Second Great Awakening, see Sydney Ahlstrom, *A Religious History of the American People,* vol. 1 (Garden City, N.Y.: Image Books, 1975), 504–697. My discussion of economic development relies heavily on the following work: Douglass C. North, *Economic Growth of the United States, 1790–1860* (1961; rpt. New York: W. W. Norton, 1966); George Rodgers Taylor, *The Transportation Revolution, 1815–1860* (1951; rpt. New York: Harper & Row, 1968); Stuart Bruchey, *The Roots of American Economic Growth* (New York: Harper & Row, 1965); and Diane Lindstrom, *Economic Development in the Philadelphia Region, 1810–1850* (New York: Columbia University Press, 1978).

2. See George M. Marsden, *Fundamentalism and American Culture* (New York: Oxford University Press, 1980) on the late nineteenth century and Charles Y. Glock and Robert N. Bellah, eds., *The New Religious Consciousness* (Berkeley: University of California Press, 1976) on the contemporary period.

3. Turner's ideas did yield the first religious histories that looked at religious development in terms of a particular environment. The classic scholarship for the frontier includes William Warren Sweet, *The Story of Religion in America* (1930; rpt. New York: Harper & Row, 1968); H. Richard Niebuhr, *The Social Sources of Denominationalism* (1929; rpt. New York: World Publishing, 1957); and Sydney Mead, *A Lively Experiment* (New York: Harper & Row, 1963).

4. *Statistics of the United States in 1860: Eighth Census* (Washington: Government Printing Office, 1866), 501.

5. It is instructive that the field of sociology, which arose independent of denominations, has a rich tradition of exploring religion within the larger American society. Not unexpectedly, seminary scholars have been one of the major groups to criticize the contextual analysis employed by sociology of religion for not reflecting "true" religious experiences.

6. For political history, see Rhys Isaac, *The Transformation of Virginia, 1740–1790* (Chapel Hill: University of North Carolina Press, 1982); Paul Kleppner,

The Cross of Culture (Glencoe, Ill.: Free Press, 1970); and Philip VanderMeer, *The Hoosier Politician* (Champaign: University of Illinois Press, 1985). For labor history, see Herbert Gutman, "Work, Society, and Culture in Industrializing America, 1815–1919," *American Historical Review* 78 (June 1973): 531–588; Bruce Laurie, *The Working People of Philadelphia* (Philadelphia: Temple University Press, 1980); and Paul Faler, *Mechanics & Manufacturers in the Early Industrial Revolution* (Albany: State University of New York Press, 1981). For women's history, see Mary Ryan, *Cradle of the Middle Class* (New York: Cambridge University Press, 1981); Nancy Cott, *Bonds of Womanhood* (New Haven: Yale University Press, 1972); and Carroll Smith-Rosenberg, "Beauty, the Beast, and the Militant Woman: A Case Study in Sex Roles and Social Stress in Jacksonian America," *American Quarterly* 23 (1971): 562–584.

7. William McLoughlin, *Revivals, Awakenings, and Reform* (Chicago: University of Chicago Press, 1978).

8. The review essays in Olivier Zunz, ed., *Reliving the Past: The Worlds of Social History* (Chapel Hill: University of North Carolina Press, 1985) illustrate the importance of modernization studies to social history.

9. Whitney Cross, *The Burned-Over District: The Social and Intellectual History of Enthusiastic Religion in Western New York* (1950; rpt. Harper & Row, 1965); Lee Benson, *The Concept of Jacksonian Democracy* (1961; rpt. New York: Atheneum Press, 1969); and E. P. Thompson, *The Making of the English Working Class* (New York: Vintage Books, 1965).

10. Paul Johnson, *A Shopkeeper's Millennium: Society and Revivals in Rochester, New York, 1815–1837* (New York: Hill and Wang, 1978). Evangelical beliefs proved attractive to these shopkeeper's because they emphasized progress, human accountability, and the promise that every Christian would internalize social habits compatible with the new economy.

11. Mary Ryan, "A Woman's Awakening: Evangelical Religion and the Families of Utica, New York, 1800–1840," in James Wilson James, ed., *Women in American Religion* (Philadelphia: University of Pennsylvania Press, 1980); Jonathan Prude, *The Coming of Industrial Order: Town and Factory Life in Rural Massachusetts, 1810–1860* (Cambridge, England: Cambridge University Press, 1983); Laurie, *The Working People of Philadelphia;* and Faler, *Mechanics & Manufacturers.*

12. Nathan Hatch, *The Democratization of American Christianity* (New Haven: Yale University Press, 1989) and Jon Butler, *Awash in a Sea of Faith: Christianizing the American People* (Cambridge: Yale University Press, 1990). Hatch, p. 12, explicitly argues that only religious issues that transcend local interests are important to American culture.

13. Randolph A. Roth, *The Democratic Dilemma: Religion, Reform, and the Social Order in the Connecticut River Valley of Vermont* (Cambridge, England: Cambridge University Press, 1987); Ferenc Morton Szaz, *The Protestant Clergy in the Great Plains and Mountain West, 1865–1915* (Albuquerque: University of New Mexico Press, 1988); Linda K. Pritchard, "A Comparative Approach to Western Religious History: Texas as a Case Study," *The Western Historical Quar-*

terly 19 (November 1988): 413–430; and George Thomas, *Revivalism and Cultural Change: Christianity, Nation-Building, and the Market in the Nineteenth Century United States* (Chicago: University of Chicago Press, 1989).

14. For an excellent account of the stages of frontier development in Ohio, see Hubert G. H. Wilhelm, *The Origins and Distribution of Settlement Groups: Ohio: 1850* (Athens: Ohio University Press, 1982). See also Solon J. and Elizabeth Hawthorne Buck, *The Planting of Civilization in Western Pennsylvania* (Pittsburgh: University of Pittsburgh Press, 1939); Thomas D. Clark, *A History of Kentucky* (New York: Prentice-Hall, 1937); and Alexander G. Flick, ed., *The History of New York,* vol. 5 (New York: Columbia University Press, 1934).

15. Frederick Jackson Turner, *The United States 1830–1850* (New York: W. W. Norton, 1935), 259. See also Helen Tanner, ed., *Atlas of Great Lakes Indian History* (Norman: University of Oklahoma Press, 1987).

16. County boundaries were extremely fluid during the early nineteenth century, but these political changes did not affect the analysis because religious variables (congregations, congregational seats, or members) and economic indicators (population, farm values, urbanization) were always compared within the same boundaries.

17. See George Bedell et al., *Religion in America* (New York: Macmillan, 1985), for a discussion of congregations in American religion, and Kevin J. Cristiano, *Religious Diversity and Social Change in American Cities, 1890–1906* (Cambridge, England: Cambridge University Press, 1987) on the use of the census for religious information. I have found county histories highly reliable on congregational organization.

18. The twenty-six counties clustered in six locations: five in the Black Swamp area of northwestern Ohio (Henry, Fulton, Wood, Lucas, and Sandusky); four in Ohio's Western Reserve (Ashtabula, Lake, Geauga, Cuyahoga); four in the Allegany (Allegheny) Forest area of New York and Pennsylvania (Potter, Pennsylvania, and Allegany, Wyoming, and Livingston, New York); six in the Redstone area of western Pennsylvania, the West Virginia panhandle, and southeastern Ohio (Washington and Greene, Pennsylvania; Brooke and Ohio, West Virginia; and Jefferson and Belmont, Ohio); three in the Hocking Valley of Ohio (Hocking, Vinton, and Athens); and four in the Cincinnati area (Hamilton, Clermont, Brown, Ohio, and Mason, Kentucky).

19. Frederick Jackson Turner, *The Significance of the Frontier in American History* (1893) edited with an introduction by Harold P. Simonson (New York: Frederick Unger, 1963), 29.

20. Unfortunately, the U.S. Census gives comparative population totals only for the first year of a decade.

21. U.S. Census 1850. Richard Wade, *The Urban Frontier* (Chicago: University of Chicago Press, 1959), p. 135, found this to be true for the major cities of the region as well: "Far from being sinks of depravity, Western cities by 1815 had become religious centers." The entire region had a slightly lower per capita congregation ratio of 1.9 churches per 1,000 people, although this was still higher than the national figure. See Linda K. Pritchard, "The Burned-Over

District Reconsidered: A Portent of Evolving Religious Pluralism in the United States," *Social Science History,* 8 (Summer 1984): 247.

22. Henry A. Ford and Mrs. Katie Ford, *History of Cincinnati, Ohio* (Cincinnati: L. A. Williams & Co., 1881), 154.

23. Ahlstrom, *A Religious History,* 555.

24. See Timothy Smith, "Lay Initiative in the Religious Life of American Immigrants, 1880–1950," in Tamara Haraven, ed., *Anonymous Americans: Explorations in Nineteenth-Century Social History* (Englewood Cliffs, N.J.: Prentice-Hall, 1971) and Wade, *The Urban Frontier,* 321.

25. Ford and Ford, *History of Cincinnati,* 154.

26. Ibid., 354.

27. J. L. Rockey and R. J. Bancroft, *History of Clermont County, Ohio* (Philadelphia: Louis H. Everts, 1880), 48–49. See Ahlstrom, *A Religious History,* vol. 2, pp. 338–339 for a discussion of the anti-mission controversy.

28. James B. Finley, *Sketches of Western Methodism* (Cincinnati: Methodist Book Concern, 1854), 105. This story was repeated in Ford and Ford, *History of Cincinnati,* 153.

29. Finley, *Sketches,* 105.

30. Wilhelm, *Ohio: 1850,* aggregated the place of birth by state or foreign country for 1850 residents of Ohio countied based on the manuscript census. SPSS Factor Analysis created five statistically significant ethnic categories: NORTH, SOUTH, WEST, BRITAIN, and GERMANY. SPSS Regression Analysis then evaluated the strength of association between these categories (independent variables) and particular religious groups (dependent variables). A hierarchical method of entry was employed, whereby the five ethnic categories were entered together and then each removed in order to determine the ethnic influence on the distribution of congregational seats across the region. For a specific discussion of the techniques, see Norman H. Nie et al., *Statistical Package for the Social Sciences* (New York: McGraw-Hill, 1975), 320–342, 468–478.

31. The number of seats reported in the 1850 census for each denomination determined the denominational strength in Ohio counties. Actual membership is impossible to determine for such a large number of congregations, and the number of seats indicates the comparative size of denominations in seventy-two counties where full census information was available.

32. The county histories gave the organizational background for sixty-two of the seventy-one congregations founded within the first decade of settlement and 134 of 168 founded in the succeeding ten years. Only congregations with the exact date of organization were used.

33. Other studies of revivalism in this region support these findings. Whitney Cross, *The Burned-Over District,* determined that Charles Finney's revivalism was most successful in the commercial towns and cities of upstate New York between 1815 and 1850, rather than in the least developed or emerging industrial areas. Furthermore, John Hammond, *The Politics of Benevolence* (Norwood, N.J.: Ablex Publishers, 1979), indicated that revivalism became associated with particular subregions in Ohio and New York, rather than primitive settlement conditions.

34. Alfred Creigh, *History of Washington County, Pennsylvania* (n.p., 1870), 47. This point has been made many times. See especially Elizabeth K. Nottingham, *Methodism and the Frontier* (New York: Columbia University Press, 1941) and T. Scott Miyakawa, *Protestants and Pioneers* (Chicago: University of Chicago Press, 1964).

35. *Ohio Railroad Guide; Illustrated, Cincinnati to Erie Via Columbus and Cleveland* (Columbus, 1854), as quoted in John A. Jakle, *Images of the Ohio Valley* (New York: Oxford University Press, 1977), 156.

36. John M. Blum et al., *The National Experience* (New York: Harcourt, Brace & World, 1963), 124.

37. Thomas Cushing, ed., *History of Allegheny County, Pennsylvania,* vol. 1 (Chicago: A. Warner & Co., 1889), 109, 450; Donald S. Wood, "A Geographical Study of the Economic and Urban Evolution of McKeesport, Pennsylvania," (M.A. thesis, Department of Geography, University of Pittsburgh, 1950), 29; and Evan Hammar, "Wilkinsburg and Edgewood: Commuter Suburbs," (Seminar paper, Department of History, Carnegie Mellon University, n.d.), 11.

38. *Commemorative Biographical Record of Northwestern Ohio* (Chicago: J. H. Beers, 1899), 170–172.

39. Lewis Cass Aldrich, *History of Henry and Fulton Counties, Ohio* (D. Mason & Co., 1888), 638 and *Commemorative Biographical Record of Northwestern Ohio,* 30.

40. Church seats help to control for the differential rates of congregational founding by denomination. For example, Protestants were more likely to have many congregations with smaller church buildings, while Roman Catholics and other liturgical denominations tended to build fewer churches with more parishioners. Even so, the direction and significance of the findings are the same when the number of congregations is used.

41. This regression analysis also employed a hierarchical method of entry. Four economic variables—total population, value of farms, value of manufacturing, and size of the largest town—were entered together (independent variables) and then each removed in order to determine how they influenced the distribution of congregational seats in various denominations (dependent variables) across the region. See Nie et al., *SPSS,* 320–342.

42. Non-evangelical groups which were not liturgical had few relationships to any developmental characteristics.

43. Although membership information was not available for all congregations, the study found 934 congregations reporting total membership between 1840 and 1860 in the twenty-six county subset. Because of the small number of counties, no statistical analysis is presented.

44. The congregational totals for Washington County were derived from county histories compiled in Creigh, *Washington County* (1870) and Boyd Crumrine, ed., *History of Washington County, Pennsylvania* (Philadelphia: L. H. Everts & Co., 1882).

45. Crumrine, *Washington County,* 510–524; Creigh, *Washington County,* 18, 94–95; and Earle R. Forrest, *History of Washington County, Pennsylvania,* vol. 1 (Chicago: S. J. Clarke Publishing Company, 1926), pp. 599–600.

46. Forrest, *Washington County,* 589–590 and Rev. Francis J. Collier, *Chartiers Church and Its Ministers* (Philadelphia: McLaughlin Brothers, 1875), 7–27.

47. Ahlstrom, *A Religious History,* 539, and the U.S. Census.

48. Ahlstrom, *A Religious History,* 541–544 and Forrest, *Washington County,* 594–595.

49. Johnson, *A Shopkeeper's Millennium* and Robert W. Doherty, "Social Bases for the Presbyterian Schism of 1837–1838: The Philadelphia Case," *Journal of Social History* 2 (1968): 69–79.

50. Curtis D. Johnson, *Islands of Holiness: Rural Religion in Upstate New York, 1790–1860* (Ithaca, N.Y.: Cornell University Press, 1989), 53–66 and Nora Faires, "Ethnicity in Evolution," (Ph.D. diss, University of Pittsburgh, 1980). See also Ryan, *Cradle of the Middle Class.*

51. Robert W. Doherty, "Sociology, Religion, and Historians," *Historical Methods Newsletter,* 6 (September 1973): 161–169.

52. Jon Butler, in *Awash in a Sea of Faith,* provides welcome attention to the ascent of bureaucratic practices within denominations during this period. See especially pp. 270–274.

53. Pritchard, "A Comparative Approach," 418, 421, and Roth, *The Democratic Dilemma,* 16, 31.

54. Szaz, *The Protestant Clergy,* 211, and Eldon G. Ernst, "American Religious History from a Pacific Coast Perspective" in Carl Guarneri and David Alvarez, eds., *Religion and Society in the American West: Historical Essay* (Lanhan, Md.: University Press of America, 1987), 3–42.

6

Sex and the Second Great Awakening: The Feminization of American Religion Reconsidered

In a provocative article first published in 1973, Barbara Welter speculated that during the nineteenth century American religion was "feminized" both in membership and theology.[1] Building upon this insight, a number of scholars have argued that the Second Great Awakening contributed to this feminization of American religion in at least three ways. First, the emotional religiosity of revivalism satisfied the psychological needs of growing numbers of socially isolated nineteenth-century women and produced overwhelming female majorities within American churches.[2] Second, the awakening was a "woman's awakening" because during this era maternal evangelism emerged as the primary means of church recruitment.[3] Third, mid-nineteenth-century American Protestantism assumed a distinctively feminine posture as ministers influenced by the rising numbers of churchwomen domesticated death and replaced their militant Calvinistic god of judgment with a meek and gentle Jesus who liberally granted eternal forgiveness and temporal abundance.[4]

As helpful as this scholarship has been in documenting that women filled the pews and served as active agents in the transformation of American Protestantism, the feminization thesis, like many revisionist theories, is oversimplistic and misleading.[5] In this essay I shall assert that nineteenth-century Protestantism was indeed feminized, but that this feminization occurred in spite of, rather than because of the revivalism of the Second Great Awakening. More specifically, I shall postulate that the awakening, both in design and consequence, was essentially an ambitious but unsuccessful attempt by nineteenth-century churchgoers to "masculinize" Protestantism without having to accommodate the Christian gospel to the growing pressures of the capitalistic marketplace. The implications of this hypothesis suggest the need for a reassessment of the standard interpretations of the origins and cultural consequences of the Second Great Awakening.[6]

To understand the relationship between nineteenth-century evangelicalism and the feminization of American religion, it first is necessary to distinguish between the proponents and opponents of the emotional religiosity associated with the Second Great Awakening. Most Christians in the early national era were evangelical in the sense that they acknowledged that propagating the gospel message was a basic religious obligation. Likewise, most early nineteenth-century Protestants agreed on the soteriological essentials, believing that God through the atoning death of Christ granted pardon and life to the regenerate, but punished the unconverted with eternal damnation. Convinced that the doctrine of atonement was the "life and soul of Christianity," early national Methodists, Episcopalians, Presbyterians, and Baptists alike expounded Anselm's "objective" version of the doctrine when they asserted that the sacrifice of Christ was necessary in order to satisfy the justice of the Father. Together they renounced Abelard's subjective theory of the atonement. According to Abelard, the death of Christ was merely an exemplary act of self-denial intended to spur humankind towards a greater devotion to a loving God. Since this notion did not require humans to recognize their sinful condition and "God's infinite love for holiness," it fell alongside the denial of the divinity of Christ as one of the two damnable heresies most frequently denounced from mainline pulpits of the era.[7] The doctrinal similarities among mainline Protestant denominations—similarities in some ways peculiar to the early nineteenth century—encouraged missionary cooperation among the various religious communities and preconditioned the nation for the possibility of regional revival.

Christians of the era differed, however, in their understanding of the nature of the conversion experience. High Church and liberal thinkers generally viewed conversion as a gradual process rather than an instantaneous event. They also frequently connected spiritual regeneration with the decision of the believer to receive church sacraments and be confirmed into a particular church. These churchgoers—generally members of Episcopal, Lutheran, German Reformed, or Unitarian congregations—often distanced themselves from and even ridiculed the aggressive and emotional religiosity associated with the awakening.[8]

In contrast, Low Church evangelicals, the primary participants in the revivals, were more willing to separate conversion from the decision to join a given fellowship. Yet, if more tolerant of conversions apart from the church, they also were more likely to insist that the believer experience a particular kind of conversion—an instantaneous experience of faith, preceded by a strong sense of personal guilt and followed by a joyful assurance of forgiveness. Viewing this conscious, instantaneous event as a prerequisite of the Christian life, these Low Church evangelicals—generally members of Methodist, Baptist, or, to a lesser degree, Presbyterian or Congregational churches—often used innovative and sometimes controversial measures calculated to provoke this type of religious experience. As proponents of the awakening, these supporters of revivalism held camp meetings and protracted town meetings; invigorated services of worship with lively choruses, lay testimonials, and extemporaneous prayer; unhesitatingly appealed to emotion as well as to reason in their religious discourses; and tolerated, if not encouraged, emotional responses to the preaching of the gospel message.

The social profile of churches that supported these new measures designed to invoke instantaneous conversions was marginally different from the social profile of the less revivalistic denominations. In general, the Unitarians and the High Church Episcopalians who condemned the revivalists generally belonged to congregations which primarily served members from economically well-to-do households. On the other hand, Low Church evangelicals such as the Methodists and Baptists generally were less likely to represent a single economic class. Their denominations included wealthy merchants and professionals, but also substantial numbers of skilled artisans and low-income free blacks or slaves. Few Protestant bodies appealed to white unskilled laborers. As a rule, the revivalistic churches embraced a larger cross section of the population than did the churches that opposed the use of the new measures in gaining new converts.[9]

This pattern of religious orientation was discernible in my study of the churches of early national Baltimore. Table 6.1 summarizes the results of an analysis of nearly three thousand Baltimore families that demonstrated at least nominal religious affiliation. With few exceptions, notably the Friends and Baptists, the study compares the occupations of the heads of households of those Baltimore families whose children were baptized during the first three decades of the nineteenth century.[10] One should note that this analysis monitors only changes within the occupation status of the head of household of nominal churchgoing families. It does not discriminate between which members of the households were religiously active in the churches of the period.

As Table 6.1 suggests, in 1800—before the debate over the proper methods of evangelism dominated the religious scene—the membership of Baltimore's Episcopal churches was evenly divided among the various social classes within the city: roughly one-third being proprietors and professionals, about one-third skilled artisans, and about one-third unskilled laborers. By 1815, however, the Episcopal denomination was underrepresented among the artisans and overproportioned among the white-collared. This trend continued, and by 1830 a clear majority of the whites who attended the Episcopal churches in the city were professionals

TABLE 6.1.   Occupations of Caucasian Churchgoers by
Denomination, 1800–1830

Denomination and year	Sample Size	White collar	Skilled artisan	Unskilled laborers
Episcopal				
1800	205	35%	32%	33%
1815	196	47	20	32
1830	232	51	22	27
Methodist				
1800	309	32	43	24
1815	232	34	44	22
1830	212	33	50	18
Presbyterian (First Church)				
1800	116	54	31	15
1815	49	65	20	14
1830	90	67	14	16
Associate Reformed				
1815	43	40	42	19
1830	41	63	32	5
All other Protestant denominations				
1800	180	24	39	37
1815	145	23	34	43
1830	113	41	37	22
Roman Catholic				
1800	187	17	33	51
1815	196	26	28	46
1830	148	28	32	39
Combined non-Roman Catholics				
1800	810	34	38	28
1815	665	38	33	29
1830	647	45	34	21
Total sample of all Caucasian churchgoers				
1800	997	31	37	32
1815	861	35	32	33
1830	795	42	34	24

or proprietors. Likewise, nearly three in four of those who attended the non-revivalistic Unitarian church were from high-status occupations, as were two in three of those who attended First Presbyterian, a church that, at least before 1825, made little use of the evangelistic methods popularized by the Methodists. A smaller proportion (four in ten in 1815 and six in ten in 1830) within the moderately evangelical Associate Reformed congregation also held high-status employment.

In contrast to these non-revivalistic or moderately evangelistic Protestants, the Methodists attracted a wide range of the city's occupational groupings. Only one in three Caucasian Methodists fell within the higher occupational groupings, while the plurality were skilled artisans. Moreover, about 35 percent of the revivalistic Methodists (as opposed to only 6 percent of the Episcopalians and Presbyterians, and virtually none of the Unitarians) were low-income and low-status blacks.[11] In short, by 1830, the Protestant congregations that opposed or only moderately sanctioned the new measures of evangelism served primarily the professional and proprietary classes. Among the major Protestant groups, only the revivalistic Methodists continued to hold a wide cross section of the entire community.

The Baltimore Methodists also were the major winners in the competition for church growth. In 1810, some five years before the most intense seasons of religious revival erupted in Baltimore, about 22 percent of the churchgoers and 30 percent of the Protestants in the city were Methodists. By 1830, the Methodists controlled a 37 percent share of the religious market, and a whopping 49 percent of the Protestant market. As the estimates presented in Table 6.2 suggest, the Methodist expansion came largely at the expense of their less evangelical Lutheran, Presbyterian, and Episcopal neighbors.[12]

Thus far, I have attempted to identify several distinctive characteristics of the primary participants within the revivals of the Second Great Awakening. I have suggested that the pro-revivalists were primarily Low Church evangelicals who emphasized the need for a conversion telescoped in time to a single datable experience, and who embraced sometimes controversial means of evangelism to reach these ends. In comparison with other Protestant churchgoers, these Low Church evangelicals represented a wider range of social and economic groupings. Moreover, the groups that adopted these more aggressive means of evangelism generally grew at a faster rate than those that relied upon parental socialization and other more traditional means of church recruitment. Correspondingly, it follows that the impact of the awakening upon the feminization of American religion should be most clearly manifested within those Low Church denominations that contributed

TABLE 6.2.   Estimated Size of Baltimore Denominations, 1790–1830

	Number of churchgoers by denominational family			Percentage of churchgoers by denominational family		
	1790	1810	1830	1790	1810	1830
Roman Catholic	900	5,550	10,000	15	25	25
Presbysterian & German Reformed	1,400	3,200	5,000	24	15	13
Episcopal	1,000	3,500	6,000	17	16	15
Methodist & United Brethren	1,200	4,900	14,500	20	22	37
Lutheran	900	3,300	1,500	15	15	4
All others	500	1,600	2,700	8	7	7

the most to and enjoyed the greatest benefits from the emotional revivalism of the era.

Recent studies of the nineteenth-century revivals have demonstrated that female converts outnumbered males by about three to two. What the interpreters of this statistic too often underplay, however, is that the significant result of these revivals was an increase in the size of the church-going male minority.[13] To illustrate, as the statistical studies of Richard Shiels, Paul Johnson, and Mary Ryan have shown, in the early nineteenth century—particularly during seasons of low-to-average church growth—women generally accounted for 70 to 80 percent of the churchgoing population. Only in times of rapid growth did this percentage dip to a mere 60 percent majority.[14]

More importantly, the gender ratio of early national denominations apparently was strongly influenced by the willingness of churches to embrace the controversial new measures of aggressive evangelism. In Baltimore, for instance, about eight in ten of the non-revivalistic Episcopal and German Reform communicants were female, while seven in ten of the marginally evangelical Presbyterian and only two in three of the highly revivalistic Methodist communicants were women. Apparently, the sex balance within Rochester, New York, churches also varied by denomination. According to Paul Johnson, between 1815 and 1838 nearly 74 percent of the Episcopalians in the city, as opposed to only 62 percent of the Presbyterians, were female.[15] Thus, while additional local studies comparing the gender profiles of early national denominations are needed to confirm the following generalizations, there exists a growing body of evidence that suggests: (1) the large majority of churchgoers from all nineteenth-century denominations was female; (2) this majority increases modestly during the course of the century; and (3) the revivalistic churches that augmented traditional patterns of recruitment with aggressive evangelistic tactics slowed but did not arrest the feminization process within religious institutions.

The ability of revivals to reach an otherwise disinterested male audience was not simply a serendipity. Post-Revolutionary clergymen—knowing all too well that women filled their pews, but men paid their salaries—genuinely feared both for the future of their churches and their profession.[16] Likewise, the faithful remnant of churchmen charged with the responsibility of raising the budget and maintaining the status of their congregations frantically sought relief from the acute problem of male declension. At this time, generally only the "fanatical" Methodists—those who embraced such disturbing measures as street preaching, protracted town meetings, camp meetings, and a host of other proven weapons of evangelism—succeeded in attracting a substantial minority of male churchgoers. Hence, frightened by their growing inability to retain male communicants, concerned ministers and laymen from the more respectable classes faced an unpleasant choice. They could continue to rely upon parental socialization and traditional means of church recruitment and see their churches become feminine institutions, or they could adopt the more dramatic techniques of the Methodists and compete for a greater share of the male market. Although few candidly confessed that they embraced the new measures simply to masculinize their churches and pay their bills, it is probable that the intense denominational competition following disestablishment, coupled with the apparent failure of traditional means of male church recruitment, drove many higher-status churches to adopt the revivalistic methods they once had ridiculed as the enthusiasm of the ignorant.[17]

The story of revivalism in early national Baltimore supports this hypothesis. Fully two decades before Charles Finney popularized his controversial new measures of evangelism, Baltimore churchgoers were sponsoring camp meetings and protracted town meetings, encouraging converts to share at public gatherings their new-found faith, and challenging the unsaved or almost saved to come to the altar or "anxious bench" for special exhortation and prayer. Before 1815, however, this evangelical activity was primarily the work of Methodists—the only Protestants in town able to boast of an active and growing male membership. By the end of the second decade of the century, other denominations began to loosen their belts of religious sophistication and adopt some of the tactics of the Methodists. Their acceptance of the new measures almost inevitably spurred both numeric growth and greater male participation.

To illustrate, after years of stagnation, during an 1818–1819 revival the Associate Reformed Church received 196 new communicants, ninety-six of whom were male.[18] Then in 1823, shortly after W. C. Walton boldly told the membership of this Third Presbyterian Church that "if we made use of the proper means, we might have a revival," this tiny congregation added sixty-three communicants to their church rolls.[19] In 1825, William Nevins of First Presbyterian responded to the suggestions of the prominent Methodist evangelist John Summerfield, and began delivering more direct, plain, and pungent messages. Shortly thereafter, a revival erupted within this prestigious congregation that replenished its declining male membership.[20] Also in 1825, John Breckenridge, upon replacing John Glendy as pastor of the decaying Second Presbyterian Church, determined to reinvigorate his near nonextant male membership. Seeking aid from local Wesleyans, Breckenridge invited Methodist laymen to testify before a newly organized weekly men's prayer breakfast, and hired an African Methodist baritone to enliven his Presbyterian services by leading the congregation in rousing camp-meeting choruses. Within two years, Second Presbyterian added as many members as it had in the previous two decades, and simultaneously reclaimed from the inactive list other former male members.[21] Although initially reluctant to embrace the vulgar piety of the "shouting Methodists," by 1830 pastors from even the most prestigious Baltimore Presbyterian congregations had accepted and institutionalized the new measures as weapons to combat the problems of male church declension.

As the bolder spirits raised their volume, they also finely tuned their message in an attempt to awaken the apathetic from their spiritual slumber. Realizing that the glitter of economic opportunity was the principal stumbling block to male church participation, early national revivalists to a greater degree than their less evangelical contemporaries condemned the too-eager pursuit of wealth as the root of all evil. Many also openly denounced the marketplace as a devourer of souls. In 1808, for instance, the Baltimore Baptist Association expressed its displeasure with certain aggressive business practices when it passed resolutions stating that Christians should not receive more than legal interest for money lent nor buy at the lowest rate and sell at the highest rate possible without regard to the value of the article purchased.[22] Baltimore Methodists and Friends expressed similar antimaterialist sentiments, and issued stern warnings of the spiritual dangers of choosing "extravagant" and "luxurious" life-styles. "Nothing is more easy than to grow rich," quipped one Methodist.

> It is only to trust nobody—to befriend none—to get everything and save all we get—to stint ourselves and everybody belonging to us—to be the friend of no man, and have no man for our friend—to heap interest upon interest, cent upon cent—to be mean, miserable and despised, for some twenty or thirty years—and riches will come as sure as disease and disappointment.[23]

The attitude of this stereotypical Methodist differed dramatically from that of another contemporary Episcopal rector who warned his flock against allowing their religious devotion from interfering with the equally godly task of providing financial security for their family.[24] Nor was this evangelical's contempt for the ethics of the emerging market economy compatible with the proclamations of later revivalists and liberals alike who made peace with the industrialists and preached a gospel of prosperity.[25] On the contrary, at least in comparision with contemporaries less committed to their evangelical mission, or with most ministers of the ensuing generation, the preachers of the Awakening emphatically insisted that the millennium was not paved with the gold of economic opportunism.

Early national preachers also differed from the more effeminate mid-century liberal clergymen described by Ann Douglas in that they placed a strong emphasis upon human accountability.[26] Far from euphemizing death, proponents of the Awakening exploited its horrors in order to arouse the negligent to spiritual decision. With great frequency, evangelicals contrasted the economic uncertainties of life with the certainties of death and judgment, and then asked, "Are you prepared to die?"[27] They endlessly forewarned of the coming judgment, depicted the eternal fires of hell, and presented parishioners with the alternatives: pardon or punishment.[28] They made funeral discourses less eulogies for the deceased than reminders to the living that death and judgment were near.[29] In short, rather than accommodating to the growing materialism of American society, the proponents of the Awakening took the offensive in a crusade to masculinize their congregations without diluting the traditional disciplinary responsibilities of church membership. The Christ they preached was a sinless Messiah slain to satisfy the wrath of a righteous God, not a divine psychologist who promised peace and prosperity to all who discovered the power of positive thinking.

While snaring its thousands, the loud, emotional, uncompromising rhetoric and religiosity of the revivalists offended many males who preferred the freedom and rationality of the workplace to the moralism and spirituality of the church. Moreover, this muscular brand of Christianity proved too violent for many nineteenth-century women. Nancy Thomson echoed the sentiments of many of her generation when she described attending an 1806 camp revival. "I went praying that God would awaken and convert my companion," she wrote, "but was very fearful that the exercises would be . . . alarming to my tender feelings. . . . I thought if I could obtain religion in a still way without much ado I would be glad . . . but [I] would rather remain without this blessing than to lose my strength or cry out as some did."[30] For many Americans of both sexes, the theology and intensity of the crusaders had little appeal. Ultimately, the American evangelicals retarded but failed to arrest the male fallout in nineteenth-century congregations.

If, as I have argued, the Second Great Awakening was functionally hostile to the feminization of the church and the consumerization of society, how then did mid-nineteenth-century American religion become so thoroughly feminized? Without attempting a definitive answer, it is apparent that this transition resulted less from the revivalism of the Awakening than from cultural and economic factors peculiar to the post-Revolutionary era. For just as increased economic activity for men distracted them from religious pursuits, the increased economic isolation of women drove them into the primary public arena open to their participation. This, at least, was the argument frequently espoused by a number of contemporary Chirstian authors who argued that women—by being socially ostracized from individualized economic pursuits—were providentially protected from the principal satanic snares obstructing church progress.[31]

Furthermore, women simply had more incentives to be religious. In an age of high maternal and infant mortality, as childbearers and mothers women were more sensitive to the realities of the grave, and hence took greater care in meeting their perceived religious obligations.[32] Likewise, although women were less susceptible than men to the noise and violence of the revivals, the process of religious conversion that was demanded by all Christian bodies was compatible with the female socialization patterns of surrender and continued submissiveness.[33]

This list could be expanded. During the early decades of the century, the religious press taught that the success of the republic and the moral health of society depended upon the ability of women to use their feminine charms to tame the ferocious instincts in man.[34] In addition, as Nancy Cott and Barbara Epstein have suggested, religious institutions preserved female values, raised female status, protected women from mistreatment in the domestic household, and by providing access to the divine, offered a degree of liberation from male authority.[35] These suppositions, it is important to note, help us understand only why nineteenth-century women were more inclined to be active in all forms of church life. None of the above supports the premise that women were uniquely suited for evangelical Christianity, or more susceptible than men to the emotionalism of the revivalists. Indeed, women dominated the pews and altars of all denominations, although particularly the more liberal ones, because churches offered them the status, satisfaction, and emotional support that many men sought in the bustling markets of a rapidly industrializing America.

In highlighting the masculine characteristics of the Second Great Awakening, I am not denying that thousands of nineteenth-century women found personal satisfaction and support from the revivals of the era. Neither am I dismissing the importance of material evangelism, or questioning the predominance of women in the early nineteenth-century Bible, tract, and missionary societies. I am suggesting, however, that the aggressive evangelistic techniques associated with the Awakening—particularly the more militant and emotional forms of religious expression—were initially accepted and ultimately institutionalized by churches from all social groupings primarily because these methods succeeded better than traditional ones in reaching an increasingly unreachable adult male population. Although only a minor corrective to the feminization literature, the implications of this reinterpretation offer valuable insights into long-standing historiographical debates.

To illustrate, a generation ago historians took the gloomy complaints of late-eighteenth-century clergymen at face value and concluded that church life in post-Revolutionary America was in an unprecedented state of decay. These historians generally viewed the Second Great Awakening as a Protestant counteroffensive against widespread religious apathy and infidelity.[36] More recently, this "low-ebb tide" theory has come under attack by studies documenting that church attendance following the Revolution was not as dismal as we once believed.[37] My own study of early national Baltimore falls within this school of revisionist thought. I argue, for instance, that while only a small minority of Baltimoreans were listed as "official" members of the local congregations, as many as four in nine Baltimore households included members who attended church at least intermittently during the final decade of the eighteenth century. This level of religious involvement, however, did not impress the clerics of the city. Baltimore clergymen from virtually every denominational family complained throughout the 1790s about the alarming state of religious declension within the city.

To explain the distance between statistical fact and rhetoric, some scholars have replaced the "low-ebb tide" thesis with a "conspiracy" theory that interprets the public jeremiads of the 1790s as strategic ploys intended to pressure churchgoers to unite under clerical leadership against the phantom forces of evil.[38] Yet, as critics have questioned, if clerical despair was only a ploy, why was it as explicit in private correspondence as in public pronouncement?[39] The hypothesis of this article offers an alternate and more persuasive resolution to the historiographical riddle. In an age of religious voluntarism, the growing gender disparity in post-Revolutionary churches troubled clergymen who recognized that it was principally adult men who paid the bills and brought status and authority to their congregations. While the prophets of doom were sincere, their jeremiads signified less a general loss in membership than a loss in those members who, at least to them, really counted.

In addition, this refinement in the feminization thesis causes us to reassess our perceptions of the causes and consequences of nineteenth-century revivalism. First, interpreting the Awakening as a masculine enterprise designed to revitalize a dwindling male churchgoing population poses a methodological dilemma for scholars attempting to explain it in terms of its peculiar appeal to nineteenth-century women. Similarly, the antimaterialism of the most revivalistic churches calls into question the assertions of the "social control" theorists who portray the evangelical united front as an unholy alliance of ministers and industrialists who exploited the power of religion to keep the masses in order and protect their personal status and wealth.[40] The popularity of nineteenth-century revivalism, I assert, had less to do with the emotional distresses of women or the conspiratorial designs of wealthy elites than it did with the problems of voluntary churches in an increasingly materialistic age. Following disestablishment, when the virgin religious market was unusually fluid, voluntary churches fiercely competed with each other for a dwindling supply of male contributors. The nature of this struggle encouraged churches to implement new strategies to enlarge their share of the population. Thus, while revivals never were as extensive as their proponents desired, they erupted primarily because churchgoers of particular denominations expected them and labored diligently to promote them.

Finally, this critique also suggests that historians have overstated the impact of the Second Great Awakening upon American culture. For underlying the patriotic and millennial rhetoric of the revivalists was the two-fold ambition: (1) to masculinize Protestantism in verve and person so that the church again could compete against the world of economic opportunity for the allegiance of the best and brightest men; and (2) to Christianize the culture so that the collective powers of individual piety could curtail the corrupting and dehumanizing pressures of the modern world. In the end, the evangelicals slowed but could not break the tide toward a female-dominated church. And in their pursuit to capture the world, they themselves became captive. By mid-century, evangelicals softened their uncompromising zeal against the too-eager pursuit of gain with the acknowledgment that the acquisition of great wealth could accomplish the greatest good. And while future generations perpetuated their denominational names and for a time their methods, mid-century Protestants replaced their original evangelical message of accountability with the promise that God would help those who helped themselves. In essence, the proponents of the Awakening, like the late nineteenth-century medievalists and orientalists described by T. Jackson Lears and the social gospelers discussed by Janet Fishburn, were antimodern dissenters who challenged the very basis of industrial capitalistic society, but in the end furthered as much as checked that which they so ardently protested. American religion along with mid-century culture was consumerized, but not as a product of the Second Great Awakening. Instead this "feminization of American culture" was a monument to the failure of the evangelicals to transform America into their vision of a masculine promised land.[41]

NOTES

1. Barbara Welter, "The Feminization of American Religion: 1800–1860," in Mary Hartman and Lois Banner, eds., *Clio's Consciousness Raised* (New York: Harper Torchbooks, 1973).
2. Nancy Cott, "Young Women in the Second Great Awakening in New England," *Feminist Studies* 3 (Fall/Winter 1975): 15–29, and *The Bonds of Womanhood* (New Haven: Yale University Press, 1977); and Amanda Porterfield, *Feminine Spirituality in America* (Philadelphia: Temple University Press, 1980). For the yearly percentages of female churchgoers within New England congregations, see Richard Shiels, "The Feminization of American Congregationalism," *American Quarterly* 33 (Spring 1981): 46–62.
3. Mary Ryan, "A Woman's Awakening," *American Quarterly* 30 (Winter 1978): 602–623, "The Power of Women's Networks," *Feminist Studies* 5 (June 1979): 66–86, and *Cradle of the Middle Class* (New York: Cambridge University Press, 1981); Ruth H. Bloch, "American Feminine Ideals in Transition: The Rise of the Moral Mother, 1785–1815," *Feminist Studies* 4 (June 1978): 100–126.
4. Barbara Epstein, *Politics of Domesticity* (Middletown, Conn.: Wesleyan University Press, 1981); David S. Reynolds, "The Feminization Controversy: Sexual Stereotypes and the Paradoxes of Piety in Nineteenth Century America," *New England Quarterly* 53 (March 1980): 96–106, and "From Doctrine to Narrative:

The Rise of Pulpit Storytelling in America," *American Quarterly* 32 (Fall 1980): 479–498; and Gayle Kimball, "Harriett Beecher Stowe's Revision of New England Theology," *Journal of Presbyterian History* 58 (1980): 64–81. Ann Douglas in *The Feminization of American Culture* (New York: Knopf, 1977) discusses a similar transition for the liberal tradition of American Protestantism.

5. Other recent publications focusing on the liberating influences of religion upon the lives of nineteenth-century women include Donald G. Mathews, "Women's History: Everyone's History," in *Women in the New World,* vol. 1 (Nashville, Tenn.: Abingdon Press, 1981); Timothy L. Smith, "Righteousness and Hope: Christian Holiness and the Millennial Vision of America, 1800–1900," *American Quarterly* 31 (Spring 1979): 21–45; Winthrop Hudson, "Early Nineteenth Century Evangelical Religion and Women's Liberation," *Foundations* 23 (1980): 151–185; Page Putnam Miller, "Women in the Vanguard of the Sunday School Movement," *Journal of Presbyterian History* 58 (1980):311–325; Joe L. Kincheloe, Jr., "Transcending Role Restrictions: Women at Camp Meetings and Political Rallies," *Tennessee Historical Quarterly* 40 (1981): 158–169; and Nancy A. Hardesty, *Women Called to Witness: Evangelical Feminism in the Nineteenth Century* (Nashville: Abingdon Press, 1984).

6. For an elaboration of these arguments, see Terry D. Bilhartz, *Urban Religion and the Second Great Awakening: Church and Society in Early National Baltimore* (Madison, N.J.: Fairleigh Dickinson University Press, 1986), 134–141.

7. For contemporary sermons on this central doctrine, see John Inglis, *Sermons of the Late Dr. James Inglis* (Baltimore, 1820), 47–60, 187–196, 197–206; William Nevins, *Select Remains of the Rev. William Nevins* (New York: 1836), 135–138, and *Sermons by the Late Rev. William Nevins* (New York, 1837), 213–216; George Roberts, *The Substance of a Sermon . . . Preached to . . . the Conference of the Methodist Episcopal Church* (Baltimore, 1807); William Wyatt, ed., *The Monument: A Small Selection from the Sermons of the Late Rt. Rev. James Kemp* (Baltimore, 1833), 91–105, 110–111; John Summerfield, *Sermons and Sketches of Sermons,* (New York, 1845), 281–286; George Lemmon, *A Sermon on the Following Words, 'This is a Faithful Saying, and Worthy of All Acceptation, that Christ Jesus Came into the World to Save Sinners'* (Baltimore, 1810); and Joseph Bend, "The Atonement of Christ with its Moral Designs," "Christ a Propitiation for the Sins of the World," "On the Satisfaction Made by Christ," "On the Sacrifice Made by Christ," "Nature, Ends, and Effects of the Death of Christ," "The Atonement of Christ with its Moral Designs," "The Fallacy of Certain Specious Doctrines Detected," MS Bend Sermons, Episcopal Diocese of Maryland (hereafter cited MdBD).

8. An excellent survey of doctrinal differences among American denominations is Arthur Carl Piepkorn, *Profiles in Belief: The Religious Bodies of the United States and Canada,* vol. 2 (San Francisco: Harper & Row, 1978). For an introduction to the psychology of religious conversion, see William James, *Varieties of Religious Experience* (New York: Longmans, Green, 1912). For a discussion of the new measures and Arminian tendencies of the Second Great Awakening, see C. C. Goen, "The 'Methodist Age' in American Church History,"

Religion in Life (Autumn 1965): 562–572; Richard Carwardine, "The Second Great Awakening in Urban Centers: An Examination of Methodism and the 'New Measures,' " *The Journal of American History* 59 (1972): 327–340; and William G. McLoughlin, *Modern Revivalism: Charles Grandison Finney to Billy Graham* (New York: Ronald Press, 1959) and *Revivals, Awakenings, and Reform* (Chicago: University of Chicago Press, 1978).

9. The pattern of segregating socioeconimc groups by denomination is well-known. For an introduction to this issue and to its impact on Christianity, see H. Richard Niebhur, *Social Sources of Denominationalism* (Cleveland: World Publishing Inc., 1929).

10. For discussion of the methodology I used in this analysis, see "Appendix A: Notes on Methodology" and "Appendix B: Vertical Categories: By Rank and Trade" in my *Urban Religion,* 142–148.

11. "Journal of the Baltimore Annual Conferences, 1800–1833," typescript located at Wesley Theological Seminary, Washington, D.C., pp. 57, 68, 77, 83, 90, 102, 114, 121, 130, 144, 154, 165, 172, 182, 190, 204, 213, 231, 238; Annie Burns, "Register of the First Presbyterian Church, Baltimore," typescripts located at the Library of Congress, Washington, D.C. (hereafter cited DLC); and "Register, St. Paul's Parish, vol. 1," located at Maryland Historical Society (hereafter cited MdHi).

12. The estimates of table 2 are summations taken from *Urban Religion,* 142–145, 157.

13. Nancy Cott identifies women as the principal participants in the revivals, and argues from this observation that revivals flourished because they satisfied the emotional needs of single women who were stranded in the cities without familial support or economic opportunity. See Cott, "Young Women," pp. 15–29. Paul Johnson in his study of Rochester, New York, notes that men increased their proportion of the communicants during revivals. The conclusion he draws from this data, however, is simply that "revivals were family experiences and that women were converting their men." See Paul Johnson, *A Shopkeeper's Millennium: Society and Revivals in Rochester, New York, 1815–1837* (New York: Hill and Wang, 1978), 102–108. In his study of New England Congregationalists, Richard Shiels also offers statistical evidence to show that evangelicals had greater success than liberals in attracting male churchgoers. However, since his focus is strictly upon the feminization process, he stops short of asserting what his evidence implies: ministers embraced the innovative and controversial new measures in an attempt to offset the growing female majorities in postrevolutionary churches. See Shiels, "Feminization of American Congregationalism."

14. Shiels, "Feminization of American Congregationalism", 46–62; and Ryan, "A Women's Awakening," 602–623. Also see Bilhartz, *Urban Religion,* 19–27, 83–99.

15. For the sex balance of Baltimore churches, see "Baltimore City Station Methodist Episcopal Records," Microfilm reel M 408; "Annual Register for the Methodist Episcopal Church on Fells Point," Microfilm reel M 411, located at the Maryland Hall of Records, Annapolis (hereafter cited MdHR); Annie

Burns, "Register of the First Presbyterian Church, Baltimore," vol. 2, typescript located at DLC, pp. 298–320; "Register of the Associate Reformed Congregation in Baltimore, 1812–1865," vol. 1, pp. 1–30, 236–266, and "Register of the First German Reformed Church, Baltimore," vol. 2, pp. 184–209, MdHR; "Trinity Protestant Episcopal Church, Register," vol. 1, pp. 48–55, and vol. 2, MS 850; and "St. Peter's Protestant Episcopal Church, Register," pp. 47–62, MdHi. The figures for Rochester were obtained by analyzing the data provided in endnote 28 of Chapter 5 in Johnson, *Shopkeeper's Millennium*, p. 189.

16. For a discussion of the problem of supporting early national clerics, see *Urban Religion*, pp. 41–44.

17. *Urban Religion*, pp. 83–99.

18. "Associate Reformed Congregation Register," MdHi, pp. 1–30.

19. W. C. Walton, *Narrative of a Revival of Religion in the Third Presbyterian Church in Baltimore* (Northampton, 1826).

20. John C. Backus, *Revivals of Religion in the Presbyterian Churches of Baltimore* (Philadelphia, 1858); William Nevins, *Practical Thoughts* (New York, 1836), pp. 91, 96.

21. Backus, *Revivals of Religion*, pp. 7–14; "Second Presbyterian Church Records, Baltimore, Volume 2," MdHi.

22. Apparently the latter point was quite controversial, for two years later the body rescinded the 1808 resolution dealing with "buying and selling." *Minutes of the Baltimore Baptist Association, Held in the City of Washington, District of Columbia, on the 14th, 15th, 16th, and 17th Days of October, 1808* (Baltimore, n.p., 1808), 9; *Minutes of the Baltimore Baptist Association Held in the Brick Meeting House, Forks of Winter's Run, Harford County, State of Maryland, on the 18th, 19th, 20th and 21st days of October, 1810* (Baltimore, n.p., 1810).

23. *Mutual Rights and Christian Intelligencer* 2 (20 August 1829): 96. For condemnations of the too-eager pursuit of wealth, see *The Christian Orator* (Baltimore, 1818), 158, 160, 212–213, 261–265; *Epistle of the London Yearly Meeting Society of Friends* (Baltimore, 1802), 2; *Epistle of the London Yearly Meeting Society of Friends* (Baltimore, 1803), 2–3; William Duke, *Observations on the Present State of Religion in Maryland* (Baltimore, 1795), 6–53; Joseph T. Smith, *Eighty Years Embracing a History of Presbyterianism* (Philadelphia: Westminster Press, 1899), 15; "Journal of the Baltimore Annual Conference, Methodist Episcopal Church, 1800–1833," typescript located at Wesley Theological Seminary, Washington, D.C. (hereafter cited as DWyT), 38, 47–48, 79, 90, 126, 207; and *The Journal and Letters of Francis Asbury*, vol. 2 (Nashville, Tenn.: Abingdon Press, 1958), 42, 45, 47, 61, 80, 83, 111, 120, and passim.

24. Joseph Bend, "Overrighteousness," MS Bend Sermons, MdBD, p. 7. For similar expressions, see Joseph Bend, "Not to be Slothful in Business, Yet to be Fervent in Spirit, Serving the Lord," MS Bend Sermons, MdBD; James Kemp, *A Sermon on the Christian Warfare Preached at the Funeral of the Rt. Rev. Dr. Claggett* (Baltimore, 1817); and William E. Wyatt, ed., *The Monument*, pp. 156–157.

25. See Donald Meyer, *The Positive Thinkers: Religion as Pop Psychology From*

Mary Baker Eddy to Oral Roberts (New York: Pantheon, 1980), especially pp. 129–207; and Robert M. Calhoon, *Evangelicals and Conservatives in the Early South, 1740–1861* (Columbia, S.C.: University of South Carolina Press, 1988), 192–198.

26. Douglas, *Feminization of American Culture*, passim.

27. For examples, see Inglis, *Sermons*, 35–46, 125–132, 169–178, 271–280; Nevins, *Sermons*, 108–110; William Nevins, *Practical Thoughts* (New York: 1836), 217; Summerfield, *Sermons*, 185–188.

28. Inglis, *Sermons*, 150–152, 241–243; Nevins, *Select Remains*, 354–355; Nevins, *Sermons*, 148–149, 239–241, 248–250, 369–370, 377–378, 401–405; Wyatt, *The Monument*, 88, 154, 161–162; Frederick Beasley, *A Sermon on Dueling, Delivered in Christ Church, Baltimore, April 28, 1811* (Baltimore, 1811), 39; and Joseph Bend, "State of the Unrighteous," and "The Fate of the Wicked Considered," MS Bend Sermons, MdBD.

29. Kemp, *Sermon on the Christian Warfare*, and "On the Death of Gen. Alexander Hamilton," July 1804, and "A Commentary on the Burial of the Dead," MdBD; Joseph Bend, "A Discourse Delivered in Christ Church Baltimore, 1798" (Baltimore, 1798), "Counsel of God and Future Glory," and "On Walking With God," MS Bend Sermons, MdBD; and Jared Sparks, *A Sermon Preached in the Hall of the House of Representatives in Congress, Washington City, March 3, 1822, Occasioned by the Death of the Hon. William Pickney, Late Member of the Senate of the U.S.* (Washington, 1822). See also Asbury's *Journal and Letters*, passim.

30. Quoted in Cott, "Young Women," 21.

31. For examples of this argument, see James Fordyce, *Sermons to Young Women* (Philadelphia, 1809), 2: 56–59; Frances E. King, *Female Scripture Characters* (Boston, 1816), 141–165; Hannah More, *Moral Sketches* (Boston, 1819), 114–119.

32. With nearly one-half of those interred in early national graveyards under ten years of age, it is clear that few parishioners escaped the pains of burying close family members. Moreover, certain evidence suggests that parental trauma following the death of children was greater for mothers than fathers. In a letter from Reverend Joseph Bend to James Kemp, and in another from a rural Methodist to Francis Asbury, two fathers casually reported the death of their children in the middle paragraphs of their letters, after first discussing more mundane news. See Annie Burns, "Cathedral Burial Records" and "Burial Records Light Street Methodist Episcopal Church," typescript at DLC; and "Register of St. Peter's Church, Baltimore, 1803–1885," and "St. Paul's Parish Register, 1776–1837," MdHi; Joseph Bend to James Kemp, November 28, 1797, MdBD; Thomas Haskins to Francis Asbury, 12 September 1791, Lovely Lane Museum, Baltimore.

33. See Barbara Welter, "The Cult of True Womanhood: 1820–1860," *American Quarterly* 18 (Summer 1966), and Kathryn Kish Sklar, *Catharine Beecher: A Study in American Domesticity* (New Haven: Yale University Press, 1973).

34. For examples, see Fordyce, *Sermons*, 1, 22–62; 2, 52–90, 110–129; *The*

Pious Parents' Present (New York, 1815); James Miltimore, *An Address to a Young Lady* (Newburyport, 1814), 12–13; *The American Lady's Preceptor* (Baltimore, 1819), 28–29, 38–42, 66–81, 279; Cardine Matilda Thayer, *Religion Recommended to Youth* (New York, 1819); Richard Watson, *An Address to Young Persons* (Boston, 1808); 34; *The Female Friend* (Baltimore, 1809); *Address to Mothers* (Simsbury, Conn.: 1817), 1; Alexander M. Proudit, *An Address to the Rising Generation* (Salem, N.Y., 1804), 33; Matthew LaRue Perrine, *Women Have a Work To Do In the House of God* (New York, 1817), 21–22; *Advice to the Fair Sex* (Philadelphia, 1803); and John Stephens, *The Advantages Which Man Derives from Woman* (Middletown, Conn., 1815).

35. Cott, *Bonds of Womanhood;* and Epstein, *Politics of Domesticity.* Also see Jan Lewis, *The Pursuit of Happiness: Family and Values in Jefferson's Virginia* (Cambridge: Cambridge University Press, 1983).

36. Among the numerous studies that adhere to this view are Leonard Woolsey Bacon, *A History of American Christianity* (New York: Christian Literature Co., 1897); William Warren Sweet, *The Story of Religion in America* (New York: Harper & Bros., 1930); Kenneth Scott Latourette, *A History of Christianity,* vol. 2 (New York: Harper & Row, 1975); Winthrop Hudson, *Religion in America,* 3d ed. (New York: Scribner, 1980); Sydney E. Ahlstrom, *A Religious History of the American People,* 2 vols. (Garden City, N.Y.: Doubleday, 1975); Charles Keller, *The Second Great Awakening in Connecticut* (New Haven: Yale University Press, 1942); David M. Ludlum, *Social Ferment in Vermont, 1791–1830* (New York: Columbia University Press, 1939); and Franklin H. Littell, *From State Church to Pluralism* (New York: Macmillan, 1971).

37. For a critique of the traditional view, see Douglas H. Sweet, "Church Vitality and the American Revolution: Historiographical Consensus and Thoughts Towards a New Perspective," *Church History* 45 (1976): 341–359. Also see Shiels, "The Second Great Awakening in Connecticut," *Church History* 49 (1980): 401–415; Stephen A. Marini, *Radical Sects of Revolutionary New England* (Cambridge: Harvard University Press, 1982), 40–59, 82–101; Donald G. Mathews, *Religion in the Old South* (Chicago: University of Chicago Press, 1977), 48–50; and Thomas O'Brien Hanley, *The American Revolution and Religion: Maryland 1770–1800* (Washington, D.C.: Catholic University Press of America, Consortium Press, 1971).

38. See Fred J. Hood, *Reformed America: The Middle and Southern States, 1783–1837* (University, Ala.: University of Alabama Press, 1980); John Boles, *The Great Revival, 1787–1805* (Lexington: University of Kentucky Press, 1972); and Martin Marty, *The Infidel: Free Thought and American Religion* (New York: World Publishing Co., 1961).

39. For examples of the prevalence of despair in private ministerial correspondence, see the manuscript letters of Joseph Bend, William Duke, and James Kemp at MdBD.

40. For a survey of the "social control" literature, see John R. Bodo, *The Protestant Clergy and Public Issues, 1812–1848* (Princeton: Princeton University Press, 1954); Charles C. Cole, Jr., *The Social Ideas of the Northern Evangelists,*

1820–1860 (New York: Columbia University Press, 1954); Charles I. Foster, *An Errand of Mercy: The Evangelical United Front, 1790–1837* (Chapel Hill: University of North Carolina Press, 1960); and Clifford S. Griffin, *Their Brothers' Keepers: Moral Stewardship in the United States, 1800–1865* (New Brunswick, N.J.: Rutgers University Press, 1960). For critiques of this interpretation, see Lois W. Banner, "Religious Benevolence as Social Control: A Critique of an Interpretation," *Journal of American History* 60 (June 1973): 23–42; William A. Muraskin, "The Social-Control Theory in American History: A Critique," *Journal of Social History* 9 (June 1976): 559–569; Lawrence F. Kohl, "The Concept of Social Control and the History of Jacksonian America," *Journal of the Early Republic* (Spring 1985): 21–34; and Robert P. Swierenga, "Physicians and Abortion Reform in the Nineteenth Century: Social Control as the New Orthodoxy," *Fides et Historia* 11 (Spring 1979): 51–59.

41. See T. Jackson Lears, *No Place of Grace: Antimodernism and the Transformation of American Culture, 1880–1920* (New York: Pantheon, 1981) and Janet F. Fishburn, *The Fatherhood of God and the Victorian Family: The Social Gospel in America* (Philadelphia: Fortress Press, 1982).

7

Women, Feminism, and

the New Religious History:

Catholic Sisters as a Case Study

Although countless observers of Western culture have remarked that women typically are more religious than men, the extent and nature of their religious presence and participation has not—until recently—been reflected in formal scholarship. Like the study of politics, religious historiography traditionally has centered on institutions and notable individuals (prmiarily clergy) and these, given the pervasively patriarchal structures of organized Judaism and Christianity, have been overwhelmingly male. That emphasis has had many consequences, most notably a serious neglect of the religious roles and contributions of women. There were differences among denominations, of course, in the precise proportion of their female membership, or in the specific responsibilities that women were permitted to fill. Still, the similarities among women's experiences are striking. Thus, although this essay focuses on American Catholicism, and specifically on members of women's religious orders, it touches on issues that are relevant to Jews and other Christians, as well.

The place of nuns within Catholicism has much in common with women's place in other Western religions.[1] Sisters are, for one thing, laypersons in a church that restricts formal power only to the ordained, who are exclusively male. At the same time, however, they are officially recognized religious *professionals* whose activities have contributed immeasurably to the development, evolution, intrinsic character, and even survival of their denomination. Thus, their lives show similarities to those of women both in faiths that were highly clericalized and stratified (in which the laity's roles generally, and those of women in particular, tended to be severely limited), and in sects where ordination was not essential to ministry (such as the pietistic groups in which gender was less likely to define an individual's ability to contribute).[2]

To be sure, sisters are formally dependent upon ordained men in ways that women of most other faiths are not: for access to the sacraments that are central to Catholic devotion and for the canonical legitimacy of their orders themselves.[3] But the nature and purpose of their lives find echoes in a wide range of religious traditions. In some, cohorts of dedicated women bear titles that testify to their commitment: Methodist, Lutheran, and Episcopalian deaconesses; Anglican nuns who emerged in the nineteenth century; and the readers, leaders, and preachers who, with or without actual ordination, pervade most of evangelical Protestantism. In addition, some of Catholic sisters' activities are undertaken by diverse Jewish and Christian (unvowed) "sisterhoods," women's missionary societies, prayer groups, and service organizations, as well as by female religious educators, writers, and artists within every denomination.[4]

In more cases than not, including the Catholic, women's ministry tended to evolve not from the demands of clerics or other male leaders, but primarily from their own perceptions and initiatives. For sisters, and for religious women generally, gender-based exclusion from official ecclesial structures (or the absence of such structures altogether) did not act as deterrents to participation but led rather to the development of independent mechanisms and avenues of service. In nineteenth-century America alone, for example, sisters founded hundreds of schools, hospitals, orphanages, and other social agencies; within them, and within the religious orders themselves, nuns enjoyed tremendous authority and autonomy from men—more, perhaps, prior to the present day, than virtually all of their female contemporaries. Through these ministries, they came into closer and more intense contact with more persons (both Catholic and non-Catholic) than their ordained brethren were likely to encounter. And throughout most of the nineteenth-century United States, where priests were scarce even in areas of heavy Catholic settlement, nuns were often their church's most visible official representatives.[5] These women, therefore, contributed substantially to the character of Catholicism in the American context. The result was a church that, however formally dominant its clerics were intended to be, always relied heavily upon a female institutional and apostolic presence.[6]

Even in this most clerical and patriarchal of denominations, therefore, the example of sisters suggests that women play various roles that—in real if not always officially sanctioned ways—are essential parts of what religion has always been all about in the American context. Thus, when scholars neglect the contributions of women, they help to perpetuate incomplete and highly inaccurate perceptions of religion's practice and significance. Fortunately, that situation is beginning to be rectified, thanks in large measure to what might be called the "new feminist religious history."[7] The discussion of nuns below is meant to exemplify that approach: to suggest the alternative vision that can be provided by explicit inclusion of woman's presence and perspective.

THE "NEW FEMINIST RELIGIOUS HISTORY" is distinguished from traditional historiography by a number of characteristics, including its critique of patriarchy, its analysis of the connection between ordination and power, its recognition of the pervasiveness and importance of unordained ministry and the roles of the laity, and its identification of transdenominational patterns. It represents a cooperative effort by (mostly female) theologians, biblical exegetes, philosophers, and feminist theorists, as well as by historians and practitioners within a broad spectrum of the social sciences. Indeed, its interdisciplinary nature and reliance on theory—rather than its reliance on quantitative methodology—is what places this scholarship most clearly within the realm of social science and the "new religious/social science history."

Generally speaking, statistical data are simply less available when it comes to women than they are for men. Many examples can be cited to illustrate the problem, but a single case from the Catholic experience will suffice. An official *Catholic Directory* for the United States has been published annually since the 1840s, and from the outset they identified every priest working in the country, the diocese where he was incardinated, his specific ministry, and his address. Even today, however, *no* comparable records are available on nuns; historically, little attempt was made to keep accurate accounts of aggregate numbers—nationally, by diocese, or by congregation. Of course, individual orders kept records, but they vary considerably in quality and reliability. Some systematically delete any mention of women who did not die as members of the community, thereby eliminating all who left either before taking vows or after profession, as well as those who remained in religious life but left their original motherhouses to establish new foundations.

Beyond problems with this sort of basic information, which makes mere *counting* a formidable (if not impossible) task,[8] the archives of different congregations may or may not contain information on parental characteristics, personal histories, and individual religious careers; gaps are particularly pronounced for orders' early years.[9] Meanwhile, if the original motherhouse burned or otherwise fell victim to natural disaster, all records, however sketchy, probably were destroyed, so reconstruction of them depended on oral tradition. Moreover, although diocesan chanceries and other repositories contain information even on men who left the priesthood (or the country), virtually nothing is known about women's communities that failed to survive or that abandoned their American foundations.[10]

Considering that Catholic sisters are among the *best* documented female cohorts, we can begin to understand the obstacles to statistical analysis of religious women generally.[11] Typically they were, after all, uncredentialed and unremunerated for what they did; it is not surprising, then, that their activities (or mere existence) are frequently undocumented and officially unremembered. Thus, most quantitative analyses of women in religion understandably tend to focus either on the relatively recent past or on fortuitously well-documented (and too often isolated and unreplicable) case studies.

To compensate for the scarcity of hard data, therefore, many social science historians of women in religion have turned to techniques of qualitative (albeit still systematic) analysis—espeically to frameworks derived from feminist theory and feminist theology—as well as to some of the methods developed for studying nonelites that have emerged from various social sciences. This literature falls into three categories. The first derives from the larger field of women's studies, and particularly women's history—bodies of literature too diverse and extensive to catalog here. More immediately pertinent, however, are the writings of historically oriented feminist theologians, such as Rosemary Radford Ruether, Elizabeth Schussler-Fiorenza, Mary Daly, Mary Jo Weaver, and Anne Carr.[12] Collectively, these scholars have explored and documented what Gerda Lerner has called the "creation of patriarchy" within the Judeo-Christian context, as well as its influence on the evolution and development of organized Western religion, its disjuncture with much of what is contained in the Hebrew and Christian scriptures (especially the Gospels), and—perhaps most significantly for students of history—the implications of this ongoing patriarchal hegemony for society generally, religion, and the lives of women over time.[13]

In addition, and complementary to this work, there has been the uncovering and rediscovery of the religious voices of women themselves. In the Christian tradition alone, for instance, a number of resources have appeared in recent years: journals like *Mystics Quarterly, Vox Benedictina,* and the *Journal of Feminist Studies in Religion;* anthologies like the first two (of three) volumes of *Medieval Religious Women* and the three-volume *Women & Religion in America: A Documenatry History* (see note 4); accessible compilations of the Gnostic Gospels and other texts excluded from the Christian Bible; and authoritative editions (and translations) from various series and publishers of writings by Hildegarde of Bingen, Julien of Norwich, Mechtilde of Hackeborn, Clare of Assisi, Catherine of Siena, Teresa of Avila, and countless more recent individuals. Based on these resources, it is clear that rich and ongoing (if long overlooked) traditions of feminine Christian spirituality were able

to evolve and flouirsh in the midst of, and despite, the dominant patriarchy. Asking how and why that occurred has opened up promising new
areas of inquiry; the pioneering efforts of scholars like Carolyn Walker
Bynum, Sharon K. Elkins, Penny Schine Gold, and others are impressive indicators of what is possible—and of how much remains to be done
to make up for literally centuries of neglect.[14]

Because the entire field of women's studies is so new, a great deal of
its energies are still being devoted to what some have called "compensa-
tory" scholarship: the identification, description, and discrete analysis of
woman's particular experience. And this essay is no exception. It
should, however, suggest some of the possibilities of the "new feminist
religious history"—not only in the light it sheds upon the particular
women discussed here, but also for the corrective it offers to the usual
images of submissive (if at all evident) women and triumphal prelates
that dominate most traditional accounts of Catholicism.

TO APPRECIATE THE IMPLICATIONS of a feminist perspective for
the study of nuns—or of placing sisters, as well as women generally,
within the larger context of Catholic historiography—one must understand what the state of the art was until very recently. The (male) author
of a post–World War II history of his order, for instance, did not think it
necessary to include sisters in his "comprehensive" *Benedictinism through
Changing Centuries,* although he published a ninety-four-page "supplement" to cover women a few years later. He introduced it by saying that "I
believe that I am rendering a service to the convents . . . since there is
hardly a single publication on the history of Benedictine nuns available."
Immediately, however, he went on to suggest why this might be the case,
as he declared: "The Benedictine nuns did not make Benedictine history.
This is not women's work." Yet, he concluded his forward by asserting
that, "in St. Benedict's sanctuary an opportunity is given [women] to
participate in the sacred Mysteries in a manner scarcely to be found
elsewhere in the world."[15]

European monks were not the only ones suffering from myopia;
American scholarship is likewise afflicted. Mary Jo Weaver has noted
that James Henesey's 1981 *American Catholics*—a work she says that
"just by mentioning 50 or 60 different women, did something no historian of American Catholicism has done"—includes just fifty (of 1300)
index items referring to women. She also remarks that Robert Trisco's
"celebratory" bicentennial volume, *Catholics in America 1776–1976,*

contains seven photographs of women and thirty of men: "significantly, buildings outnumber women by two to one."[16]

Weaver's examples are typical. And yet anyone who wishes to look for it can readily find a plethora of publications about nuns: the legacy of a sizable cadre of sister-scholars who began to write around the turn of the twentieth century. These women existed largely because of internally inconsistent church policies that on the one hand directed nuns to obtain professional training comparable to that of their secular counterparts, and that on the other prohibited their admission to nearly all Catholic institutions of higher learning, which were operated by and for men. Thus, sisters were impelled to open their own colleges (if only to train their own members), and to send prospective professors for graduate degrees (to state or non-Catholic private universities, until Catholic ones reluctantly opened their doors to women) in order to secure the necessary credentials.[17] Since most congregations could spare such talented individuals for only a couple of years of full-time study, if that, most theses were written while their authors were "on the job," usually at an academy or college connected with the motherhouse. The result is a massive amount of research from community archives, which collectively reveals a great deal about nineteenth- and early-twentieth-century sisters. And even more historiography was produced in the aftermath of Vatican II, as sisters were asked to "rediscover and explore their foundresses' charisms" during the process of community renewal.[18]

There are several problems with this work, however—and with the dozens of biographies of "Mother Foundress," and volumes produced to commemorate orders' "jubilee" years. Even the best of it is community-specific; only six American works prior to 1980 attempted to deal in a serious manner with more than a single congregation.[19] More critically, much of the writing, even that done under academic auspices, consists of unimaginative narrative, tedious chronicling, triumphalism, flowery piety, or some combination of these.[20]

If one reads enough of this material, however, one learns to recognize such rhetoric as the specialized jargon of pre–Vatican II religious life, and one learns to read between the lines. Repeated references to "eccentric" clerics, for example, become recognizable as euphemisms for parochial tyrants with frequently bizarre theological opinions, while discreet allusions to "trials" and "the cross" would signify anything from financial woes to long-term persecution by a local bishop. These interpretations are confirmed by drawing connections between older accounts and those published within the past couple of decades, as well as by primary materials in community archives.[21] And what begin to emerge are *patterns:*

indisputable replications of experiences that transcended time, locale, ethnicity, ministry, or personality. Not only had many of these never been identified as patterns before, but the incidents that comprised them were often covered up or evaded in the official (and sometimes even oral) histories of individual communities, because they did not seem to coincide with what traditional, pious tomes had indicated was normal or appropriate for religious life.

Nuns, after all, were supposed to be docile, submissive, self-effacing, and unworldly—the epitome of the feminine within a world of patriarchal hegemony.[22] Like men in religious orders, sisters were bound by vows of obedience, but—unlike monks, friars, and clerics regular—vowed women ultimately were governed not by one of their own members, but by a male "ecclesiastical superior." Thus, for women, the "call" of obedience and demands to suppress one's own will at the demand of higher authority (as virtually every congregation's Rule put it: "the voice of the superior is the voice of God"), were expanded and intensified by the pressures of patriarchy. Through daily spiritual reading, usually from their own Rule, martyrologies and "edifying" tomes like Thomas à Kempis's *Imitation of Christ,* the virtues of humility, patient suffering, and reverence for priests were drummed repeatedly into sisters' ears. "Distrust your knowledge and be set on nothing whatsoever," a typical peroration read. "Hold to nothing against the decision of a priest . . . always submitting your judgment to [him]. . . . [B]e assured that in spite of all you may know or remember, it is far more probable that it is you who are in error." Another declared that nuns should "suffer cheerfully inconveniences, contradictions, scoffings, calumnies, and other mortifications . . . remembering that our Savior, who was innocence itself, endured far greater sufferings and even prayed for those who crucified him."[23]

Precepts like these suggest that women's congregations were supposed to be oases of pliability and unassertiveness. Yet the most pervasive pattern I encountered within women's religious orders was that of *conflict.* Disputes among sisters were frequent, and usually centered on one or more of three sources of tension: class, ethnic antagonisms, and the increasingly disparate visions of European superiors and women from their communities who were missioned in the United States.[24] These issues are well worth exploring. But the rest of this essay focuses upon a second kind of conflict: gender-defined confrontations between women and men. Incidents of this sort were more common than those involving only nuns; indeed, they occurred without exception in every one of the approximately 175 communities on which I have done any research.[25]

FRICTION BETWEEN PRELATES AND SISTERS was rooted in a combination of at least four factors: (1) the generic clericalism that afflicted all nineteenth-century relationships between priests and the Catholic faithful,[26] (2) the patriarchy that explicitly delimited woman's place within the Roman communion,[27] (3) evolving notions of authority within the Catholic hierarchy (culminating in the 1870 declaration of papal infallibility, Rome's condemnation of the so-called "Americanist heresy" in 1899, and the 1917 codification of canon law), and (4) the peculiar ecclesial ambiguity in which apostolic communities of women had developed since the sixteenth century. The first two of these need not be explicated here. Regarding the others, it should be noted that the legitimacy of "active" sisters—as opposed to strictly contemplative "nuns"—was not officially recognized by the church until the promulgation of *Conditae a Christo* in 1900. But for over three centuries prior to that, apostolic orders evolved irregularly but relentlessly, tolerated and even encouraged for reasons of social and religious ministerial necessity. In practical terms, although some received recognition from Rome, all their existence required as approbation by a diocesan bishop. And because there were no formal canonical guidelines for such congregations until 1901, there were no clearly defined limits to the authority that local prelates could exercise over those under their jurisdiction.[28]

Meanwhile, during the very years (comprising most of the nineteenth century) that women's orders were establishing themselves in this country, and during which the status of apostolic sisters everywhere was acquiring de facto legitimacy, the American hierarchy was struggling to define and assert its authority and autonomy within a church structure that was becoming increasingly "Romanized." The issues involved are too complex to explore even superficially in this essay.[29] But an important repercussion of the struggle was that, in the face of ongoing efforts by the Vatican to restrict their hegemony, U.S. bishops sought to maintain as much control as they could in areas where Roman challenges were not immediately forthcoming. One such sphere encompassed those congregations of nuns who owed their very existence to diocesan approbation. Thus, it is not surprising that, in constitutions they drafted for such groups, the prelates who served as their ultimate "ecclesiastical superiors" retained tremendous power for themselves. As a typical religious Rule declared:

All the Monasteries of Sisters, in this Diocese, according to Apostolic Privileges, are placed under the Bishop; and the Bishop can and ought to rule and govern such Monasteries according to the Constitutions of the Order, and to visit, correct, and reform them, both in the heads and members. He can appoint, depose, change, and transfer the Sisters, Prioresses, Sub-Prioresses, and other officials, and can make such ordinances as he shall judge to be salutary, according to the Spirit of God, and even enforce them by penalties. The ordinances of the Bishop endure forever, or until revoked by equal authority. The Bishop, being the proper and immediate Superior of the Sisters, they are all bound humbly and devoutly to obey him, according to the Rule and Constitutions. The Bishop has the power to fix the interpretation of the Rule and Constitutions, in case of ambiguity; which interpretations, although they have not the force of constitutions, are yet to be held and observed by subjects.[30]

Now, it must be understood that everything in a sister's training and mode of life served to reinforce the primacy of obedience and humility, and stressed the spiritual rewards that would accrue to those who embodied those virtues. A nun's ingrained inclination was to submit to all authority, and most especially to that of clerics. Why, then, did conflict between vowed women and ordained men run rampant through nineteenth-century American Catholicism?

"Conflict" here does not mean mere minor grumblings, privately held opinions, or niggling complaints and criticisms, although there were certainly plenty of these—and their cumulative effect cannot be underestimated.[31] Instead, the issue that needs to be addressed is more serious: what could lead women, thoroughly indoctrinated in the precepts of institutionalized (even "God-ordained") clericalism and patriarchy, and inclined to accept its validity, to openly, knowingly, and sometimes fiercely act in defiance of those norms? What were the consequences of such behavior and why, given the likely repercussions, did so many sisters persist in their "defiance"? And what did all of this mean for the development of religious life and Catholicity in America—and for the place of women within that tradition, and in that Church?

At the root of virtually every instance of conflict were two seemingly irreconcilable but equally compelling concepts: integrity and power. Women religious—particularly those chosen by their sisters for positions of leadership, and most especially the founders of orders—believed it was their sacred responsibility to safeguard the integrity of their congregation's Rule and charism[32] from any source of threat, including clerics who were their juridical superiors. Most clerics, on the other hand, felt just as certain that their authority/hegemony was unchallengeable by any "inferior," especially female ones.[33] Often compounding the tension was the fact that the vast majority of bishops and ecclesiastical superiors were secular priests, and thus had no direct personal experience with religious life in any form, much less that of the sisters under their jurisdiction.[34] Nonetheless, these prelates possessed the authority to control almost every aspect of what went on in an order of nuns, from the secular and mundane (such as the design of women's habits and headgear) to the most deeply spiritual, from the most petty to the most profound.

The first attempt in this country to exercise that authority occurred in the eighteenth century; its perpetrator was John Carroll, the first American bishop, and its target was the first women's community. Carroll, already the de facto leader among the handful of Catholic clergy then resident in the United States, was elected in 1789 by his fellow priests to be their Ordinary and, hence, became "founder of the American hierarchy." As several scholars have pointed out, this process, combined with Carroll's initiative in the rejection of a mere Vicar Apostolic to preside over his country's church, left his immediate successors in the episcopacy with a legacy that included "a strong sense of collegiality" among their ranks that would not dissipate entirely until the beginning of the twentieth century. But historians have noted as well that Carroll also "had a strong sense of what it meant to be an ordinary bishop of a diocese": an understanding that clearly included the exercise of fairly extensive power over underlings.[35] It was this latter trait that would bear most directly on sisters' experience—an experience that began within a year of Carroll's consecration to the See of Baltimore with the arrival in Maryland of four Carmelite nuns.

This first conventual foundation within the original borders of the United States was atypical at least in one respect: no other exclusively contemplative order of women would be established prior to 1875.[36] But it *was* representatively American in that its members almost immediately found themselves involved in disagreement with their Ordinary. Pleading the exegencies of circumstances in his missionary domain, Carroll initiated a petition to Rome for authority to dispense these sisters from the strict rule of enclosure and contemplation to which they were vowed, so as to enable them to operate a school. Permission was soon forthcoming; the Bishop transmitted it enthusiastically to the nonplused cloistered daughters of St. Teresa who, in the quaint words of John Gilmary Shea, "were loth to swerve from the rule under which they had lived, and did not avail themselves of the permission." To his credit,

Carroll did not press the point, and the Carmeliltes maintained their practice of prayer and reparation throughout the remainder of his episcopacy.[37] Thus, this first instance of conflict was resolved with relative ease and amicability—a result that would not always prevail for the hundreds of congregations that followed. Indeed, Carroll's acceptance of the nuns' refusal to go along with his plan for them to become teachers may well be attributable to his own background as a Jesuit—a group which, while he was a member, itself suffered the effects of external interference, culminating in its suppression by Pope Clement XIV in 1773.[38]

Carroll's experience as a religious-order priest was unusual, and would be shared by fewer than 15 percent of his pre-1917 successors in the American hierarchy. In other respects, the Carmel case illustrated many factors that *would* become habitual in the United States over the years. To begin with, Carroll assumed the right to ask for abrogation of an essential element of the sisters' form of religious life; Rome's endorsement of this proposal confirms both the validity of his assumption of such a right and the lack of concern in both Baltimore and the Vatican with soliciting or considering the *nuns'* wishes. It also foreshadows the countless occasions in which the practical necessities of a mission territory would be cited to justify clerical interference.[39]

Moreover, even a prelate's status as a religious did not guarantee sympathy for the needs or desires of vowed women—even if both cleric and nuns belonged to the same order. Consider the St. Catharine (Kentucky) Dominicans, for example. Eager to open an academy (which they did) shortly after they were founded in 1822, but lacking the wherewithal to do it, the samll band of pioneer sisters persuaded Father Pius (Richard) Miles, O.P., of neighboring St. Rose Priory, to sign a note on their behalf for a $2,000 debt; as women, the sisters were legally unable to sign for it on their own. In 1828, however, the sympathetic prior was replaced by a Spaniard, Raphael Muños, who had never met uncloistered sisters in Europe and who did not like the idea of them in the least—especially when he discovered that his newly assumed office carried with it responsibility for the loan guaranteed by his predecessor. Thus, he advised the women to disband and, when they did not heed his advice, proceeded to take steps to disband them without their consent. In this, he received at least tacit encouragement from Edward Fenwick, Provincial of the Dominican men and simultaneously Bishop of Cincinnati, who wrote to the Dominican Master General on Muños's behalf. In the face of this "indefensible harassment," the dozen or so nuns remained firm; in a secret ballot, they unanimously agreed to stay together, and to "take the consequences of their vote." After an hour of prayer, Mother Angela Sansbury led them across a field to St. Rose's, where they confronted Muños: "The note for $2,000 is our debt which we intend to pay." And pay they did, within just a couple of years. Muños, meanwhile, was replaced by a Kentucky native, Father Stephen Montgomery. With his help, the community was incorporated under an act of the state legislature in 1839. As an incorporated entity (even though all its officers were women), sisters could enter into contracts without relying on male clerics to sign for them; never again would St. Catharine's suffer the threat of dissolution.[40]

The first Benedictine women in America were not as lucky with their finances—or with so quickly finding a brother within their own order as supportive as Stephen Montgomery. Tradition has it that, when they got to this country and appeared at the newly established (male) St. Vincent's Abbey, Pennsylvania, a cynical lay brother muttered: "Here comes trouble."[41] This may establish the anonymous brother as one of the great prophets of 1852—but maybe he just knew his abbot, Boniface Wimmer. Wimmer, who had invited the women to come to America, immediately forced them to adopt ministries and prayer rituals completely at odds with their original charism—and, not incidentally, stole their money.

Wimmer settled the three Bavarian women into a convent that, five years earlier, the School Sisters of Notre Dame had abandoned as hopeless. Appalled by conditions there and by her total financial dependence upon the abbot, the twenty-seven-year old Mother Benedicta Riepp—correctly concerned about the very survival of her sisters—petitioned for a donation to the *Ludwig-Missionsverein* (the LMV, a Bavarian philanthropy for support of German Catholic missions in the United States). Although the LMV sent her two grants of 8000 and 3000 florins, Riepp never saw any of the money. European officials, following accepted procedures, sent the funds to her Ecclesiastical Superior, Boniface Wimmer. They were explicitly designated for the women's use, but Wimmer simply decided that he needed the money more than they did; eventually, he used it to purchase the land in Minnesota on which St. John's University and Abbey (both for men) now stand. By 1857, Riepp decided that, if she could not escape from Wimmer's technical jurisdiction, it would not be so oppressive at a distance. Thus, she went to St. Cloud, Minnesota, with six other sisters. The long-term legacy of her refusal to remain under Wimmer's thumb included what became the two largest Benedictine communities of women in the world, St. Benedict's (Minnesota) and St. Scholastica (Kansas)—both established when the St. Cloud mission disbanded in 1863—as well as eleven more descendant foundations.[42]

Both the Benedictine example and that of St. Catharine's indicate the vital relationship between money and the exercise of power; without independent financial resources, nuns were dependent upon potentially autocratic clerics for their material well-being, as well as for the integrity of their way of life.[43] In contrast, nuns with independent resources of their own had great success in resisting priestly interference. Thus, Mother Katharine Drexel, heir to the fortune of her father (a partner of J. P. Morgan) and founder of the Sisters of the Blessed Sacrament for Indians and Colored People, was able to maintain direction over both her community's life-style and its missions. Likewise, a group of Oblate priests threatened to assume total control over a San Antonio, Texas, school and orphanage complex to which they had been assigned as pastors. It had been erected by Mother Margaret Mary Healy-Murphy, the wealthy widow of a former slaveholder who founded the Sisters of the Holy Ghost and Mary Immaculate; she was able to persuade the bishop to restrict the men's jurisdiction to the purely sacramental—when she reminded him that it was *her* money that both paid for the buildings and provided for the clerics' salaries![44]

But although money provided women like Drexel and Healy-Murphy with a substantial degree of independence, wealth was not an essential prerequisite for orders seeking to maintain their autonomy. The experience of Benedicta Riepp shows that even indigent sisters had some options. Stated simply, nineteenth-century American nuns were in a seller's market; more people wanted their services than the available personnel were able to satisfy. Thus, those who found themselves in untenable situations could identify other prelates who needed teachers, nurses, or whatever, and could thereby escape the purview of particularly oppressive clerics. This was a course that numerous congregations would follow over the years. For example, the Sisters of Charity of Leavenworth, Kansas, had moved from Nashville when a new head of the Tennessee diocese began making impossible demands of them. To find a more hospitable location, their founder merely presented herself at a regional meeting of bishops in St. Louis and asked who needed help. Likewise, a band of Kentucky Franciscans transferred their headquarters to Clinton, Iowa, during the particularly oppressive regime of Bishop William George McCloskey. And countless communities simply closed down individual missions in order to escape from the problems of working under "eccentric" pastors.[45]

Moving to escape from difficulties was not always feasible, however, especially when a congregation was well established in an area and possessed considerable property.[46] Besides, some congregations were stubborn, and believed they had as much right to be in a particular place—*and* to maintain the integrity of their own identity—as did the prelate who officially ruled there. Such was the case with the Sisters of Charity of Nazareth, another early Kentucky foundation, established in 1812. Their first Ecclesiastical Superior, Father (later Bishop) Jean-Baptiste David, had come to Kentucky from Emmitsburg, Maryland, where he had unsuccessfully tried to persuade Mother Elizabeth Bayley Seton to unite the community she established in 1809 with the French-based Daughters of Charity. The Nazareth group had based its Rule on Seton's, retaining changes she had made in the French Daughters' constitution, which contained a number of restrictions unsuitable for conditions in the United States.[47] Like Seton, the group in Kentucky—all of whose original members were native-born Americans—understood that at least some practices developed in the Old World were unworkable in the New. Nonetheless, David hoped that he could accomplish in Nazareth what he had failed to do in Maryland: the merger of "his" sisters with the European order.

By 1840, opportunity seemed to present itself. Seton was dead, and maneuvers by some Vincentian priests in Emmitsburg were underway that would amalgamate her foundation with the Daughters in 1850. David's plan was to begin by joining Nazareth to Emmitsburg, so that the sisters there would also be subsumed by the French congregation. As soon as the Kentucky sisters, led by their founder, Mother Catherine Spalding, learned of his intention, they began actively to resist it. They argued that *they,* not the foreign-born David, were best able to determine the mode of life appropriate to their particular setting. After a series of verbal and written negotiations between nuns and prelates, Spalding prepared a petition that every professed member of her congregation signed; among other things, it asserted that "it was much better for both our happiness and spiritual good that we should exist always as . . . a separate and distinct body. . . . Surely religion in Kentucky can be more extensively and effectively served by us as we now exist."[48] In the face of the pressing needs that their services were meeting in the Bardstown area, both Bishop Flaget and David (now the coadjutor) felt it necessary to acquiesce to their resistance.

ALTHOUGH EACH EXAMPLE above ended more or less successfully from the sisters' perspective, not all instances of conflict produced such results. And even when they did, the women involved often suffered greatly. This becomes clear when one looks at traumas that perdured for years, and sometimes decades—and whose effects have not entirely dissipated today. A number of community leaders were deposed, and entire congregations placed under interdict or more casually deprived of the sacraments by autocratic (or simply unthinking) prelates whose reasons for imposing such severe sanctions were sometimes petty, often vindictive, and frequently indicative of their resentment that "mere women" would assert themselves in opposition to any *man*'s wishes or directives (even one proven to be in the wrong).

Of the petty variety, for instance, is an 1871 entry, two days before Christmas, in the diary of Mother Hyacinth Oberbrunner of the Racine (Wisconsin) Dominicans: "No Holy Communion today. Father didn't give it to us because we were not good."[49] This incident is typical of many that could have been cited; what it suggests is that provision or denial of the sacraments—one of the principal foundations of Catholic piety—could be used by clerics as a disciplinary device to wield control over those they were presumably ordained to serve. The explicitly destructive possibilities of sacramental aggression are made clearer by examination of what happened between Kentucky's Sisters of Loretto, Texas's Sisters of Divine Providence, and their respective bishops.

Catherine Connor was removed from her position as Mother General of Kentucky's Sisters of Loretto after an 1895 ecclesiastical investigation she had initiated into the authoritarianism of Louisville Bishop George William McCloskey ended with a verdict upholding all her charges.[50] Bishop Thomas Byrne of Memphis, who conducted the inquiry, decided that, although McCloskey would no longer serve as the women's Ecclesiastical Superior, it was necessary to "begin the new era" with completely clean slates on both sides of the battle line. So, on 21 March 1896—without consulting anyone in the Loretto community—Connor was summarily deposed.

Her replacement, Mother Praxedes Carty, was hardly a shrinking violet, and soon found herself battling with her predecessor's nemesis. For while McCloskey's power had been restricted substantially, he was more than willing to use whatever was left to make life miserable for the Lorettines. In 1904, when Carty was away from the motherhouse, the bishop removed John Elder, overseer of the convent property, from a room he had occupied for twenty-five years in the spacious chaplain's residence. When Carty returned, she told him to move back immediately, because their insurance required the building to be lived in at all times, and the chaplain was frequently absent. Two days later, while the chaplain was away, a neighboring priest arrived with the news that McCloskey had placed the entire congregation under interdict for disobeying his order. Not until more than two weeks passed, and the Trappist Abbot of nearby Gethsemane, Edmund Obrecht, made a special trip to Washington to inform the Papal Nuncio of what had happened, was the unjustified interdict countermanded.[51]

McCloskey, who had become biship in 1869, lived five more years after the interdict, never relenting in his persecution of Carty's order. The archivist at the time labeled her account of an incident in November 1908 as "OUR BELOVED BISHOP'S last dig"; she concluded it by noting that: "before another November comes, our dear Bishop and exerciser is dead, and Mother General Praxedes is one of the chief mourners at his funeral."[52]

Many female leaders other than Connor were deposed by bishops whom they managed to antagonize, and several were not only removed from office but also banished from their communities.[53] One was Mother Theresa Maxis Duchemin, a "free woman of color" (the first U.S.-born black nun) who began her career as a sister in 1829 as one of the first four members of the black Oblate Sisters of Providence (Baltimore), and who in 1845 founded what would become three independent communities of *white* nuns: the Sisters, Servants of the Immaculate Heart of Mary (or IHMs, in Monroe, Michigan, and Scranton and Philadelphia, Pennsylvania). She left Michigan for Pennsylvania when John Neumann was still bishop there, hoping that he (a member of the Redemptorist order that had guided both the Oblates and the IHMs in their early years) would be able to help her stop alterations in the IHM customs that the sisters' austere and rigid midwestern Ecclesiastical Superior, Edward Joos, tried to impose. Shortly after Duchemin went East, however, Neumann died, and his successor was the particularly autocratic James Wood. Wood and Michigan Bishop Peter Paul LeFevre considered this woman too difficult to deal with, and in the mid-1860s agreed jointly to ban her from residence in, or even communication with, any of the three motherhouses she had founded. Duchemin spent eighteen years in Canadian exile with the Grey Nuns of Ottawa. Only in 1885, after both bishops and Joos had died, was she able to return to one of her "homes (that in Philadelphia)," where she died in 1892.[54]

Although Duchemin spent nearly two decades apart from her sisters, she was never actually expelled from her order. That was the fate of others, however, including Mother St. Andrew Feltin, founder and superior of the Texas Congregation of Divine Providence (CDP). In 1886, Bishop John Claude Neraz of San Antonio first deposed her, and then ousted her and a companion from the community when they subsequently left the diocese with the permission of Feltin's successor—but not *his*. Neraz, after all, was their ultimate Ecclesiastical Superior; two years earlier, he had used deceptive means to force the separation of the small band of women in Texas from the European congregation which had missioned them to the United States in 1866. And when the immigrant nuns became "independent," their bishop, of course, acquired unrestricted juridical control over them.

Even before 1884, however, Feltin had become angry about various untoward demands (among other things, to do cooking and housekeeping tasks in the rectories, without remuneration and in violation of the sisters' Rule) that priests were making of the sisters who taught in their parochial schools. She tried repeatedly to stop the clerics, but they complained to the bishop about her interference in "their" parishes; a group of them announced that they would withhold the sacraments from any CDP until "that woman" was no longer in office. Apparently valuing the contentment of his priests more than the integrity of the nuns' charism, Neraz called Feltin before an ecclesiastical court, where she was found guilty of several now-undocumentable charges. Then the bishop deposed her, and demanded that the CDPs elect a new superior. Despite their Ecclesiastical Superior's unequivocal order, however, the sisters unanimously reelected Feltin on the first two ballots they held. Only when Feltin asked them to do so did the women finally choose someone else (Sister Florence Walter); that balloting was a precursor to the fidelity that the CDPs extended to Felton during the eighteen years of her exile, which began a few weeks after Mother Florence was installed. As soon as Neraz died, in 1894, Walter invited her predecessor back to San Antonio, but Feltin felt herself unable to leave the new responsibility she had assumed in 1886: supporting and educating the seven half-orphaned children of her alcoholic brother in Mission San José, California. She never gave up the dream of returning to the convent (throughout the years of exile, she kept her habit clean and ready to wear). Finally, in 1901, all the children were on their own, and Feltin returned to Texas. Like the IHM's Theresa Maxis Duchemin, Mother St. Andrew Feltin—and the sisters she had left behind—suffered through an eighteen-year separation.[55]

THESE ACCOUNTS SUGGEST that certain types of incidents were sufficient to push sisters over the brink—to impel them to go against all of their training in the religious life, as well as their faith's entire clerically premised ecclesiology—and stand up to "Father." Personal comfort was not a sufficient cause; indeed, that was often something nuns were willing to bargain away in order to achieve their principal objectives. Neither was mere personal vindication, or material happiness, as the cases of Mother St. Andrew and Mother Catherine Connor reveal.

It is obvious that women were able to be disciplined and rendered submissive by the sacramental requirements of their religion; perhaps the most effective threat that could be used against them was denial of those means to grace. To combat such tactics required assistance from sympathetic clerics. Thus, Mother Praxedes owed the lifting of the Lorettine interdict to a Trappist abbot, while Mother St. Andrew, in the absence of such an ally, was forced into a process that led to her exile.

What was shared by virtually all the women discussed here was a fierce determination to fight for what they perceived as the essence of their religious life: preservation of their right to follow their particular Rule and to live out their distinctive charism. To achieve this end, individuals were willing to sacrifice their positions, and even membership in their own communities. After examining the lives of pioneers like Mother Benedicta Riepp, Mother Catherine Connor, and Mother St. Andrew Feltin—as well as Duchemin, Carty, Spalding and others whose stories are better known but are not included here—it is difficult to overestimate what such women were willing to undergo for what they believed.

As the example of Abbot Obrecht (through the assistance he provided to the Sisters of Loretto) confirms, of course, not all clerics were oppressive in their relationships with sisters; not every bishop was a William George McCloskey. Still, patriarchy was the fundamental factor that defined relationships between nineteenth-century nuns and clerics. So one can sympathize with, if not entirely endorse, the contention of the feisty old "Nun of Kenmare," Margaret Anna Cusack, convert and founder of the Sisters of St. Joseph of Peace, who died, as she had been born, a Protestant. As she wrote in the U.S. edition of her memoirs, written shortly after she left her order and before her self-imposed exile from Catholicism, "The crushing hand of ecclesiastical despotism stifles every cry of suffering or complaint. . . . I know that Roman Catholics will cry out with indignation, and Protestants with amazement, when I say that the sisterhoods in the Roman Catholic church have often succeeded, not because of the help of the church, but in the face of its determined, and, I might say, often cruel opposition."[56]

NOTES

1. Although the terms "sister" and "nun" traditionally had distinct meanings in canon law, this essay reflects the widely followed practice of employing them interchangeably. Similarly, the technical differences between terms like "order,"

"congregation," and "community," will also be ignored and the words will be used synonymously.

2. For general discussion of both the similarities and differences, see my "Women and American Catholicism, 1789–1989," in *Perspectives on the American Catholic Church, 1789–1989*, ed. Virgina Geiger and Stephen Viccio (Westminster, Md.: Christian Classics, 1989); and various essays in *Women and Religion in America: A Documentary History*, ed. Rosemary Radford Ruether and Rosemary Skinner Keller, 3 vols. (San Francisco and New York: Harper & Row, 1981–1986).

3. Judith Anne Barnhiser, "A Study of the Authority Structures of Three Nineteenth-Century Apostolic Communities of Religious Women in the United States," (Ph.D. diss., Catholic University of America, 1975 [CUA Canon Law Studies No. 487]); and Lynn Marie Jarrell, "The Development of Legal Structures for Women Religious Between 1500 and 1900: A Study of Selected Institutes of Religious Life for Women," (Ph.D. diss., Catholic University of America, 1984).

4. Mary Sudman Donovan, *A Different Call: Women's Ministries in the Episcopal Church, 1850–1920* (Wilton, Conn.: Morehouse-Barlow, 1986); Herman L. Fritschel, *A Story of One Hundred Years of Deaconess Service* (Milwaukee, Wis.: Lutheran Deaconess Motherhouse, 1949); Frederick S. Weiser, *Love's Response: Lutheran Deaconesses in America* (Philadelphia: United Lutheran Publications, 1962); Frieda Marie Kaufman (founder in 1908 of the Mennonite deaconesses at Bethel, Kansas), *Inasmuch as I Am a Deaconess, I Will Glorify My Ministry* (North Newton, Kans.: Deaconess Committee Western District Conference, 1947); Elizabeth M. Lee, *As Among the Methodists: Deaconesses Yesterday, Today, and Tomorrow* (New York: Board of Missions of the Methodist Church, 1963); Ruthe Esther Meeker, *Six Decades of Service: 1880–1940—A History of the Woman's Home Missionary Society of the Methodist Episcopal Church* (New York: The Society, 1969); Noreen D. Tatum, *Crown of Service: A Story of Woman's Work in the Methodist Episcopal Church, South, from 1878–1940* (Nashville, Tenn.: Parthenon Press, 1960); and the three volumes of Ruether and Keller, *Women and Religion in America*.

5. A recent survey of extant sources reveals that in 1820 there were 270 sisters in the United States and 150 priests; in 1830, the figures were 448 and 232; in 1840, 902 and 482; while the figures on priests are standard ones taken from the most authoritative Catholic directories of each period, this survey represents a more detailed and complete count of sisters than any available up to now. Catherine Ann Curry, "Statistical Study of Religious Women in the United States," unpublished manuscript prepared for Mr. George C. Stewart, Jr., June 1989. To give one specific example of the larger presence of sisters than priests, during the Civil War, 640 nuns served as nurses in military hospitals, while only 84 priests served as chaplains (During the Spanish-American War, there were 282 nurses and 13 priest-chaplains.) Mary Ewens, "The Leadership of Nuns in Immigrant Catholicism," in Ruether and Keller, eds., *Women & Religion in America*, 2: 102.

6. This theme is been developed more fully in my other work. See also the various essays in *Women in the Catholic Community,* special double issue of *U.S. Catholic Historian* 5 (Summer/Fall 1986): 241–418; and in *American Catholic Women: A Historical Exploration,* ed. Karen Kennelly (New York: Macmillan, 1989).

7. Earlier work in the period since World War II, particularly by scholars like Marty, Gaustad, Hudson, and Ahlstrom, has contributed to a larger appreciation of the laity and to correction of the overly clerical perspective of much previous writing on American religion. Still, even those authors tend to overlook much of what women have done—and their focus has been overwhelmingly Protestant. Within Catholic historiography, even that which explicitly downplays clericalism, similar gaps in the coverage of women are also evident: e.g., James Hennesey, *American Catholics: A History of the Roman Catholic Community in the United States* (New York: Oxford University Press, 1981); and Jay P. Dolan, *The American Catholic Experience: A History from Colonial Times to the Present* (Garden City, N.Y.: Doubleday, 1985). See also Mary Jo Weaver, *New Catholic Women: A Contemporary Challenge to Traditional Religious Authority* (San Francisco & New York: Harper & Row, 1985), chap. 1, and "Feminist Perspectives and American Catholic History," *U.S. Catholic Historian,* 5 (1986): 401–410.

8. Curry, note 5, is the best available compilation of gross membership figures, by decade, diocese, and order, but it is unpublished and still in preliminary form. See its "preface" for the difficulties of compiling such data.

9. See, for example, the statistical tables (and the unavoidable gaps in them) in Barbara Misner, "A Comparative Social Study of the Members and Apostolates of the First Eight Permanent Communities of Women Religious Within the Original Boundaries of the United States, 1790–1850," (Ph.D. diss., Catholic University of America, 1980).

10. Mary Christina Sullivan, "Some Non-Permanent Foundations of Religious Orders and Congregations of Women in the United States (1739–1850)," *Historical Records and Studies,* 31 (1940):7–118.

11. See my "Women's Religious Community Archives: A Historian's Perspective," paper delivered at the 1987 meeting of the Society of American Archivists, New York; and "Research into the History of American Sisters: A Progress Report," *American Catholic Studies Newsletter* (Fall 1986). See also Evangeline Thomas, *Women Religious History Sources: A Guide to Repositories in the United States* (New York: R.R. Bowker, 1983). The entries in Thomas, which is the standard reference for the location and contents of sisters' archives, suggest the incompleteness of information and the lact of organization that characterizes many of these repositories.

12. Representative works include Rosemary Radford Ruether, *Sexism and God-Talk: Toward a Feminist Theology* (Boston: Beacon, 1983), *New Woman, New Earth: Sexist Ideologies and Human Liberation* (New York: Seabury, 1975), *Womanguides: Readings Toward a Feminist Theology* (Boston: Beacon, 1985), and *Women-Church: Theology and Practice of Feminist Liturgical Communities* (San Francisco: Harper & Row, 1985); Elizabeth Schussler-Fiorenza,

In Memory of Her: A Feminist Theological Reconstruction of Christian Origins (New York: Crossroad, 1983); Mary Daly, *Beyond God the Father* (Boston: Beacon, 1973), *The Church and the Second Sex* (New York: Harper Colophon, 1975), *Gyn/Ecology* (Boston: Beacon, 1978), and *Pure Lust* (Boston: Beacon, 1984); Weaver, *New Catholic Women;* and Ann Carr, *Transforming Grace: Christian Tradition and Women's Experience* (San Francisco & New York: Harper & Row, 1988).

13. For an overview of other works, and thinkers, in this field, and for insights into other religious traditions, see by way of introduction: Anne Carr, "The New Feminist Theology: A Review of the Literature," *Religious Studies Review,* 3 (1977): 203–212, "Theological Anthropology and the Experience of Women," *Chicago Studies,* 19 (1980): 113–128, and "Is a Christian Feminist Theology Possible?" *Theological Studies,* 43 (1982): 279–297; *Religion and Sexism: Images of Women in the Jewish and Christian Traditions,* ed. Rosemary Radford Ruether (New York: Simon & Schuster, 1974); *Womanspirit Rising: A Feminist Reader in Religion,* ed. Carol P. Christ and Judith Plaskow (San Francisco: Harper & Row, 1979); *Women's Spirit Bonding,* ed. Janet Kalven and Mary I. Buckley (New York: Pilgrim Press, 1984); most of the essays in *Beyond Domination: New Perspectives on Women and Philosophy,* ed. Carol C. Gould (Totowa, N.J.: Rowman & Allanheld, 1983); *Women of Faith in Dialogue,* ed. Virginia Ramey Mollenkott (New York: Crossroad, 1987); and several of the essays in *Women, Religion and Social Change,* ed. Yvonne Yazbeck Haddad and Ellison Banks Findly (Albany: State University of New York Press, 1985).

14. Caroline Walker Bynum, *Jesus as Mother: Studies in the Spirituality of the High Middle Ages* (Berkeley and Los Angeles: University of California Press, 1982), and *Holy Feast and Holy Fast: The Religious Significance of Food to Medieval Women* (Berkeley and Los Angeles: University of California Press, 1987); Sharon T. Elkins, *Holy Women of Twelfth-Century England* (Chapel Hill: University of North Carolina Press, 1988); Penny Schine Gold, *The Lady and the Virgin: Image, Attitude, and Experience in Twelfth-Century France* (Chicago: University of Chicago Press, 1985); and Haddad and Findly, eds., *Women, Religion and Social Change,* parts 1 and 2.

15. Stephanus Hilpisch, O.S.B., *History of Benedictine Nuns,* trans. M. Joanne Muggli, O.S.B. (Collegeville, Minn.: St. John's Abbey Press, 1958; the German original appeared in 1951), pp. v–vi.

16. Weaver, *New Catholic Women,* 1–3. In two working papers, Hennesey has supplemented his coverage of sisters' history by noting the large amount of recent research in that area: "American Catholic Bibliography 1970–1982," Cushwa Center Working Paper Series 12, No. 1 (Fall 1982), and "Supplement to American Catholic Bibliography 1970–1982," Cushwa Center Working Paper Series 14, No. 1 (Fall 1983).

17. The first "sisters' institute" at Catholic University, for example, was held in the summer of 1911.

18. Elizabeth Kolmer, *Religious Women in the United States: A Survey of the Influential Literature from 1950 to 1983* (Wilmington, Del.: Michael Glazier,

Inc., 1984), and "Catholic Women Religious and Women's History: A Survey of the Literature," in *Women in American Religion,* ed. Janet Wilson James (Philadelphia: University of Pennsylvania Press, 1980), 127–139; Barbara Misner, "Historiography of Women's Religious Communities in the 19th Century," paper delivered at the 1982 Conference on Perspectives on American Catholicism, University of Notre Dame; and the bibliography in *Women Religious History Sources,* ed. Evangeline Thomas (New York: R. R. Bowker Co., 1983), 143–68.

19. Mary Regina Baska, *Congregation of St. Scholastica: Its Foundation and Development* (Washington: Catholic University of America Studies in American Church History, vol. 2, 1935); M. Teresa Austin Carroll, *Leaves from the Annals of the Sisters of Mercy,* 4 vols. (New York: O'Shea, 1881–1895); Elinor Tong Dehey, *Religious Orders of Women in the United States,* rev. ed. (Hammond, Ind.: Conkey, 1930); Joseph B. Code, *Great American Foundresses* (New York: Macmillan, 1929); Mary Ewens, *The Role of the Nun in Nineteenth-Century America* (Ph.D. diss., University of Minnesota, 1971; published New York: Arno, 1978); and Misner, "The First Eight Permanent Communities."

20. As historian Barbara Misner has put it, such literature was "characterized chiefly by a desire to edify and inspire, and there is often more hagiography than apologetics. (One might suspect there were vocation directors behind the projects.)" Misner, "Historiography of Women's Religious Communities," 2. See, for example, the books by Code and Dehey, cited above.

21. Thompson, "Women's Religious Community Archives" and "New Approaches to the Historical Study of American Catholic Sisters," the latter the keynote paper delivered at the Lilly Foundation Conference on Women Religious and History, Cushwa Center, University of Notre Dame, October 1987. In a field such as this, where primary research by "outsiders" has only recently been made possible, personal contact and confidence is essential. As more than one sister-archivist admitted to me, "We had to feel that we could trust you before we would reveal what *really* happened to us in the early years." Fortunately, like most of today's nuns, archivists are prodigious readers and energetic "networkers"; after a while, I found that my reputation had preceded me, and— with four exceptions—not only was I was given access to everything I asked for, but files "I really shouldn't show you" were pulled out with increasing frequency and candor.

22. See my "Women and American Catholicism." See also Mary Ewens, *The Role of the Nun in 19th-Century America,* and "Removing the Veil: The Liberated American Nun," in *Women of Spirit,* ed. Rosemary Ruether and Eleanor McLaughlin (New York: Simon & Schuster, 1979), 256–278; Karen Kennelly, "Ideals of American Catholic Womanhood," and Colleen McDannell, "Catholic Domesticity, 1860–1960," in Kennelly, *American Catholic Women,* 1–16, 48–80; and McDannell, *The Christian Home in Victorian America, 1840–1900* (Bloomington: Indiana University Press, 1986).

23. "On Distrust of One's Own Light," Art. XX, *Constitutions of the Sisters of Divine Providence,* 1883, p. 80, Sisters of Divine Providence Archives, Melbourne, Ky.; *Regulations for the Society of the Sisters of Charity, of the United*

States of America, for the Mother-House of Nazareth, Kentucky (Cincinnati, 1877), p. 5.

24. See my "Sisterhood and Power: Class, Culture, and Ethnicity in the American Convent," *Colby Library Quarterly* (Fall 1989).

25. Much of what follows was originally presented as: "'Father' Didn't Always Know Best: Nuns versus Clerics in Nineteenth-Century American Catholicism," paper delivered at the 1987 meeting of the Social Science History Association, New Orleans; see also my "To Serve the People of God: Nineteenth-Century Sisters and the Creation of an American Religious Life," Cushwa Center for the Study of American Catholicism, University of Notre Dame, Working Paper Series 18, No. 2 (delivered 26 February 1987).

26. Consider, for instance, this statement by the first bishop of a diocese that, according to its most recent historian, "has a heritage of lay leadership": "No matter what the acquirements of a layman, no matter how much a scholar, no matter how much worldly and scientific knowledge he may have, even as a profound theologian, he is not a teacher. He has no authority to teach because . . . he does not participate in the divine mission to teach all nations." Bishop Patrick A. Ludden, in David O'Brien, *Faith and Friendship: Catholicism in the Diocese of Syracuse, 1886–1986* (Syracuse: Catholic Diocese of Syracuse, 1987), 110 ["lay leadership" statement on the back cover].

27. Thus, Pope Leo XIII declared in 1896 that "woman is by divine counsel and decree of Holy Church, formally excluded from what directly regards the Adorable Body of Christ;" she could not "pass the limits of the Holy of Holies," and had "no part in the act, by which, enveloped in a mysterious cloud of faith and love, the Man-God daily renews upon the altar the divine Holocaust of Calvary." Instead, her sanctity was to be achieved through "the labor of her hands, which have prepared the sacred vestment and linens and provided all that pertains to the divine sacrifice." Joseph P. Chinnici, *Living Stones: The History and Structure of Catholic Spiritual Life in the United States* (New York: Macmillan, 1989), 151. See also Ann Taves, *The Household of Faith: Roman Catholic Devotions in Mid-Nineteenth-Century America* (Notre Dame, Ind.: University of Notre Dame Press, 1986).

28. Apostolic, or "active," congregations are those that engage in ministries such as teaching, nursing, or social work; they differ from the contemplative mode of religious life, in which members devote themselves almost entirely to prayer—and which was the normative type of religious life for women (the only type accorded recognition in canon law) until 1900. Jarrell, "Legal Structures for Women Religious" is the best short account of the canonical development of active communities. See also Elizabeth Rapley, *The Devotes: Women & Church in Seventeenth-Century France* (Montreal: McGill-Queen's University Press, 1990); Barnhiser, "A Study of Authority Structures"; and Mary Ann Donovan, *Sisterhood as Power: The Past and Passion of Ecclesial Women* (New York: Crossroad, 1989).

29. See Gerald P. Fogarty, *The Vatican and the American Hierarchy from 1870 to 1965* (Wilmington, Del.: Michael Glazier, 1985), and Fogarty, ed., *Patterns of*

Episcopal Leadership (New York: Macmillan, 1989); James Hennesey, *The First Council of the Vatican: The American Experience* (New York: Herder & Herder, 1963); Thomas T. McAvoy, *The Great Crisis in American Catholic History, 1895–1900* (Chicago: Henry Regnery, 1957); *The Catholic Priest in the United States: Historical Investigations*, ed. John Tracy Ellis (Collegeville, Minn.: St. John's University Press, 1971); and *The Papacy and the Church in the United States*, ed. Bernard Cooke (Mahwah, N.J.: Paulist, 1989).

30. *The Rule of St. Augustine, and the Constitutions of the Sisters of Penance of the Third Order of St. Dominic, Forming the American Congregation of St. Catharine of Siena, of the Diocese of Louisville, Ky.* (Louisville: Courier Journal Job Printing Company, 1892), 157–158; St. Catharine (Kentucky) Dominican Archives. See also Mary Patricia Green, *The Third Order Dominican Sisters of Saint Catharine of Siena, Saint Catharine, Kentucky: Their Life and Their Constitutions, 1822–1969* (St. Catharine, Ky., 1978).

31. Virtually every archive, for instance, contains "circular letters" from community leaders to members in the field, repeatedly reminding them to refrain from criticism (even within convent walls) of priests with whom they had to work.

32. "Rule" is technically synonymous with constitution but in popular usage, particularly prior to 1900, it was commonly used to signify all established practices that an individual community followed, including specific devotions, modes of address and interaction, and other cutsoms (normally recorded in a Customary that, unlike a constitution, did not require episcopal approbation). "Charism" refers to the spirit that makes a particular community unique; it generally derives from the special insights, inspiration, spirituality, and objectives of the founder, as well as from the circumstances of time, place, and culture that surrounded an order's founding.

33. Taves, *Household of Faith*, 102–106; Chinnici, *Living Stones*, esp. chaps. 3, 6, 9, 11, and 13; and my "Women and American Catholicism."

34. Since Ecclesiastical Superiors changed frequently, it is impossible to calculate precise figures for them. But only 14.9 percent of American bishops prior to 1917 (44 of 296) have ever been members of religious communities—and several of these belonged to the Sulpicians or similar societies that actually were associations of secular priests and not technically the same as congregations of friars, monks, or canons regular, in which members took religious vows and so forth. Figures derived from data in John Hugh O'Donnell, *The Catholic Hierarchy of the United States, 1790–1922*, Catholic University of America Studies in American Church History, vol. 4 (Ph.D. diss., 1922); and Joseph Bernard Code, *Dictionary of the American Hierarchy* (New York: Longmans, Green, 1940).

35. Quotations from Gerald Fogarty, "Theologians and the Magisterium," *Seminaries in Dialogue*, 16 (1987): 11, 10. See also Fogarty, *The Vatican and the American Hierarchy;* and James Hennesey, "An Eighteenth Century Bishop: John Carroll of Baltimore," *Archivum Historiae Pontificae* 16 (1978): 171–204.

36. The congregation of Visitation Nuns, founded officially in 1816 from among some "Pious Ladies" already teaching in Georgetown, D.C., has consistently been engaged in education and, therefore, has never been under papal enclosure.

Successful foundations of Poor Clares and the Benedictine Sisters of Perpetual Adoration (Clyde, Mo.)—the latter, again, subject merely to episcopal enclosure—were both begun in 1875. See Misner, "The First Eight Permanent Communities," 18ff; Dehey, *Religious Orders of Women in the United States,* 50ff, 531ff, 638ff; and Sullivan, "Non-Permanent Foundations."

37. John Gilmary Shea, *Life and Times of Most Rev. John Carroll* (New York, 1888), 386. See also Charles Warren Currier, *Carmel in America: A Centennial History of the Discalced Carmelites in the United States* (Baltimore, 1890); and Misner, "First Eight Permanent Communities," 14–18. As Misner notes (p. 18), the nuns eventually were forced to submit to "practical requirements" and opened a school when they moved their convent from Port Tobacco to Baltimore in 1831; it remained open for twenty years.

38. As Shea put it: "Himself trained to a religious life, and feeling as the great blow of his life the decree which exiled him from it, [he] could not press these pious women to adopt a course repugnant to them." *Carroll,* p. 386.

39. The impact of such interference upon one order is analyzed in Judith Sutera, *True Daughters: Monastic Identity and American Benedictine Women's History* (Atchison, Kans.: Mt. St. Benedict, 1987).

40. Green, *Third Order Dominican Sisters of . . . St. Catharine, Ky.;* Monica Kiefer, *Dominican Sisters, St. Mary of the Springs: A History—Log Cabin Days in Kentucky* (Columbus, Ohio: priv. published, n.d.).

41. This tradition is recorded, among other places, in Anon., *One Hundredth Anniversary of The Benedictine Sisters, 1852–1952* (St. Joseph's Convent, St. Marys, Elk County, Pa.: priv. printed, no date, pages unnumbered).

42. Principal sources for this case include the Sisters of St. Benedict Archives, St. Joseph, Minn.; M. Incarnata Girgen, *Behind the Beginnings: Benedictine Women in America* (St. Joseph, Minn.: priv. published, 1981)—a collection of translated, original documents; Sutera, *True Daughters;* and Jerome Oetgen, *An American Abbot: Boniface Wimmer, O.S.B., 1809–1887* (Latrobe, Pa.: St. Vincent's Archabbey Press, 1976).

43. See Sutera, *True Daughters,* esp. chaps. 10 and 11, for the Benedictines' struggle to recapture their monastic identity, which continues even today.

44. Consuela Marie Duffy, *Katharine Drexel: A Biography* (Cornwell Heights, Pa.: Mother Katharine Drexel Guild, 1965); Mary Immaculata Turley, *Mother Margaret Mary Healy-Murphy: A Biography* (San Antonio: priv. published, 1969); and my "Philemon's Dilemma: Nuns and the Black Community in Nineteenth-Century America—Some Findings," *Records of the American Catholic Historical Society of Philadelphia,* 96 (1986): 3–18. Healy-Murphy's community is now known as the Sisters of the Holy Spirit and Mary Immaculate.

45. Julia Gilmore, *Come North: The Life of Mother Xavier Ross, Foundress of the Sisters of Charity of Leavenworth* (New York: McMullen Books, 1951), and *We Came North* (St. Meinrad, Ind.: Abbey Press, 1958); Clyde F. Crews, "American Catholic Authoritarianism: The Episcopacy of William George McCloskey, 1868–1909," *Catholic Historical Review,* 70 (1984): 560–580; [anon.] *Picture History of the Sisters of Saint Francis of the Immaculate Conception of the Blessed*

Virgin Mary, Clinton, Iowa (priv. printed, n.d.), and letter from Sister Eileen Smith, OSF, (archivist) to M. S. Thompson, 20 June 1989; as well as countless references in published histories and archival materials for every congregation about closed missions.

46. In many cases, even where religious orders had paid for their property, its title was retained in the name of the "church"—which, canonically speaking, might mean the bishop himself as *corporation sole.* Orders with pontifical status (which few nineteenth-century women's congregations enjoyed) were supposed to be exempt from such diocesan claims but, even in those cases, nineteenth-century U.S. bishops individually and collectively tried (unsuccessfully) to assert some financial claim. Gerald P. Fogarty, "The Bishops versus Religious Orders: The Suppressed Decrees of the Third Plenary Council of Baltimore," *The Jurist,* 33 (1973): 384–398.

47. Among provisions deemed inappropriate (or impossible to follow) in the United States were the prohibition against teaching boys or caring for male orphans, and the fact that the Daughters were forbidden to accept payment for any of their services. The French Rule and the revisions made at Emmitsburg by Elizabeth Seton are in Ellin Kelly, *Numerous Choirs: A Chronicle of Elizabeth Bayley Seton and Her Spiritual Daughters,* vol. I (Evansville, Ind.: Mater Dei Provincialate, 1981), 243–282. See also Kelly, "The Rule of St. Vincent DePaul and American Women's Religious Communities," paper presented at the Cushwa Center Conference on Perspectives on American Catholicism, Notre Dame, Ind., November 1982.

48. Petition in the Nazareth Archives.

49. Mother Hyacintha Oberbrunner's Diary, vol. I, 23 December 1871, Archives of the Racine Dominicans (I am grateful to Sr. Suzanne Noffke for providing the English translation from the German).

50. The incidents involving the Sisters of Loretto and McCloskey will be developed extensively in my forthcoming history of American sisters (*The Yoke of Grace: American Nuns and Social Change, 1808–1917,* to be published by Oxford University Press). They are documented by literally thousands of pages of relevant material in the Sisters of Loretto Archives, Nerinx, Ky. See also my " 'Father' Didn't Always Know Best," and "Loretto, the Vatican and Historical Irony," *NCAN News* [newsletter of the National Coalition of American Nuns], December 1986; Crews, "American Catholic Authoritarianism," and Florence Wolff, *From Generation to Generation: The Sisters of Loretto, Their Constitutions and Devoltions: 1812–Vatican II* (Louisville, Ky.: priv. published, 1982).

51. Technically, of course, an interdict is an extremely severe sanction; under normal circumstances it is rarely employed. There is reason to suspect, moreover, that McCloskey knew his use of it was unjustified; Abbot Obrecht believed this to be the case, but charged that the bishop used it anyway, knowing that it would take time for the sisters to appeal to higher authority for its removal. Given the centrality of the sacraments to the sisters' spiritual welfare, it was an effective weapon in the prelate's ongoing war with them. And McCloskey was not the only bishop in the isolation of missionary America to take advantage of

U.S. nuns' relative powerlessness and difficulty of access to the higher ecclesiastical authorities who could protect them; Bishop Michael Heiss of La Crosse imposed an interdict on the Sinsinawa (Wis.) Dominicans, and Bishop Celestine de la Hailandière of Vincennes (Ind.) excommunicated Mother Theodore Guerin of the Sisters of Providence, and occasionally threatened to excommunicate the entire community. Edmund Obrecht to Praxedes Carty, 27 and 29 June and 9 July 1904, Sisters of Loretto Archives, Nerinx, Ky.; M. Mileta Ludwig, *Right-Hand Glove Uplifted: A Biography of Archibishop Michael Heiss* (New York: Pageant Press, 1968), 446ff; and M. Theodosia Mug, *Life and Life-Work of Mother Theodore Guerin* (New York: Benziger Bros., 1904), chap. 25.

52. Sister Antonella, in the last of dozens of folders containing material on Bishop McCloskey in the Loretto Archives.

53. Mother Catherine Connor was never banished from her order, but her final years were nonetheless sad and spent in a sort of internal exile. Although she approved of some changes that Byrne made in the congregation's constitution, especially those limiting the power of the Ecclesiastical Superior, she could not accept the continued necessity of *any* such official (an outsider, and a man) at all. Furthermore, she became irate over several changes Byrne made in the Lorettine Manual of Prayers, which she judged to be well outside his legitimate purview as temporary advisor and "custodian." Because she refused to go along with either of these things, Connor was removed from the local superiorships of two missions to which she was assigned after her deposition and was forbidden, even though duly elected, from serving as a delegate to the general chapter. She died in 1901, in obscurity and with her reputation under a cloud that has never entirely dissipated. See Wolff, *From Generation to Generation;* my "Loretto, the Vatican and Historical Irony," and numerous painful references to Connor in the Mother Praxedes Papers, Sisters of Loretto Archives.

54. I told this story in greater detail in "A Gusty Woman of Vision," *Catholic Sun* (Syracuse, N.Y.), 24 Feb.–1 March 1988, pp. 6–7. See also my "Philemon's Dilemma;" and Margaret Gannon, "Mother Teresa Maxis Duchemin, I.H.M.: Let Your Heart Be Bold" (unpublished mimeograph, 1984); Joseph B. Code, "Mother Theresa Maxis Duchemin," *America* (22 Dec. 1945): 317–20; [anon.] *Thou, Lord, Art My Hope: The Life of Mother M. Theresa, a Pioneer of the Sisters, Servants of the Immaculate Heart of Mary* (Lancaster, Pa.: Dolphin Press, 1961); Immaculata Gillespie, *Mother Theresa Maxis Duchemin* (New York: Kenedy & Sons, 1945); and Rosalita Kelly, *No Greater Service: The History of the Congregation of the Sisters, Servants of the Immaculate Heart of Mary, Monroe, Michigan, 1845–1945* (Detroit: priv. published, 1948).

55. This account is told at greater length in my " 'Father' Didn't Always Know Best," and is based largely on a combination of CDP oral tradition, scanty archival sources, and two books: Mary Generosa Callahan, *History of the Sisters of Divine Providence, San Antonio, Texas* (Milwaukee, Wis.: Bruce Press, 1955); and Angelina Murphy, *Mother Florence: A Biographical History* (Smithtown, N.Y.: Exposition Press, 1980), as well as a February 1986 interview with Callahan. Sister Janet Griffin, CDP, a historian at Our Lady of the Lake Univer-

sity (San Antonio), is currently at work on a biography of Feltin. The reason that the archival resources are sketchy is that Bishop Neraz ordered all of Feltin's papers destroyed when she was deposed; all that survived were the council minutes that subsequently recorded the balloting for her (CDP Archives, San Antonio).

56. Margaret Anna Cusack, *The Nun of Kenmare, An Autobiography* (Boston: Ticknor and Co., 1888), 404–405.

8

Religion and Immigration

Behavior: The Dutch Experience

Economics explain the "why" of immigration but religion largely de-
termines the "how" of immigration and its effects. Although most
immigrants left their homelands in the hope of economic betterment,
religious institutions facilitated the move, guided the newcomers to certain destinations, and shaped their adjustment in the new land. Religion
was the very "bone and sinew" of immigrant group consciousness and
the "focal point" of their life.[1] One of the first scholars to recognize this
was Oscar Handlin, who wrote in *The Uprooted* (1951) that "the very
process of adjusting immigrant ideas to the conditions of the United
States made religion paramount as a way of life."[2] A few years later,
Henry S. Lucas, in a masterful study of the Dutch, observed that "for
years religion determined the pattern of Dutch settlement in America."[3]
The church community was a "shelter in the time of storm," a provider
of benevolent and charitable services, an emplyoment agency, and the
center of social and cultural life. The newcomers embraced it with a
fervor unknown even in the Old Country. Attacks from without by
nativists reinforced ethnoreligious group solidarity, and even internal
conflicts between Americanizers and anti-Americanizers served to define the boundaries of the community.[4] In turn, the receiving communities were shaped by the interaction of successive waves of immigrant
groups, each with its unique religious heritage.

The motives of overseas immigrants were as varied as the immigrants
themselves, but economic factors were certainly paramount. Radical,
political, religious, and cultural motives were secondary except in special
circumstances such as the pogroms against Jews in Russia in the 1880s; the
failed political revolutions in Germany and France in 1848; and the desire
for religious liberty among Mennonites, Quakers, Haugean Lutherans,
Dutch Reformed Seceders, and other free-church movements.

Whatever forces instigated the migration outflow to North America,
religious communities and their leaders played crucial roles in the move
itself and in determining the ultimate destinations. The churches as
institutions created immigration organizations, clerical and lay leaders
personally promoted and participated in it, and the church communities
created a supportive emotional and psychological environment in the
sending and receiving areas. Immigrants faced a personal crisis due to a

sense of loss, rootlessness, and social degradation; but religious faith offered stability and helped resolve tensions.

Religiously based immigrant aid societies commonly helped members to emigrate. As early as the 1700s, for example, Jewish synagogues in The Hague and Amsterdam provided grants for paupers in their communities to immigrate to America.[5] A century later ultra-Calvinists, who had seceded from the Netherlands Reformed Church, formed organizations such as the Utrecht-based Christian Association for Emigration to North America, led by Seceder clerics and lay patrons. At least a dozen Seceder clerics themselves emigrated with some or all of their congregations.[6] Dutch Catholics were somewhat less organized and the church hierarchy opposed overseas emigration, but several mission-minded priests founded emigration societies such as the Nederlandsche Catholijke Kolonies and the U.S.-based Catholic Colonization Society. American priests organized the latter in 1911 to prevent the dispersion of coreligionists by planting colonies.[7]

American churchmen with ethnic roots also assisted immigrants. At the outset of the Dutch Calvinist migration in the mid-1840s, the Reverend Isaac N. Wyckoff of the (Old) Dutch Reformed Church of Albany, New York, formed the Protestant Evangelical Holland Emigration Society, which became the model for a similar New York City organization.[8] Subsequently, Reformed immigrant congregations in the Midwest established common revolving loan funds, derived from annual levies on the entire membership, to provide passage money for eligible relatives who were chosen by lot. The sponsored family pledged to settle in one of the participating church colonies and to repay the loan with a small interest charge as soon as possible.[9] Dutch churches and synagogues also established benevolent and burial societies, health and accident funds, and insurance cooperatives, all mandated by the law of charity.

Not only did churches directly promote and fund immigration, but they created ethnic colonies where religion gave "form and substance" to community life. Religious solidarity provided an even stronger bond than ethnic identity alone, and ensured the long-term success of nearly all church-centered colonies. Dutch Calvinists especially, it was said, "stick together not primarily on the bases of ethnicity or nationalism but on the basis of their religion."[10] Consequently, the Dutch Reformed were indifferent to their Catholic, Jewish, or secularist countrymen even when they lived in close proximity in the cities.[11]

While immigrant religion ensured cultural maintenance, it also led to conflict both within and without. Some ethnoreligious communities were racked with theological controversies carried from the Old Country as part of their cultural baggage. Recent studies of Dutch Reformed and Norwegian Lutheran schisms illustrate the divisive nature of such an inheritance.[12] Monolithic churches, such as the Roman Catholic, with hierarchical ecclesiastical structures had to deal with lay challenges to clerical authority.[13] Every immigrant settlement also faced new conflicts stemming from the internal pressures of Americanization and external intergroup rivalries and conflicts with the dominant (usually New England Protestant) host society.[14]

While religion provided continuity for the immigrants by bridging the Old and New Worlds, which made gradual adjustment to American culture possible and even bearable, at the same time every group had battles between the conservative "slow Americanizers" and the liberal "fast Americanizers."[15] The traditional forces believed that "language saves faith" and "in isolation is our strength." Liberals advocated rapid language changeover and the desirability of becoming "good Americans" in every respect.[16]

Multiethnic religious groups like the Catholics and Jews struggled with endemic nationality conflicts—the Sephardic versus Ashkenazic Jews in the early nineteenth century and the German against East European Jews later in the century. Other classic examples are the Irish and German struggles in American Catholicism at mid-nineteenth century and at the turn of the twentieth century and the South and East European challenge to the more assimilated northern European Catholics.[17] While a few immigrants were secularists, for the vast majority ethnicity and religion were so closely intertwined as to be indistinguishable.[18] As Jay Dolan noted about New York:

> In New York Irish and German parishes were located within walking distance of one another, but they were as distinctive as German beer and Irish whiskey. They reinforced the ethnic differences of the people and enabled neighbors to build cultural barriers among themselves. As the center of their religious life the neighborhood parish exhibited the piety of the people, and the differences in piety proved to be more striking than the similarities of the urban environment.[19]

If religion strongly influenced the process of immigration and subsequent adjustment to American life, it is necessary to differentiate the effects of religion per se from the equally powerful forces of national identity. For immigrants from countries dominated by one religion, such as Irish, Italian, Belgian, or Czech Catholics, nationality and religion were interwoven. Which beliefs and practices arose from religious identity and which from national identity? Was the puritanical streak among

Irish Catholics in America a product of traditional Irish rural life, or religious defense against American Protestantism, or both? Did Dutch Calvinists in America seemingly revel in theological disputes and schisms because they were Dutch or because they were Calvinists?

One possible method to employ to address this differentiation problem is to study immigrants from countries such as the Netherlands and Germany where religions were regionally segmented, and to compare to immigrant behavior of the different religious subgroups. Dutch emigration in the nineteenth century affords such a research opportunity. Reformed and Roman Catholic emigrants can be identified and traced from their communities of origin to their communities of destination in the United States. Nearly sixty-two thousand Hollanders emigrated in the years 1835 to 1880, with more than 90 percent going to the United States, and for each family or single adult who departed overseas, the official records compiled by government officials specify religion or denominational affiliation. Additionally, the emigration records report more than a dozen other personal facts about the household, including age, sex, and occupation of the family head or single adult; family composition; social class; taxe status; presumed reason for emigrating; intended destination; place of last residence; and year of departure.[20]

All of the extant Netherlands emigration records in the years from 1835 through 1880 have been converted into computer files, which contain the name and full information on each registered emigrant household or single adult.[21] The emigration records have been augmented by U.S. population census records of Dutch-born nationals in 1850, 1860, and 1870.[22] Finally, by the process of record linkage the two record series were merged to create a third comprehensive file containing pre- and post-migration biographical information. These three individual-level files permit one to compare the emigration and adjustment patterns of Catholics and Protestants within the same nationality group. This may enable us to assess the role of religion, as distinct from nationality (or ethnicity), in shaping the total immigration experience.

The cycles of Dutch emigration closely paralleled the general northern European pattern, with the first high point from 1846 to 1857, a trough during the American Civil War, a second peak from 1865 to 1873, followed by a low during the economic crisis of the mid 1870s, and then another high point in the 1880s. Thus, during the period of interest here, 1835 to 1880, there were two complete up and down cycles and the beginning of a third up cycle.[23]

The first emigration era began in the mid-1840s in conjunction with a widespread agricultural crisis caused primarily by the failure of the potato crop for several years. In addition to the food problem, religious dissension in the 1830s within the privileged *Hervormde* (Reformed) church, which had been accompanied by police suppression of dissenters and seceders, strengthened the emigration mentality already strong among rural peasants who had long suffered from poverty and over-crowding.[24] Cheap lands in America and improved means of transportation to reach there provided an irresistible lure. Beginning in 1846, some twenty thousand persons emigrated within a decade. More than one-fourth were Seceders. Among both Calvinists and Catholics, families and religious groups emigrated in large numbers, led by their preachers and priests. This group migration was primarily a reflection of harsh religious and economic conditions.

The religious factors in Dutch emigration are evident both in the Old Country and in the New. At home, Catholics were more reluctant to emigrate and fewer did so. In America, Catholics settled in cities mainly and assimilated more rapidly than Protestants. Catholics were less prone to emigrate because of cultural and clerical pressures against it, as well as regional differences.[25] One of the earliest brochures that warned against emigrating came from the pen of a "Catholic citizen" and was published in 1846 in the Catholic center of 's Hertogenbosch. The pamphlet's inflammatory title, "Think Before you Start! A cordial word to my Countrymen concerning the illness in our Fatherland called 'Emigration,' " is sufficient to indicate the strident nature of the text. The desire to emigrate, said the writer, is a "strange disease" that afflicts "a blind crowd," who in the mistaken hope of getting away from "cares and troubles" will instead find a hard, lonely, and despised life in the United States.[26]

Catholics comprised 38.3 percent (10,700) of the Dutch population in 1849 but made up only 17.3 percent of the total emigrants in the years through 1880 (see Table 8.1). Hence, to match their share of the population, over twice as many Catholics should have emigrated. Seceders, on the other hand, were heavily overrepresented, particularly in the first wave, which followed on the heels of bitter government repression in the 1830s. Seceders comprised 48.7 percent (11,400) of all Dutch emigrants in the years 1845 to 1849, yet they formed only 1.3 percent of the total population in 1849. The new liberal constitution of 1848, which granted complete religious freedom, sharply reduced the Seceder propensity to emigrate. Nevertheless, Seceders numbered 18.4 percent of the emigrants, but they claimed only 3 percent of the Dutch populace in 1869. Thus, six times as many Seceders departed the fatherland as their share of the total population. *Hervormde* church members were also overrepresented but by only 7 points. They numbered 54.8 percent of the population in 1849 but comprised 61.7 percent (38,200) of all emigrants.

FIGURE 8.1.   Provinces of the Netherlands, Showing the
Percentage of Emigration by Religion, 1835–1880,
and the Percentage Over- or Under-represented
According to the 1849 Census

SOURCE: Table 1; 1849 Census (*Volkstelling*) of the Netherlands.

TABLE 8.1.   Religion* by State, 1850, 1860, 1870: Dutch Immigrants and Their Children

State	Protestant								Catholic							
	1850		1860		1870		1850–70		1850		1860		1870		1850–70	
	N	%	N	%	N	%	N	%	N	%	N	%	N	%	N	%
IL	204	100.0	884	100.0	2,881	92.3	3,969	94.3	0	0.0	0	0.0	239	7.7	239	5.7
IN	28	100.0	382	67.8	745	76.6	1,155	73.9	0	0.0	181	32.2	227	23.4	408	26.1
IA	1,053	93.9	3,372	93.4	5,598	92.2	10,023	92.8	68	6.1	237	6.6	473	7.8	778	7.2
KA	0	0.0	0	0.0	22	0.0	22	100.0	0	0.0	0	0.0	0	0.0	0	0.0
MI	3,325	98.7	8,882	97.6	17,278	98.0	29,485	98.0	42	1.3	221	2.4	342	2.0	605	2.0
MN	0	0.0	224	36.4	551	25.4	775	27.8	0	0.0	392	63.6	1,622	74.6	2,014	72.2
MO	0	0.0	30	3.4	78	4.9	108	4.0	202	100.0	849	96.6	1,515	95.1	2,566	96.0
NE	0	0.0	0	0.0	110	100.0	110	100.0	0	0.0	0	0.0	0	0.0	0	0.0
NJ	312	100.0	1,311	95.3	3,833	98.0	5,456	97.4	0	0.0	64	4.7	79	2.0	143	2.6
NY	1,281	46.5	3,956	52.8	5,567	174.7	10,804	61.0	1,473	53.5	3,530	47.2	1,889	25.3	6,892	38.9
OH	81	22.3	580	29.6	787	26.9	1,448	27.6	283	77.7	1,378	70.4	2,137	73.1	3,798	72.4
WI	904	54.2	3,966	57.7	5,730	57.3	10,600	57.2	163	45.8	2,904	42.3	4,274	42.7	7,941	42.8
	7188	71.7	23587	70.7	43180	77.8	73955	74.4	2831	28.3	9756	29.3	12797	22.2	25384	25.6

SOURCE: Robert P. Swierenga (compiler), *Dutch Households in U.S. Population Censuses, 1850, 1860, 1870: An Alphabetical Listing by Family Heads* (Wilmington, Del., 1987).

*See note 40, Ch. 8, for a description of the method for determining religion.

As Figure 8.1 displays, Calvinists overshot and Catholics undershot their proportion of the population in every province except Drenthe, where the pattern was reversed. But Drenthe had an insignificant number of emigrants and can safely be ignored.[27] Catholic emigrants, on the other hand, were heavily underrepresented in the three urban provinces (Noord Holland, Zuid Holland, and Utrecht), which indicates that urban Catholics were less prone to emigrate than rural. In the traditional Catholic provinces of Noord Brabant and Limburg, Catholic emigrants were underrepresented by only 5 percent and 1 percent, respectively. These regional differences in the propensity to emigrate are worthy of further study, but the salient fact remains that Calvinists were more willing than Catholics to leave the fatherland.

This Catholic-Seceder disparity in emigration raises the question of causation. Both were religious minorities in the society as a whole; yet Catholics were far more reluctant to emigrate. What factors might explain this pattern?[28] The Dutch Catholics were the most traditional cultural group in the country. They had the largest families, were least likely to move away from ancestral lands, and were most willing to obey religious leaders. Significantly, Catholic clerics generally discouraged emigration because it threatened to disrupt religious supervision and instruction and might lead to the loss of social control. Only a few clerics, notably Father Theodore Van den Broek, actively recruited emigrants and this was done under the cloak of promoting missionary enterprise. Van den Broek had already established a mission outpost among the Menominee Indians near Green Bay, Wisconsin, and he sought to build a Christian community there.

Yet Van den Broek was well aware of the risks to the faith. In an 1847 emigration pamphlet, he warned that in America the numerous Protestant sects may fight each other but they "stand side by side against the Catholics; . . . so it is desirable that all Catholic immigrants remain together and chose no other places except where they find their spiritual leaders."[29] Some five hundred Dutch Catholics responded to Van den Broek's appeals, and in the following decades another one thousand to fifteen hundred persons followed. By 1880, there were at least three Dutch parishes in northern Wisconsin—Green Bay, Little Chute, and DePere. But this was only a fraction of the more than ten thousand Dutch Catholic immigrants in these years. The rest scattered widely.[30]

The cultural and institutional forces discouraging Catholic emigration were reinforced by economic developments. The Catholic Netherlands was in the upland, sandy-soil region where traditional small-scale farming remained the norm. The introduction of commercial fertilizers and land reclamation projects in this region enabled fathers to subdivide their farms among their sons or to open new ones on reclaimed lands. However, in the diluvial, sea-clay regions of the Protestant north and southwest, a different farming pattern developed. There the cash-grain farmers mechanized their operations, consolidated their holdings in the quest for efficient large-scale production, and cut their labor costs by laying off farm workers. These excess laborers had few alternatives but to leave farming and move to the large cities or emigrate to America where cheap land beckoned.

Another economic factor in the low Catholic emigration rate was that the sandy-soil farmers were heavily engaged in the home production of textiles as part of the textile industry in the region.[31] Home industry augmented their farm income and provided a greater measure of stability against fluctuating food prices. After 1865, when the textile industry modernized by shifting production from farm cottages to urban factory centers such as Eindhoven, Tilburg, Geldrop, and Helmond, sons and daughters of farmers could go to the nearby towns and cities for work and still remain within a predominantly Catholic culture. Catholic peasants thus had more attractive economic alternatives than did Protestant farm workers in the north and west.

In brief, the emerging industrial growth in the textile centers of southeastern Noord Brabant and Limburg in the third quarter of the nineteenth century served as urban magnets to attract families and single workers from the surrounding rural areas. The only major emigration from Noord Brabant, therefore, originated in the northeastern part of the province that was farthest removed from the new textile centers.

The timing of Protestant and Catholic emigration also differed (see Table 8.1). Both Catholic and Seceder emigration was heavier in the first wave from 1846 through 1856 and fell off in the decades after 1856. The pattern of the *Hervormde* emigration was the reverse—low in the early phase but gaining momentum over the decades, until the second half of the 1870s when 71 percent of all emigrants were *Hervormde,* whereas they numbered only 55 percent of the Dutch population.

The Seceders began to depart in large numbers in 1846, one year earlier than did the Catholics, and over forty-eight hundred Seceders left by 1849, 41 percent of the whole. Once the Catholic outflow started in earnest in 1847, these too departed steadily, with the heaviest movement in 1850–1854 and 1865–1870, mainly originating in the provinces of Noord Brabant and Gelderland. In the interim years of 1857 to 1865, the adjoining province of Limburg first began contributing emigrants, sending out more than half of all Catholic emigrants during the Civil War era. In the postbellum decades (1865–1880), the overall Catholic proportion declined to about 14 percent. Improved economic conditions at home and job opportunities across the border in Germany dampened the enthusiasm to emigrate. Thus, Catholic emigration was more important before 1865 than in the postwar decade.[32]

Another difference is that a higher proportion of Catholic emigrants settled in the United States than did the majority of Protestants, many of whom—all non-Seceders—went to Dutch colonies in Southeast Asia and South America, or to South Africa. The Seceders, however, had the highest rate of America-centeredness, averaging 98.6 percent; while 90.4 percent of the Catholic emigrants went to the United States, compared to 88.9 percent of the Reformed. Seceders and Catholics, the former a new religious minority and the latter a traditional minority, had suffered sufficiently as second-class citizens to dissuade them from emigrating *within* the empire, if equal opportunities beckoned elsewhere.

Just as the emigration patterns differed between Protestants and Catholics, so did the settlement behavior in the United States.[33] The Dutch Catholics established very few immigrant colonies, in distinction from the Calvinists, and especially the Seceders, who formed ethnic enclaves wherever they settled, whether in rural areas or major cities. Also, over one-third of the Catholic emigrants settled in cities and towns (above five thousand population), compared to only one-quarter of the Seceders. Thus, the Dutch Catholics and Calvinists in America distanced themselves from one another.

The only lasting Dutch Catholic colony of the mid-nineteenth century was in the Green Bay area, especially southward along the Fox River Valley at Little Chute and Hollandtown.[34] Many Dutch Catholic immigrants, however, went to the larger cities along the established transportation routes to the Midwest: Cincinnati and Saint Louis from the South, and from the East coast Rochester, Buffalo, Cleveland, Detroit, Bay City, Chicago, Milwaukee, and Green Bay. In these places, all Catholic centers with institutional infrastructures in place, Dutch Catholics readily worshipped and intermarried with Catholics of other nationalities, especially Germans, Belgians, and Irish. As historian Henry S. Lucas says:

> The common bond of faith made it possible for them to live happily with people who were not Dutch. . . . Dutch Catholics did not tend so markedly to settle in Dutch communities, but scattered, were speedily assimilated, and so left few distinctive traces.[35]

Cincinnati, Chicago, and Grand Rapids were notable exceptions. The Dutch Catholics in Cincinnati, four hundred strong, had by 1854 established their own parish with a Dutch-speaking priest, Father Johannes

Van De Luijtelaar. In Chicago's Kensington district on the far southside, the only Dutch parish in the city, Saint Willebrord, was organized in the early 1890s and totaled two hundred families in the era of World War I, when a Dutch-born cleric, Father J. A. Van Heertum, O.P., pastored the parish. Saint Joseph's Parish on the near southwest side of Grand Rapids was founded in 1887 to serve some seventy Dutch families in the Furniture City. Under the leadership of the Dutch-speaking priest, Henry Frencken of 's Hertogenbosch, who served the parish from 1887 to 1906, the church grew to one hundred twenty families by 1915. Dutch-language services ceased in 1906, however, when Father Frencken returned to the Netherlands, and the parish gradually lost its ethnic solidarity.

These Dutch Catholic urban churches were three of only twenty-five congregations nationwide that were primarily Dutch, according to historian Jacob Van Hinte, but they had no mutual connections and all were short-lived. In 1920, there was only one Dutch-nationality parish and three in 1940. Even the concentrated Fox River Valley Catholic settlements failed to maintain a Dutch ethnic flavor after World War I, except for the two small villages of Hollandtown and Little Chute that still celebrate their annual *Schut* (shooting) festival, which is of Brabantine origin. By contrast, there were five hundred Dutch Calvinist congregations in the 1920s and most continue to the present day.[36] Thus, a feeling of religious solidarity not only led to group migration but to successful colonization. In the words of the Dutch immigration expert, Jacob Van Hinte: "What held the colonists together was the powerful bond of religion—a bond that showed itself to be stronger, in many aspects, than the one of ethnic identity. It was the power of religious conviction," Van Hinte continued, "that must be credited for the success of nearly all of these colonies and that made them into the foci of the Dutch presence in America."[37] In short, as Lucas succinctly summarized the matter, "religion encouraged dispersal" for Dutch Catholics, because the Catholic churches were everywhere, but religion cemented together Dutch Calvinists.[38]

Calvinists, especially Seceders, in contrast to Catholics, preferred settling in isolated rural colonies or forming Dutch neighborhoods in major cities where they could preserve their faith. Most of the Calvinists settled in southwestern Michigan, southeastern Wisconsin, northern Illinois, central Iowa, western New York, and northern New Jersey. Urban concentrations could be found in Grand Rapids, Kalamazoo, Chicago, Milwaukee, Rochester, Buffalo, Albany, and Paterson. As of 1850, more than three-fourths of the Protestants lived in colonies, whereas less than a third of the Catholics did so. Twenty years later, in 1870, after further emigration as well as internal migration, the proportions remained virtually unchanged.[39]

The geographical distribution by state of Dutch immigrants illustrates these patterns (see Table 8.2).[40] Catholic Dutch comprised over 95 percent of the Dutch-born in Missouri (in Saint Louis City and Bollinger County), over 70 percent in Ohio (in Cincinnati, Cleveland, and Toledo) and Minnesota (widely scattered but mainly in and around Minneapolis-Saint Paul in Carver County and at Saint Cloud in Benton County), and around 40 percent in New York (New York City and Brooklyn, Rochester, Buffalo, Auburn, Albany, Troy) and Wisconsin (Green Bay and environs, Racine and Milwaukee).

However, Protestants predominated by over 95 percent in Michigan (the southwest sector) and New Jersey (Passaic County [Paterson] and Bergen County [Lodi]), over 90 percent in Iowa (Pella and the Mississippi River cities), Illinois (Chicago area), Kansas (Ottawa County), and Nebraska (Lancaster County). In Indiana (northern part), Protestants made up nearly 75 percent of Dutch-born. In Wisconsin, Protestants ranged over 55 percent (in Sheboygan, Milwaukee, and the southeastern sector generally) and they were over 60 percent in New York City and along the Erie Canal route.

In general, both Protestant and Catholic Dutch favored the Great Lakes region, but the Protestants did so the most (63.5 percent), while 21.8 percent of the Protestants stayed in the East and 28.2 percent of the Catholics went west of the Mississippi River into Missouri and Minnesota (see Table 8.3).

In terms of the size and type of settlement areas, Protestant and Catholic Dutch also favored rural communities, but the Seceders, who had the highest rate of family migration, were most rural with 73.4 percent. Catholics were next in selecting rural locations (65.3 percent), and the *Hervormde* were the least rural (59.1 percent). Catholics had the highest propensity to settle in large cities (over twenty-five thousand) at 17.3 percent, with *Hervormde* a close second at 16.9 percent, whereas only 9.4 percent of Seceders resided in large cities. Reformed immigrants had the highest proportion living in medium and small cities (24 percent). These figures are averages for the thirty-five year period from 1835 to 1870.

The reasons for these settlement patterns in the first plantings of the mid-nineteenth century are many, but they can be classified as idiosyncratic, cultural, and structural. Individuals often directed immigrants to particular places for their own economic, religious, or cultural reasons. Pioneer immigrants sent home letters about America to attract their

TABLE 8.2. Religion by Year, Total Netherlands Emigrants, 1835–1880

YEAR	REFORMED			SECEDER			CATHOLIC			JEWISH			OTHER		
	#	Era Total	Era %	#	Era Total	Era %	#	Era Total	Era %	#	Era Total	Era %	#	Era Total	Era %
1835	0			6			17			0			0		
1836	0			3			10			0			0		
1837	0			1			0			0			0		
1838	1			0			0			0			0		
1839	9			0			0			0			0		
1840	1			0			1			0			0		
1841	0			5			0			0			0		
1842	8			7			8			0			0		
1843	35			7			32			0			0		
1844	98	152	44.8%	65	94	27.7%	25	93	27.4%	0	0	0.0%	0	0	0.0%
1845	221		(0.4%)	178		(0.8%)	110		(0.9%)	0		(0.0%)	6		(0.0%)
1846	371			744			195			0			14		
1847	871			2297			339			26			19		
1848	880			779			450			21			46		
1849	1023	3366	34.8	711	4709	48.7	330	1424	14.7	18	65	0.7	19	104	1.1
1850	348		(8.8)	77		(41.3)	327		(13.3)	27		(11.2)	10		(9.9)

Year														
1851	580			118			492			11			13	
1852	765			60			283			56			15	
1853	812			152			565			18			78	
1854	2459	4964	58.8	402	809	9.6	642	2309	27.3	68	180	2.1	67	183	2.2
1855	1389	(13.0)		342	(7.1)		300	(21.5)		21	(31.0)		11	(17.4)	
1856	1300			311			263			5			28	
1857	1198			142			244			50			21	
1858	778			28			294			12			25	
1859	303	4968	68.7	11	834	11.5	87	1188	16.4	28	116	1.6	44	129	1.8
1860	772	(13.0)		9	(7.3)		47	(11.1)		6	(20.0)		24	(12.2)	
1861	460			37			127			2			7	
1862	330			21			338			10			17	
1863	327			8			668			0			13	
1864	486	2375	60.1	46	121	3.1	169	1349	34.2	1	19	0.5	25	86	2.2
1865	1218	(6.2)		167	(1.1)		164	(12.6)		14	(3.3)		31	(8.2)	
1866	2502			273			375			16			42	
1867	2740			827			513			25			74	
1868	1931			488			475			16			48	
1869	2320	10711	69.7	505	2260	14.7	518	2045	13.3	15	86	0.6	70	265	1.7
1870	1194	(28.0)		191	(19.8)		366	(19.1)		7	(14.8)		24	(25.2)	

TABLE 8.2. (continued)

YEAR	REFORMED			SECEDER			CATHOLIC			JEWISH			OTHER		
	#	Era Total	Era %	#	Era Total	Era %	#	Era Total	Era %	#	Era Total	Era %	#	Era Total	Era %
1871	1189			279			330			50			37		
1872	2435			542			439			26			30		
1873	2667			636			555			23			59		
1874	807	8292	68.1	128	1776	14.6	125	1815	14.9	2	108	0.9	38	188	1.5
1875	471		(21.7)	52		(15.6)	116		(16.9)	2		(18.6)	22		(17.8)
1876	225			22			75			0			30		
1877	172			10			45			3			17		
1878	203			7			20			0			4		
1879	635			61			65			1			4		
1880	1687	3393	71.0	639	791	16.6	169	490	10.2	0	6	0.1	21	98	2.1
		(8.9)			(6.9)			(4.6)			(1.0)			(9.3)	
Total	38,221		61.7	11,394		18.4	10,713		17.3	580		0.9	1053		1.7

N. A. = 611

SOURCE: Robert P. Swierenga, *Dutch Emigrants to the United States, South Africa, South America, and Southeast Asia, 1835–1880: An Alphabetical Listing by Household Heads and Independent Persons* (Wilmington, Del, 1983).

TABLE 8.3.   Religion* by Geographic Region, Protestant and
                  Catholic Dutch, 1870

Religion	Great Lakes[a]		Midwest[b]		East[c]	
Protestant	27,421	63.5	6,359	14.7	9,400	21.8
Catholic	7,219	56.4	3,610	28.2	1,968	15.4

SOURCE: Same as table 2.
NOTE: See note 40, ch. 8, for description of the method for determining religion.
[a]Great Lakes=Illinois, Indiana, Michigan, Ohio, Wisconsin
[b]Midwest=Iowa, Kansas, Missouri, Minnesota, Nebraska
[c]East=New Jersey, New York

countrymen. Dutch Catholics went to the Green Bay area because a Dutch priest had begun an Indian mission station there. Other Catholic Dutch settled in large cities that had social and religious institutions in place. Seceders followed their "dominies" to sparsely settled regions in order to establish homogeneous colonies. *Hervormde* Dutch sometimes sought out descendants of the Old Dutch in New York and New Jersey or they settled among those who had followed the frontier westward to the Great Lakes.

Given the historic Protestant-Catholic division in the Netherlands, it was to be expected that Protestants deliberately avoided Catholic-dominated areas such as northern Wisconsin and cities like Cincinnati and Saint Louis. But apart from the religious consideration, most Dutch in the mid-nineteenth century avoided hot climates and open prairies (both unknown in the Netherlands). The major exception was the Pella, Iowa, colony of the maverick Seceder cleric, Hendrik P. Scholte, who led some nine hundred followers to the prairies. Once the settlers adapted to the new environment, their sons and daughters in the 1870s and 1880s founded many other prairie settlements in northwestern Iowa, eastern South Dakota, southwestern Minnesota, and eventually the Pacific Northwest. The Dutch pioneers usually located near major waterways and markets, and they desired areas such as the forest lands of Michigan and Wisconsin that had exploitable natural resources for the cash-hungry settlers.

The geographical and institutional differences had a significant impact on marital assimilation. Already in the initial immigrant population (i.e., 1840–1870), Dutch Catholics had a higher intermarriage rate than did Protestants. The difference is apparent as early as 1850, only a few years after emigration began, which indicates that some Catholics had married non-Dutch spouses even before emigrating. These were mainly neighboring Flemish Belgians, plus a few German Catholics. In 1850, 32.1 percent of married Dutch-born Catholics had non-Dutch spouses, compared to only 5.2 percent among Protestant Dutch. In 1860, the Catholic outmarriage rate had risen to 43.7 percent and in 1870 to 45.6 percent, whereas Protestant intermarriage rates were 9.9 percent in 1860 and 13.2 percent in 1870. On average, the Dutch Catholics in the United States were four to five times as likely as Protestants to have non-Dutch spouses.

An even more dramatic picture of Catholic outmarriage emerges when the 1870 census figures are differentiated by couples married before immigration or before the first census enumeration after immigration, and couples married after being reported as single in the first census enumeration after arrival. The latter are mainly Dutch-born children of Dutch parents who were minors at the time of immigration. Among Protestants, 9.8 percent of first generation couples outmarried by 1870 compared to 24.3 percent of the next generation. But among Catholics, 37 percent of first generation couples married non-Dutch spouses and an overwhelming 69.9 percent of their unmarried children selected non-Dutch spouses. Clearly, the less isolated Catholic communities and the international nature of the Roman church broke down the ethnic identity of Dutch Catholics more rapidly than Protestants.

When Dutch Catholics and Protestants did outmarry, the nativity of their choices again differed dramatically. Over 80 percent of the Catholic non-Dutch marriage partners were foreign-born (in order, German, Belgian, Irish, and French), whereas Protestants intermarried with native-born Americans half the time by 1870. Most of the native-born were children of Dutch-born parents, so the Protestant rate of outgroup marriages was actually lower in 1870 than the 13 percent reported. When Dutch Protestants married non-Dutch, they were often fellow religionists, German Calvinists from the Dutch border regions of Hannover and Ost Friesland.

The explanation for the high Catholic outmarriage was the "mixed parish." In the Diocese of Green Bay between 1875 and 1900, where all the parishes were of mixed nationality, ten out of fifty-eight parishes included a substantial number of Dutch. Four of the ten Dutch parishes were mixed English and German; two included English, German, and French; one English, German, and Bohemian; one was simply Dutch and Flemish; and two were Dutch and German.[41]

These mixed parishes, created out of needful compromise, were plagued with problems of language, customs, worship liturgies, and weak institutional loyalties. Most evolved into single nationality or territorial parishes. The immigrant groups, except those that resided in transplanted colonies, experienced a series of transformations. First they worshipped in an "alien" parish or became part of a mixed congregation, and finally when their numbers multiplied, they established their own parish. Over time, however, unless the congregation was nourished by a steady stream of new immigrants from the mother country, it reverted again to a mixed parish. The U.S. immigration restriction laws following World War I often caused such a reversion.

For millions of immigrant Catholics the nationality parish and parochial school were surrogate associations for the communal village they left behind. Ethnoreligious institutions relieved their emotional stress, protected them from the dominant Protestant world, and facilitated their transition to American life. As James Olson aptly noted: "Church newspapers, parish sodalities and confraternities, parochial schools, emigrant aid and mutual benefit societies, and religious associations dedicated to particular shrines and patron saints reconstructed the community that had died."[42] In the decades before World War I, more than 80 percent of the children of East European immigrants attended parish schools using or teaching native languages. Church, school, and societies provided cultural continuity and became the social and emotional center of the neighborhood. In the minds of most inhabitants, the parish and neighborhood melded together.[43]

However, a strong ethnic parish could retard but not prevent the slow movement toward a "Roman Catholic melting pot." Language was the first to go, even though its maintenance was the major function of the nationality parish. Then the immigrant press declined. Culturally, the patriarchal family and hierarchical church governance weakened and even national loyalties disappeared through intermarriage.[44]

The role of religion in promoting or retarding assimilation depended on modes of settlement, church institutional structures, and theological traditions. Transplanted churches and nationality parishes ensured the survival of European languages and cultures for three or more generations. Protestants, such as Dutch Calvinists, German Missouri Synod Lutherans, and Norwegian Haugean Lutherans, tended to establish homogeneous rural colonies more than did Roman Catholics, and the Protestant ethnics preserved their cultural ways longer. To what extent this was an artifact of settlement patterns rather than ecclesiastical structures is not always clear. William Petersen attributed the "imperfect integration" into American society of the Dutch Protestant colonies in Michigan and Wisconsin after more than one hundred years to the "efforts of the Orthodox Calvinist ministers to keep their flocks together," whereas Roman Catholics assimilated rapidly "principally because there was no separate Dutch Catholic Church.[45] Lucas noted that "Reformed principles" gave the Calvinists their conception of life and "helped them to organize their social and economic activities."[46]

A group that assimilated even faster than Dutch Catholics were Dutch Protestants who settled away from the colonies and joined Presbyterian and other English-speaking churches. These persons deliberately chose the "fast track" to acculturation and quickly jettisoned their Dutchness. German Forty-Eighters, the so-called "secular-club" liberals, followed the same path. They deliberately abandoned German culture in favor of the American democratic system. Wherever the Forty-Eighter influence was greatest, they promoted rapid assimilation. By contrast the so-called "church Germans," who were less cosmopolitan in their mental outlook and religiously conservative, formed "language islands" throughout the United States centered around church and creed. Lutherans clung to their various synods (Missouri, Wisconsin, etc.) and Catholics to their dioceses, priests, and bishops.[47]

Theological tenets also influenced the rate of assimilation. Churches with a prophetic (or pietistic) theology that stressed individual conversion and a life of benevolence ("good works") made it easier for members to shuck off old cultural patterns and to adopt new ones. The converts personally appropriated their faith and enlisted in the social-reform crusades of the Second Great Awakening, eventually appropriating the American individualistic success ethic. Churches with an orthodox theology or priestly hierarchy, on the other hand, stressed cultural maintenance and were therefore inherently countercultural and even anti-American.[48] Dutch Calvinists even had a theological rationale for cultural separation, the doctrine of the "antithesis," which held that believers' religious value systems were squarely opposed to those of unbelievers. The power of resistance to Americanization inherent in this key doctrine of Calvinist orthodoxy proved to be the pioneers' most valuable asset. As Adriaan J. Barnouw remarked: "For, thanks to that same power, they were able to withstand the trials and hardships of the life that awaited the first settlers in the forests of Michigan and the prairies of Iowa. Calvinism, thanks to the fervor with which it inspires the faithful, is a great builder of colonies."[49] A tight theological and ecclesiastical system certainly slowed the process of assimilation and sustained a secure fortress mentality. As Barnouw observed: "The stubbornest resistance to Americanization is offered by the most orthodox believers."

Religious faith and theology, in short, were crucial to the existence of ethnic enclaves, led to resistance against nearby "out-groups," and strengthened commitments to the church community. The immigrant church also cushioned the shock for newcomers on a personal level and facilitated their gradual adjustment to the new society.[50]

The thrust of current immigration research is that religious affiliation significantly influenced the entire resettlement process—the decision to emigrate, the direction of the emigrant stream, and the subsequent adjustment and adaptation in the new homeland. But religious forces operated within a common context. Economic forces primarily spurred emigration among lower and middle classes in all religious communities, although with greater or lesser intensity. Immigrants of all religious affiliations overwhelmingly chose the United States as their destination, but dissenting religious minorities were the most America-centered because of the proffered freedoms. All immigrants relied on family resources and information networks in the first instance and created family migration chains. Catholic and Jewish immigrants likely experienced a greater uprooting than did Protestants and they assimilated more readily. The international character of Catholicism and Judaism weakened national identities and ethnic feelings, at the same time that transplanting church-centered colonies maintained their language and institutional life, and carved out new daughter colonies when expansion became necessary after the mother colony reached saturation.[51] Religion was truly the "bone and sinew" of immigrant group life and determined its form and character.

NOTES

1. Randall M. Miller, "Introduction," in Randall M. Miller and Thomas D. Marzik eds., *Immigrants and Religion in Urban America* (Philadelphia: Temple University Press, 1977), xv; and John Bodnar, *The Transplanted: A History of Immigrants in Urban America* (Bloomington: Indiana University Press, 1985), 144–168.

2. Oscar Handlin, *The Uprooted* (New York: Grosset and Dunlap, 1951), 117. Sociologists and psychologists of the postwar decades assumed that faith was irrelevant to the successful adjustment of immigrants. See, for example, Abraham A. Weinberg, *Psychosociology of the Immigrant: An Investigation into the Problems of Adjustment of Jewish Immigrants into Palestine Based on Replies to an Enquiry among Immigrants from Holland* (Jerusalem: Israel Institute of Folklore and Ethnology, 1949), 20, and L. J. Menges, *Geschiktheid voor Emigratie. een onderzoek naar enkele Psychologische Aspecten der Emigrabiliteit* (The Hague, Staatsdrukkerij- en Uitgeverijbedrijf, 1959), 104.

3. Henry S. Lucas, *Netherlanders in America: Dutch Immigration to the United States and Canada, 1789–1950* (Ann Arbor: University of Michigan Press, 1955).

4. James D. Bratt, *Dutch Calvinism in Modern America: A History of a Conser-*

vative Subculture (Grand Rapids, Mich.: Eerdmans, 1984); Andrew T. Kopan, "Greek Survival in Chicago: The Role of Ethnic Education 1890–1980," in Peter d'A Jones and Melvin G. Holli, eds., *Ethnic Chicago* (Grand Rapids, Mich.: Eerdmans, 1981), 95.

5. Bertram Wallace Korn, *The Early Jews of New Orleans* (Waltham, Mass.: American Jewish Historical Society, 1969), 13.

6. Lucas, *Netherlanders in America,* chaps. 3–5.

7. J. Stellingwerff, *Amsterdamse Emigranten: onbekende brieven uit de prairie van Iowa, 1846–1873* (Amsterdam: Buijten & Schipperheijn, 1975), 15; Jacob Van Hinte, *Netherlanders in America: A Study of Emigration and Settlement in the 19th and 20th Centuries in the United States of America,* Robert P. Swierenga, general ed., Adrian de Wit, chief trans. (Grand Rapids, Mich.: Baker Book House, 1985), 729–730; and Mary Gilbert Kelly, *Catholic Immigrant Colonization Projects in the United States, 1815–1860,* United States Catholic Historical Society Monograph Series 17 (New York: United States Catholic Historical Society, 1939).

8. Van Hinte, *Netherlanders in America,* 131.

9. Ibid., 390.

10. Lucas, *Netherlanders in America,* 473, 579, 315.

11. An example of this is Bastiaan Broere, a devout Calvinist in West Sayville, Long Island, who deliberately avoided any contact with two neighboring Dutch families because "they would offend us with their ungodly language." Van Hinte, *Netherlanders in America,* 315.

12. Bratt, *Dutch Calvinism;* John Gjerde, "Conflict and Community: A Case Study of the Immigrant Church in the United States," *Journal of Social History* 19 (Summer 1986): 681–692; and Dolores Ann Liptak, *European Immigrants and the Catholic Church in Connecticut* (New York: Center for Migration Studies, 1987).

13. Dennis J. Clark, "The Irish Catholics: A Postponed Perspective" in Miller and Marzik, *Immigrants and Religion,* 48–68; Henry B. Leonard, "Ethnic Conflict and Episcopal Power: The Diocese of Cleveland, 1847–1870," *Catholic Historical Review* 62 (July 1976): 388–407; Timothy L. Smith, "Lay Initiative in the Religious Life of American Immigrants, 1880–1950," in Tamara K. Hareven, ed., *Anonymous Americans: Explorations in Nineteenth Century Social History* (Englewood Cliffs, N.J.: Prentice-Hall, 1971), 214–249; and Jay P. Dolan, *The Immigrant Church: New York's Irish and German Catholics, 1815–1865* (Baltimore: Johns Hopkins University Press, 1975).

14. Clark, "Irish Catholics"; Rudolph J. Vecoli, "Prelates and Peasants: Italian Immigrants and the Catholic Chruch," *Journal of Social History* 2 (Spring 1969): 228–251; Jed Dannenbaum, "Immigrants and Temperance: Ethnocultural Conflict in Cincinnati, 1845–1860," *Ohio History* 87 (Spring 1978): 125–139; and Nora Faires, "The Evolution of Ethnicity: The German Community in Pittsburgh and Allegheny City, Pennsylvania, 1845–1885" (Ph.D. diss., University of Pittsburgh, 1981). Faires argues for a dynamic concept of ethnicity, which suggests that churches played a greater role among immigrants in America than

they did in the homeland (see pp. 66–68). See also Sylvia June Alexander, "The Immigrant Church and Community: The Formation of Pittsburgh's Slovak Religious Institutions, 1870–1914" (Ph.D. diss., University of Pittsburgh, 1980).

15. Miller, "Introduction," viii; Andrew M. Greeley, *The Catholic Experience* (New York: Doubleday, 1967), 22–23, and passim.

16. James S. Olson, *Catholic Immigrants in America* (Chicago: Nelson Hall, 1987), 186; and Jay P. Dolan, "Philadelphia and the German Catholic Community," in Miller and Marzik, *Immigrants and Religion,* 71.

17. Clark, "Irish Catholics;" Dolan, "German Catholic Community;" Olson, *Catholic Immigrants,* 101–125.

18. Harry S. Stout, "Ethnicity: The Vital Center of Religion in America," *Ethnicity* 2 (April 1975): 204–224; Martin E. Marty, "Ethnicity: The Skeleton of Religion in America," *Church History* 41 (March 1972): 5–21; William J. Galush, "Faith and Fatherland: Dimensions of Polish-American Ethnoreligion, 1875–1975," in Miller and Marzik, *Immigrants and Religion,* 84–102; Timothy L. Smith, "Religion and Ethnicity in America," *American Historical Review* 83 (December 1978): 1155–1185, esp. 1181; and James D. Bratt, "Religion and Ethnicity in America: A Critique of Timothy L. Smith," *Fides et Historia* 12 (Spring 1980): 8–17.

19. Dolan, *Immigrant Church,* 44.

20. A thorough description of this source is in Robert P. Swierenga and Harry S. Stout, "Dutch Immigration in the Nineteenth Century, 1820–1877: A Quantitative Overview," *Indiana Social Studies Quarterly* 28 (1975): 7–34.

21. Robert P. Swierenga, comp., *Dutch Emigrants to the United States, South Africa, South America, and Southeast Asia, 1835–1880: An Alphabetical Listing by Household Heads and Independent Persons* (Wilmington, Del.: Scholarly Resources, 1983).

22. Robert P. Swierenga, comp., *Dutch Households in U.S. Population Censuses, 1850, 1860, 1870: An Alphabetical Listing by Family Heads,* 3 vols., (Wilmington, Del.: Scholarly Resources, 1987).

23. Robert P. Swierenga, "Dutch Immigration Patterns in the Nineteenth and Twentieth Centuries," in *The Dutch in America: Immigration, Settlement, and Cultural Change,* ed. Robert P. Swierenga (New Brunswick, N.J.: Rutgers University Press, 1985), 27–32. For more details on Dutch immigration, see Robert P. Swierenga, "Dutch," in *Harvard Encyclopedia of American Ethnic Groups,* ed. Stephan Thernstrom (Cambridge, Mass.: Harvard University Press, 1980), 284–295.

24. Robert P. Swierenga, "Local-Cosmopolitan Theory and Immigrant Religion: The Social Bases of the Antebellum Dutch Reformed Schism," *Journal of Social History* 14 (1980): 113–135.

25. H. Blink, "Immigratie in Amerika en Emigratie uit Europe in Verband met de Economische Toestanden," *Vragen Van Den Dag,* 30 (1910), 630; Henry van Stekelenburg, "Tracing the Dutch Roman Catholic Emigrants to North America in the Nineteenth and Twentieth Centuries," in *Dutch Immigration to North America,* ed. Herman Ganzevoort and Mark Boekelman,

(Toronto: Multicultural History Society of Ontario, 1983), 66. Lucas, *Netherlanders in America*, 213, contests this point unconvincingly and also greatly overestimates Catholic emigration.

26. *Verzint eer gij begint! Een hartelijk woord aan mijne landgenooten, over de in ons Vaderland heerschende ziekte ganaamd: Landverhuizing* ('s Hertogenbosch, 1846).

27. The few Drenthe Catholics emigrated from the isolated Catholic region of Nieuw-Schoonebeek immediately adjacent to the German border.

28. The data on this section on Roman Catholic emigration is described in greater detail in Robert P. Swierenga and Yda Schreuder, "Catholic and Protestant Emigration from the Netherlands in the 19th century: A Comparative Social Structure Analysis," *Tijdschrift voor Economische en Sociale Geografie*, 74 (1983): 25–40.

29. Henry S. Lucas, "De Reize naar Noord-Amerika van Theodorus J. Van den Broek, O.P.," *Nederlandsch Archief voor Kerkgeschiedenis* 41 (1955), 96–123. An English translation by E. R. Post and D. F. Van Vliet, entitled "The Journey to North America of Theodorus J. Van den Broek, O.P., is in the Heritage Hall Archives, Calvin College, Grand Rapids, Mich. The quote is on p. 115 of the Dutch version and p. 25 of the English version.

30. Lucas, *Netherlanders in America*, 223–25.

31. Yda Schreuder, *Dutch Catholic Immigrant Settlement in Wisconsin, 1850–1905* (New York: Garland Publishing Co., 1990). See also by the same author "Emigration and the Decline of Traditional Industries in mid-nineteenth-century Europe," *Immigration History Newsletter* 17 (May 1985): 8–10, and "Dutch Catholic emigration in the mid-nineteenth century: Noord-Brabant, 1847–1871," *Journal of Historical Geography* 11 (1985): 48–69.

32. Yda Schreuder and Robert P. Swierenga, "Catholic Emigration from the Southern Provinces of the Netherlands in the Nineteenth Century," Working Paper No. 27, Netherlands Interuniversity Demographic Institute (Voorburg, 1982), 15–17, 46.

33. H.A.V.M. van Stekelenburg, "Rooms Katholieke landverhuizers naar de Vereenigde Staten," *Spiegel Historiael*, 12 (1977): 681–689; idem, "Dutch Roman Catholics in the United States," *Dutch in America*, ed. Swierenga, 64–75; Lucas, *Netherlanders in America*, 213–225, 444–459; Van Hinte, *Netherlanders in America*, 555–557; and Irene Hecht, "Kinship and Migration: The Making of an Oregon Isolate Community," *Journal of Interdisciplinary History*, 8 (Summer 1977): 45–67.

34. The role of family networks in the founding of Little Chute is documented in Yda Schreuder, "Dutch Catholic Immigrant Settlement in Wisconsin, 1850–1870," in *Dutch in America*, ed. Swierenga, 105–124. For the role of the Dominican Order at Amsterdam in this settlement, see Kelly, *Catholic Immigrant Colonization Projects*, 183–185, 270–272; and Frans H. Doppen, "Theodoor J. Van den Broek: Missionary and Emigration Leader: The History of the Dutch Catholic Settlement at Little Chute, Wisconsin," *U.S. Catholic Historian*, 3 (1983): 202–225.

35. Lucas, *Netherlanders in America,* 214. See also Van Stekelenburg, "Dutch roman Catholics in the United States," 73–74.

36. Van Stekelenburg, "Dutch Roman Catholics in the United States," 72; Van Hinte, *Netherlanders in America,* 856–857. The information on Saint Joseph's Parish was provided by Dr. Dennis W. Morrow of the Grand Rapids Diocesan Archives.

37. Van Hinte, *Netherlanders in America,* 579.

38. Lucas, *Netherlanders in America,* 459. For details see 492–506.

39. This estimate is derived from *Dutch Households in U.S. Population Censuses.*

40. The religious variable in tables 8.1, 8.2, and 8.3 is determined by classifying each township and city ward in the United States census file as to the "primary religious orientation" of its Dutch immigrant population according to one of five categories: Protestant, Catholic, Jewish, mixed, and unknown. The designation is based on several factors. The most reliable is the religion in the Netherlands of all families and individuals in the United States census that were linked with the Netherlands Emigration records. Secondary evidence was the family and given names common in the locality, the presence of ministers or priests, the nationality of marriage partners, occupation, and other social and cultural clues. The tables only include the first two categories, Protestant and Catholic.

41. Olson, *Catholic Immigrants,* 105.

42. Ibid., 113.

43. Ibid., 114–15, 117, 125.

44. Ibid., 185–293, 203, 215–217. However, as late as the 1960s survey data showed that ethnicity was yet the strongest factor in differential church attendance rates and support for parochial schools among Catholics. See Harold J. Abramson, "Ethnic Diversity Within Catholicism: Comparative Analyses of Contemporary and Historical Religion," *Journal of Social History,* 4 (Summer 1971): 354–388, esp. 360–361.

45. William Petersen, *Some Factors Influencing Postwar Emigration from the Netherlands* (The Hague: Martinus Nijhoff, 1952), 65–66.

46. Lucas, *Netherlanders in America,* 473.

47. Gunther Moltmann, "German Emigration to the United States During the First Half of the Nineteenth Century as a Social Protest Movement" in Hans L. Trefousse, ed., *Germany and America: Essays on Problems of International Relations and Immigration* (New York: Brooklyn College Press, 1980), 104–136, esp. 126–127; Frederick Luebke, "The Immigrant Condition as a Factor Contributing to the Conservatism of the Lutheran Church—Missouri Synod," *Concordia Historical Institute Quarterly,* 38 (April 1965): 19–28; and Jon Gjerde, *From Peasants to Farmers: The Migration from Balestrand, Norway, to the Upper Middle West* (Cambridge, England: Cambridge University Press, 1985), 157, 160–165.

48. J. J. Mol Develops this intriguing line of argument in "Churches and Immigrants: (A Sociological Study of the Mutual Effect of Religion and Immigrant Adjustment)," *R.E.M.P. Bulletin* (Research Group for European Migration Problems), 9 (May 1961): 11–15. Mol (pp. 54–55) also cites S. N. Eisenstadt,

The Absorption of Immigrants (Glencoe, Ill.: Free Press, 1955), 217–218, who notes that in the founding of Israel (1945–1948) the majority, who were strongly Zionist-oriented immigrants, assimilated more rapidly than the minority of secularists who emigrated for economic reasons. The Zionists readily discarded their former cultural traditions in favor of Zionist ideals and goals.

49. A. J. Barnouw, "Dutch Americans," in Frances J. Brown and Joseph Slabey Roucek, eds., *Our Racial and National Minorities: Their History, Contributions, and Present Problems* (New York: Prentice Hall, 1937), 143–144. Cf. Mol, "Churches and Immigrants," 11, for whom I am indebted for the Barnouw article.

50. Mol, "Churches and Immigrants," 17.

51. This is also the conclusion of a study of the differential process of assimilation of Dutch Calvinists and Catholics in Canada in the twentieth century. See Joe Graumans, "The Role of Ethno-Religious Organizations in the Assimilation Process of Dutch Christian Reformed and Catholic Immigrants in South Western Ontario" (M.A. thesis, University of Windsor, 1973). Graumans found that "Calvinists build their own Church and Church-related organizational structures in Canada, whereas the Catholics join existing Canadian Catholic organizations" (p. ii). Unfortunately, Graumans did not investigate intermarriage rates by nativity or ethnicity between the two populations. He did, however, find that 88 percent of the Calvinists and 77 percent of Catholics preferred a marriage partner of the same religion for their children, so we can assume that the Calvinists would marry Dutch Reformed while the Catholics, as a minority group, would be unlikely to do so (p. 71).

JONATHAN D. SARNA

9

Seating and the American Synagogue

One can learn much about the history of the American synagogue by looking at where members of the congregation sat.[1] Seating patterns mirror social patterns. In determing where to sit, people disclose a great deal about themselves, their beliefs, and their relationships to others. Outside of etiquette books, however, seating patterns are rarely written about, much less subjected to rigorous study. Although it is common knowledge that American synagogue-seating patterns have changed greatly over time—sometimes following acrimonious, even violent disputes—we still have no full-scale study of synagogue seating (or church seating, for that matter), certainly none that traces the subject over time. This is unfortunate, for behind wearisome debates over how sanctuary seats should be arranged and allocated lie fundamental disagreements over the kinds of social and religious values that a congregation should project and the proper relationship between a congregation and the larger society that surrounds it. As we shall see, changes in American synagogue-seating patterns reflect far-reaching changes in the nature of the American synagogue itself.

This study of seating patterns focuses on one ramified aspect of American synagogue seating: the allocation of seats and the resulting shift from stratified to free (unassigned) seating. Like the tumultuous debate over mixed seating, the controversy over free seating reflects the impact of American equality and democracy on synagogue life.[2] American society was conflicted with regard to its goals: some considered equality of opportunity the ideal, others looked for equality of condition. Furthermore, egalitarian ideals, however defined, clashed ever more forcefully with the reality of social inequality and the desire of the newly rich to engage in "conspicuous consumption."[3] These disputes—the one a conflict over ideals, the other a clash between ideals and realities—affected religious institutions no less than society at large. Changing synagogue-seating patterns reflected these disputes and provide an illuminating case study of how American religion and society have historically interacted.

THE EARLIEST SYNAGOGUES did not apparently face the problem
of where people should sit. Most worshippers either stood wherever
there was room or sat on an available floor rug. Some seats have turned
up in archeological excavations of synagogues, but they are believed to
have been reserved for officers, elders, and dignitaries; others could
presumably sit where they pleased. To be sure, one rabbi in the Babylonian Talmud teaches the wisdom of setting aside a "fixed place" for one's
prayers, but he does not spell out how these places ought to be arranged
relative to one another. What we do know is that in order to promote
business, the great Alexandrian synagogue, existing even in Second Temple times, arranged seating by occupation ("goldsmiths by themselves,
silversmiths by themselves," etc.), making it easier for travelers to find
their fellow craftsmen. Rabbi Judah's vivid description of this synagogue
suggests that it was unique; the more common practice was for the elders
to sit up front while the masses sat "all jumbled together."[4]

Stratified seating found recognition in Jewish legal codes, and in post-
Temple times it became the norm in Jewish communities around the
world. Sometimes, synagogue officials assigned seats and assessed their
occupants depending on what they could pay. At other times, they sold
seats for fixed prices or auctioned them off to the highest bidder. Either
way, the "best people"—those with the greatest wealth, learning, age,
or prestige—ended up occupying the best seats, those along the eastern
wall and closest to the front. Those possessing lower status, including
the young and the newly arrived in town, occupied seats that were
somewhat less choice. The worst seats in the hall were reserved for those
who could afford to sit nowhere else. Seating inside the synagogue thus
mirrored social realities outside in the community. People worshipped
alongside those of their own kind.[5]

WHEN JEWS CAME TO AMERICA, they found that very similar
patterns prevailed among the local churches:

> In the goodly house of worship,
> where in order due and fit,
> As by public vote directed,
> classed and ranked the people sit,

Mistress first and good wife after,
clerkly squire before the clown,
From the brave coat, lace embroidered,
to the gray frock shading down.[6]

In colonial New England, most town churches assigned a "proper" place to every member of the community based on complicated, controversial, and at times capricious sets of standards that predictably aroused no end of squabbling. "The bulk of criticism . . . ," Robert I. Dinkin observes, "was directed less at the system as a whole than at the specific arrangements made by the various seating committees. Most people did not seem to have disliked the idea of seating as long as they were able to obtain a coveted spot for themselves." Similar patterns of assigning seats appear to have been the rule in other colonies as well, although specific evidence is lacking.[7]

The practice of assigning seats declined only after the American Revolution, being gradually replaced by systems of pew rental and pew sale. This was a bow to republican ideology, for it did away with hereditary privileges and made seats equally available to all who could pay. The new procedure also bespeaks the development in America of a less rigidly defined social order: people no longer had a fixed position in a seating hierarchy. Yet relative stratification based on wealth continued. The house of worship, like the community at large, accepted social inequalities as inevitable, but believed that everyone should have an equal chance to move up.[8]

THE EARLIEST AMERICAN SYNAGOGUE, New York's congregation Shearith Israel, founded in the seventeenth century, mirrored this church pattern, which also happened to be the method of financing employed by the Sephardic synagogue (Bevis Marks) in London. The congregation carefully allocated a seat to each member, and each seat was assessed a certain membership tax in advance. What happened in 1750 was typical: The minutes recount an agreement "to appoint four proper persons to rate the seats for the year and appoint each person a proper place for which seat he shall now pay to the present parnas [president] the sum annexed to his seat." Members of the wealthy Gomez family enjoyed the most prestigious seats and paid the highest assessments. Others paid less and sat much further away from the holy ark. Considerable revenue was produced by this system, but it also generated a great deal of bad feeling. The congregation's early minutes are strewn with complaints from those dissatisfied with their seats, some of whom, we learn, were "seating themselves in places other than those assigned."[9]

Seating in the women's gallery proved particularly troublesome, perhaps because the gallery held fewer places and the difference between a good and bad seat there was far more pronounced. Interestingly, women did not necessarily sit in the same rank order as their husbands, and sometimes acquired status on their own independent basis. In the minutes of Mickve Israel Congregation in Savannah, Georgia, for example, one woman lay claim to a high-status pew by virtue of being the eldest married woman among the congregants. Front-row seats in the women's gallery of Shearith Israel in New York were similarly reserved for married women, despite vociferous protests from members who were single.[10]

In its constitution of 1805, Shearith Israel, bowing to the demands of American religious voluntarism, abandoned its system of assigned seats and assessments, and committed itself to a system of pew rent. Under this procedure, the trustees assigned different values to different seats and then leased them on a first-come, first-served basis. This allowed for freedom of choice, since a wealthy person could opt to lease a poor seat and a poor person could save up to lease an expensive one. In practice, however, social stratification within the synagogue continued, albeit in less specific and more muted fashion. Where before seats reflected each individual's precise social ranking, now they only offered an approximate picture of the community's economic divisions.[11]

We possess a detailed description from Congregation Mikveh Israel in Philadelphia of how this system of leased pews actually worked. Seats in the synagogue's women's gallery were divided into three categories (termed, quite appropriately, "classes,") from the front seats ("inner range") to the back. In 1851, a three-year lease to a "first class" seat went for sixty dollars with an additional annual assessment of eight dollars, while second- and third-class seats could be leased for thirty dollars and twenty dollars with annual assessments of four dollars and three dollars. Leftover seats could be rented on an annual basis for ten, six, or four dollars. Men's seats were divided into five categories, with a three-year lease costing one-hundred, sixty, forty, thirty, or twenty-five dollars, depending on the seat's "class," and additional annual assessments of fourteen, nine, seven, four, or three dollars. Leftover men's seats could be rented at twenty, twelve, nine, six, or five dollars. Seats in the back ("the sixth and seventh ranges") were neither leased nor rented "but reserved for strangers or persons unable to take seats." As non-seatholders, those in the back were separated from everybody else and marked as outsiders.[12]

The difference here between the price of men's and women's seats is particularly fascinating. Not only were men more socially stratified than women (five classes as opposed to three), but men of every class level were superior (in terms of what they paid) to women of their class, and even men with seats in the lowly fifth class paid more overall than women of the third class. This may reflect real differences between what men and women earned, but is more likely an indication of women's inferior synagogue status. Since women had to sit upstairs and were denied synagogue honors, they were charged less than the men were.

Over time, some synagogues experimented with alternative means of allocating seats. The system pioneered by New York's Temple Emanu-El in 1847 whereby seats were sold in perpetuity—a practice well-known in Europe—proved particularly popular, for it raised a large fund of capital "up front" to pay off building debts. In 1854, when Emanu-El moved into its 12th Street Temple, the sale of seats at auction yielded $31,000. A similar sale fourteen years later, when the temple moved up to Fifth Avenue and 43rd Street, yielded "100,000 over and above the cost of the building and the lots." While those with lesser means could still rent seats at Emanu-El and remain members, only pew owners could serve as officers. In some other synagogues that sold pews, renters could not be members at all but were classified as nonvoting seatholders.[13]

Regardless of whether synagogues sold seats or rented them, assigned seats or not, assessed members once or continually solicited them throughout the year, they all depended on seat revenues for a large percentage of their upkeep. Survival dictated that the best seats be given to those who supported the synagogue most liberally. What Edna Ferber found in Appleton, Wisconsin, at the beginning of the twentieth century was thus true of most synagogues:

> Seating was pretty well regulated by the wealth and prominence of the congregation. In the rows nearest the pulpit sat the rich old members, their sons and daughters and grandchildren. Then came the next richest and most substantial. Then the middling well-to-do, then the poorest. The last rows were reserved for strangers and . . . "Russians."[14]

Some synagogues did set aside a few seats for prominent members (government officials, scholars, writers, etc.) who lacked means but were felt to merit front-rank status on account of their social prestige. Others, however, found this to be undemocratic and divisive. One synagogue actually banned the practice in its constitution, declaring that every seat would henceforward be offered for sale, "in order to avoid unnecessary trouble to the Board of Directors and to give more satisfaction to *all* the members of the Congregation." Even here, those too poor to pay for a seat were not completely excluded from synagogue life. As secondary or nonmembers, however, they were expected to know their place. If they sought to occupy vacant pews owned by more affluent congregants, they ran the risk of being forcibly ejected.[15]

SYNAGOGUES AND CHURCHES were hardly to blame for the existence of inequalities in America. Nor were they to blame for the fact that, far too frequently, America's wealthy only made donations of urgently needed funds in return for conspicuous rewards in social status. Still, the intrusion of social and class distinctions into the hallowed domains of sacred institutions troubled many Americans, particularly those who interpreted the country's democratic ideals in egalitarian terms. "As Americans perceive it," James Oliver Robertson has pointed out, "the tendency of American history is toward classlessness. The Revolution was fought to destroy privilege. American reform, since the Jacksonian era, has been motivated by the desire to perfect equality and democracy. . . . In American myth, America *is* a classless society. If it can be shown not to be, then something is wrong and needs to be put right."[16]

Stratified seating so obviously contradicted the goals of egalitarian democracy that opposition to it should not prove surprising. Already in the immediate post-Revolutionary era, when "people on a number of fronts began to speak, write and organize against the authority of mediating elites, of social distinction and of any human tie that did not spring from volitional allegiance," free seating on a first-come, first-served basis became the general rule in many of the new and frontier churches, notably among the Methodists (except in New England) and the Disciples of Christ.[17] Growing experience with "classlessness" both in the public schools, where rich and poor sat side by side, and on the railroads where, in the astonished words of one immigrant Jewish observer, "everyone sits together in one car—for there is only one car of one class for all—rich and poor, master and slave together in one body," made stratified seating in houses of worship seem even more incongruous. Yet at the same time, the realities of economic inequality in America were becoming increasingly profound. Urban geography, clubs, resorts, and the entertainment world all reflected a heightened awareness and acceptance of social and class divisions. In spite of noble ideals and symbolic bows to classlessness, rich and poor in America were actually growing ever further apart.[18]

This paradox—the disjunction between ideal and reality—posed an obvious dilemma for churches and synagogues. Should they maintain the class and status distinctions that many congregants considered proper, or should they champion egalitarian ideals, even at the risk of imperiling their own financial security? The move from assigned seats to sale of seats salved some consciences by opening up pews to anyone with the means to pay for them, but it did nothing about the underlying problems of social inequality itself. Periodically, aggrieved members spoke up on this issue and called for reforms on the frontier church model.[19] However, large-scale changes did not come about until the rise of the Social Gospel movement in the late nineteenth century. Then, concern about the "unchurched" poor, fear of the urban masses, renewed dedication to social justice, and a resulting surge of religious activism lent new weight to the free-pews movement. Free seating won adoption both in many liberal Protestant churches and in many Catholic churches.[20] For the first time, it also won adoption in an American synagogue.

CALLS FOR FREE SEATING in the synagogue first rang out early in the Social Gospel era in connection with appeals for more democracy in Jewish life and more aid to the poor and unaffiliated. In 1882, the year that William S. Rainsford originated his free "institutional church" at New York's St. George's Episcopal Church, Myer Stern, secretary of Temple Emanu-El in New York, advocated the creation of a totally free synagogue—all seats unassigned and available without charge—for "those of our faith who are eager to worship with us, but whose circumstances through misfortune and various causes are such as to prevent their hiring pews or seats either in our or any other temple or synagogue."[21] Ray Frank, the remarkable woman preacher whose sermons pricked the consciences of Jews throughout the West, later assailed the whole system of making "stock" of synagogue seats. "If I were a rabbi," she declared in 1890, "I would not sell religion in the form of pews and benches to the highest bidder." She then documented some of the system's worst abuses.[22] Rabbi Isaac Moses of Chicago had come to the same conclusion, and in 1896 attempted to found a congregation based upon this new plan. Attacking the "undemocratic" nature of the synagogue—which, he felt, kept many Jews unaffiliated, and limited the rabbi's independence—he offered full membership to all, "regardless of their annual contributions," with dues payments only "to be such as each individual member feels that he or she is justified in making."[23] Nothing came of this effort, but in 1898 Rabbi William Rosenau of Baltimore, less radical than Moses but equally concerned about the large number of those too poor to afford seats, proposed a different solution: "Every congregation ought to set aside a certain number of pews, not in the rear of the temple, or in the galleries, but in all parts of the auditorium, so that no lines of distinction be drawn between the rich and the poor at least in the house of God."[24]

Since changes in the internal arrangement of a synagogue are easier to propose than to effect, particularly when they have economic implications, assigned seating of one sort or another remained the rule. At Temple Beth El in Detroit, Michigan, however, an unanticipated problem developed. Although a new temple had been erected on Woodward Street in a growing section of town, nobody envisaged that membership would grow as rapidly as it did, increasing at a rate of more than 25 percent a year. The task of assigning seats equitably to all members and their families under these conditions proved impossible. There were enough seats to accommodate those who actually came and worshipped on any given Sabbath, but not enough to accommodate those who had rights to particular seats and wanted them to remain unoccupied even when they themselves were not present. As a result, in September 1903, the congregation voted that seats in the new building would remain temporarily unassigned, available to all on a first-come, first-served basis, while the board of trustees decided what to do. Pragmatic rather than ideological considerations motivated this decision, and nobody expected it to have a lasting effect. But in fact, a historic change had taken place.[25]

Formerly, Beth El had offered members the choice of buying seats, renting them, or having a seat assigned to them from the pool that remained. Those who chose either of the first two options paid both their annual assessment of dues, levied on every member by the board of trustees on a sliding scale based on ability to pay, and an additional sum representing their purchase or rental fee. Everyone else received seats commensurate with their dues assessment. This was a cumbersome and somewhat inequitable system that many members opposed. But the board of trustees finally recommended that it be reinstated in the new synagogue; otherwise, the board feared, the congregation's rapidly rising budget would not be met. The recommendation was greeted with a barrage of criticism and spawned a vigorous congregational debate. Some members wanted all seats sold. Some wanted all seats rented.

Some wanted an end to the system of assessments. All agreed to search for a compromise that would seat as many people as possible, as equitably as possible, without threatening the congregation's income. Meeting followed meeting while seats in the new temple remained open and unassigned. Finally, after every other proposal failed to win approval, the new status quo was made permanent. On 27 April 1904, "the unassigned pew system was unanimously concurred in by those present at a large and enthusiastic meeting of the congregation." Higher assessments ensured that the lost revenue from seat income would be more than made up.[26]

ALTHOUGH UNASSIGNED SEATING came to Beth El by accident ("sheer force of circumstances"), and the plan won permanent adoption largely by default, ideological considerations played a significant part both in the debate over the issue and in the justifications that followed it. What began as a practical measure ended up serving a symbolic purpose—a sequence that paralleled what had earlier happened in the movement from separate to mixed seating. In this case, proponents used free seating as evidence of Judaism's concern for "justice, equality and fraternity."[27]

Rabbi Leo Franklin of Beth El, casting himself as the Jewish apostle of free seating, took the lead in trumpeting the system's virtues and defending them against all critics. To him, the system came to be identified as something "essentially Jewish," as "nearly ideal as human institutions can be." "In God's house all must be equal," he maintained, echoing Social Gospel rhetoric: "There must be no aristocracy and no snobocracy." Franklin lambasted as "fundamentally wrong, unjust and unJewish" the contention that those who contributed more to a synagogue deserved disproportionate rewards. He insisted that the finances of the congregation could remain strong without special pews for the rich so long as a graduated dues-assessment system was in effect. He even assured frightened synagogue regulars that "practical experience" demonstrated that most people could "occupy the same seats the year round, even under the unassigned system." As for free seating's benefits, he pointed out that besides equality of opportunity the system encouraged people to come to temple on time and to bring their families. It ended the "abomination of having rented seats unoccupied while perhaps dozens of poor men and women are compelled to stand in the aisles or lobbies." And it made it easier to accommodate guests who no longer had to sit in specially set aside areas, apart from regular members.[28]

Franklin was convinced that free seating's virtues would win it wide acceptance within the American Jewish community, bringing glory to all Jews and introducing a greater degree of "practical idealism" into the synagogue. Even in his own congregation, however, he met with repeated challenges. Various resignations attended the first acceptance of the free-seating plan, including that of Seligman Schloss, one of Beth El's most distinguished members and an ex-president (who later withdrew his resignation). According to one source, "a large percentage" of the other elderly members, including some of the congregation's leading benefactors, were no less adamant in seeking to prevent the plan from ever taking effect.[29] They insisted that status considerations played no part in their opposition, and that they simply wanted some guarantee that they would find a seat somewhere in the sanctuary, even if they came late. They also complained about being forced to scurry around the whole synagogue searching out members of their family who would no longer be found in one place. A proposal to set aside several rows for the elderly did not molify the malcontents. Indeed, "nothing outside of the complete waiver of the principle involved would satisfy them." The fact that opponents used financial leverage to put pressure on the congregation added to the belief that their demands were motivated by more than just disinterested concern for those whom free seating inconvenienced.[30]

Rhetoric aside, it seems apparent that the Beth El dispute actually saw two conflicting and widely accepted American principles colliding head on: belief in equality and recognition of natural inequalities.[31] Rabbi Franklin's supporters recognized inequalities but sought to promote visible equality. They thus both encouraged "religious fellowship," believing that "every man . . . deserves an equal place with every other," and continued to recognize inequalities for purposes of dues assessment.[32] By contrast, opponents of free seating sought one *or* the other. Either all should contribute equally and enjoy equal access to all seats, or all should contribute unequally and be rewarded in the same fashion. While to Rabbi Franklin unassigned seating represented a blow against class divisions and support for the highest values that America and Judaism had to offer, to his opponents the same system exuded injustice and violated the basic principles of equity. At a deep level, the dispute had as much to do with symbols as with substance.

In the end, the two sides compromised. In the congregation, as in the country at large, egalitarian ideas and natural inequalities both won recognition. Free seating thus remained the policy of the congregation alongside the system of dues assessments. At the same time, in return for their agreement to pay their substantial arrears and remain at Beth El, dissident members won the status concessions that they had sought. The three malcontented ex-presidents, for their "long and appreciated services and contributions to the cause of the Temple," each had three seats assigned to them for as long as they lived. Seligman Schloss promptly selected a choice location: "in the easterly row of benches, in the seventh bench from the pulpit, on the western end." The other dissidents won the right to have up to four seats always reserved for them "in the center section of the auditorium" for "up to fifteen minutes after the time set for the commencement of services."[33]

EVEN BEFORE THE DISPUTE at Beth El was settled, leading Reform rabbis from around the country had spoken out in favor of free seating as an expression of social justice. Rabbi Emil Hirsch of Chicago, the leading exponent of social justice within the Reform Movement, called it "the ideal plan" for synagogues to adopt. Rabbi Henry Berkowitz of Philadelphia recommended free seating to his own congregation. Others, according to Leo Franklin, wrote to him privately expressing admiration for what he had done. Many promised to watch the experiment carefully.[34]

The rabbi who expressed the greatest immediate interest in free seating was young Stephen Wise, then still at Temple Beth Israel in Portland, Oregon. Wise had taken over the Portland ministry in 1900, and had from the start firmly allied himself with the aims of the Social Gospel movement. He achieved spectacular success, tripled his congregation's membership, and brought the congregation into financial health for the first time, building a surplus of $4,000. Given this financial cushion, he issued, in 1904, his first call for a "free synagogue" in which members could sit where they choose and pay what they choose. As opposed to Beth El, where free seating had come first and justifications later, Wise began with his principles: each man paying what he can afford, all equal in the eyes of the Lord. He also displayed a greater degree of consistency than Rabbi Franklin had, for he attacked both stratified pews and stratified dues at the same time.[35]

Wise's free synagogue experiment, begun in 1905, achieved success. The experiment succeeded again when Wise moved back to New York and opened his Free Synagogue (now the Stephen Wise Free Synagogue) in 1907. There, free seating on a first-come, first-served basis represented a "token and symbol" of other freedoms: freedom from fixed dues, freedom of the pulpit, and freedom of opportunity for all—women included—to become Temple members and officeholders. Drawing (without credit) from the ideas of previous Jewish and Christian critics of stratified seating, Wise established the most compelling case yet for the relationship between free seating, Jewish ideals, and American ideals. He made free seating part of his solution to the twin problems of the fast-waning influence of the synagogue, and the fast-growing number of urban Jews who belonged to no synagogue at all. The values he espoused through synagogue seating were the values he proclaimed to society at large: "freedom, hospitality, inclusiveness, brotherhood, [and] the leveling of the anti-religious bars of caste."[36]

For all of its idealistic appeal, however, the free-synagogue idea failed to take hold nationwide; in the absence of a particularly charismatic rabbi it proved impractical. In Philadelphia, for example, the venerable Sephardic congregation Mikve Israel, after moving into a new synagogue building in 1909, decided to keep its old edifice in the poorer section of town "open all the year around absolutely free to worshippers." But it soon found the cost of this to be prohibitive. When free-will offerings did not reach expectations, the project had to be abandoned. Mickve Israel Congregation in Savannah faced the same problem in 1913: Although it tried to become a free synagogue, economic considerations forced it to abandon the experiment after only one year.[37]

By contrast, free seating combined with some system of required dues posed far less of an economic threat, served as a visible symbol of social-justice ideals, and, in time, did succeed. To take just a few examples, Temple Israel in Memphis instituted free seating in 1918, Rodef Shalom Congregation in Pittsburgh in 1920, Temple Israel in Boston in 1922, and Congregation Beth Israel of Houston in 1927. By 1940, nearly two hundred synagogues had adopted some form of free seating, and many more assigned seats only for the high holidays. The free-seating movement continued to spread, especially during the war years when it was associated with the effort to strengthen democracy at home. By the 1960s, even many old-line synagogues had abandoned assigned seating, replacing it with a new "fair share" system that, by assigning dues on the basis of income rather than seat location, ensured that "democratization" would not result in any loss of revenue from the wealthy. Although statistics are lacking, impressionistic evidence suggests that free seating, while not ubiquitous, is now predominant across the spectrum of American Jewish life, in Reform, Reconstructionist, Conservative, and Orthodox synagogues alike.[38]

IF FREE SEATING produced more visible equality in the American synagogue, it failed to produce perfect equality. Wealthy congregants were still more likely than their poorer counterparts to be recognized from the pulpit or to serve as synagogue officers, and they soon found alternative means to engage in conspicuous consumption: by leaving their names on synagogue plaques, for instance, or by staging lavish congregational parties to celebrate significant family milestones. Moreover, even with free seating rich and poor did not necessarily sit side by side. Instead, as Samuel Heilman found, synagogue goers naturally tended to sit by their friends, usually people similar in occupation, education, and religious outlook to themselves. As a result, congregational seating patterns often continued to mark status, power, and authority within the synagogue community, albeit far more subtly. "Seating patterns," Heilman concluded, "are not simply physical arrangements but reflect social belongingness."[39]

The rise of free seating is nevertheless a revealing and significant development in American synagogue history. First of all, it sheds light on how, under American influence, the synagogue experienced change. Seating by social rank, and later any pattern of assigned seating that emphasized differences based on wealth, became in the eyes of many American Jews an affront to America's democratic ethos. Although stratified seating had characterized synagogues for centuries, American cultural values in this case exerted a much stronger pull. The reason, I think, is that free seating, unlike mixed seating of men and women, was not actually incompatible with Jewish tradition. Furthermore, free seating permitted the synagogue to display a measure of patriotic piety, and had the added advantage of using seats more efficiently. Most important of all, perhaps, experience suggested that the change could be implemented without serious financial loss. As a result, it was hard to oppose. Rabbis like Leo Franklin and Stephen Wise, by investing free seating with deeper Jewish significance, made the process of adjustment even easier. By implementing free seating, congregants could now view themselves not only as better Americans but as better Jews as well.

Second, free seating is significant as an illustration of a noteworthy and little-studied type of Jewish religious innovation that was debated largely on the local congregational level, rather than becoming a major point of contention between the different American Jewish religious movements. Although Reform Jews, who traditionally emphasized social justice, pioneered free seating, I have found no evidence that Orthodox and Conservative Jews were ideologically opposed to it. Moreover, within the Reform Movement itself some leading temples (like Temple Emanu-El of San Francisco and Isaac M. Wise Temple of Cincinnati) maintained traditional patterns of stratified seating long into the twentieth century. Free seating thus spread on a congregation-by-congregation basis, and was decided in each case by balancing egalitarian ideals against pragmatic realities: Would loss of seat income be balanced by increasing dues? Would existing seatholders insist on their property rights? Would wealthy members transfer their membership elsewhere? The answers to such questions had far more to do with whether free seating would be adopted than denominational affiliation did—a reminder that the diversity of American synagogue life cannot be explained on the basis of intra-Jewish politics alone.[40]

Third, free seating demonstrates the impact on American Jewish life of ideas generally associated with the Protestant Social Gospel. Nathan Glazer wrote in *American Judaism* about "the failure of a Jewish 'social gospel' to develop among Reform Jews," and his words have been widely echoed. But in fact, Social Gospel concerns—translated into Jewish terms and stripped of their Christological rhetoric—received considerable attention in American Jewish circles, and influenced not only the Reform movement and synagogue life, but also the whole relationship between American Jews and East European Jewish immigrants. The subject as a whole requires further study and cannot be pursued here. What we do learn from free seating, however, is that even specific Social Gospel causes had their American Jewish analogues.[41]

Finally, free seating is significant for what it teaches us about the ongoing tension between realism and idealism in American Jewish life. Free seating, as its supporters plainly admitted, represented a kind of utopia, an exalted vision of classless democracy where people from different walks of life dwelt harmoniously side by side. Realistically speaking, however, the synagogue could not survive under such conditions; unless wealthier members contributed more than poorer ones, no synagogue could pay its bills. This was the synagogue's version of what Murray Friedman calls the "utopian dilemma," the clash between romantic idealism and pragmatic self-interest. The result, as we have seen, was a compromise.[42]

NOTES

1. Samuel C. Heilman, *Synagogue Life* (Chicago: University of Chicago Press, 1976), 36.

2. Jonathan D. Sarna, "The Debate Over Mixed Seating in the American Synagogue," in Jack Wertheimer, ed., *The American Synagogue: A Sanctuary Transformed* (New York: Cambridge University Press, 1987), 363–394.

3. The expression, of course, was popularized by Thorstein Veblen in *The Theory of the Leisure Class* (1912; rpt. New York: Mentor, 1953), 60–80. For an

illuminating historical analysis of the idea of equality, see R. R. Palmer, "Equality," in *Dictionary of the History of Ideas* (New York: Scribner, 1973), 2:138–148.

4. Samuel Kraus, *Korot Bet HaTefilah BeYisrael* (New York: Ogen, 1955), 251; Babylonian Talmud, Tractate Berakhot, 6b; Tosefta Sukkah 4:6.

5. *Tur;* and see Isserles gloss on *Shulkhan Arukh* OH 150:5; Salo W. Baron, *The Jewish Community: Its History and Structure to the American Revolution* (Philadelphia: Jewish Publication Society, 1945), 2, 130–131; Kraus, *Korot,* 252–256; *Encyclopaedia Judaica* (Jerusalem: Keter Publishing, 1972) 15:593.

6. Quoted in Robert J. Dinkin, "Seating the Meeting House in Early Massachusetts," *New England Quarterly* 43 (1970): 450.

7. Ibid., 459.

8. On stratified seating, see also Ola Elizabeth Winslow, *Meetinghouse Hill, 1630–1783* (New York: W. W. Norton, 1972), 142–149; Peter Benes and Philip D. Zimmerman, *New England Meeting House and Church, 1630–1850* (Boston: Boston University Press, 1979), 55–56; David H. Fischer, *Growing Old in America* (New York: Oxford University Press, 1977), 38–40; and for nineteenth-century Catholicism, Jay P. Dolan, *The Immigrant Church* (Baltimore: Johns Hopkins University Press, 1975), 49–52.

9. *Publications of the American Jewish Historical Society* 21 (1913), 62; see also 81–84, 154–155; 27 (1920): 28; David and Tamar de Sola Pool, *An Old Faith in the New World* (New York: Columbia University Press, 1955), 199, 270–273; and Rachel Wischnitzer, *Synagogue Architecture in the United States* (Philadelphia: Jewish Publication Society, 1955), 12–13.

10. Saul J. Rubin, *Third to None: The Saga of Savannah Jewry 1733–1983* (Savannah, Ga.: Congregation Micke Israel, 1983), 52; Pool, *An Old Faith,* 272.

11. Hyman B. Grinstein, *The Rise of the Jewish Community of New York, 1654–1860* (Philadelphia: Jewish Publication Society, 1945), 479–83; Pool, *An Old Faith,* 299.

12. *At a special meeting of the Board of Managers of K.K.M.I., held on Sunday June 8th, 1851 . . . the following Resolutions were adopted and ordered to be printed* [Broadside] (Philadelphia, 1851), copy in Klau Library, Hebrew Union College, Cincinnati, Ohio. On the traditional position of women in the synagogue, see Carol H. Krinsky, *Synagogues of Europe* (New York: MIT Press, 1985), 28–31.

13. Grinstein, *The Rise of the Jewish Community of New York,* 482–483; *New Era* 4 (1874): 131.

14. Edna Ferber, *A Peculiar Treasure* (New York: Literary Guild, 1939), 74.

15. *Montefiore Congregation Constitution* (Las Vegas, N. Mex.: 1898), 11, copy in American Jewish Archives, Cincinnati, Ohio. For an example of a seating plan where social prestige played a role, see *Canadian Jewish Archives* 1 (August 1955), 16. On the poor, see Pool, *An Old Faith,* 273. Compare Krinsky's description of the London Great Synagogue's "large pew where the poor were kept to prevent their mingling with those who could pay for seats and for building maintenance," *Synagogues of Europe,* 417.

16. James O. Robertson, *American Myth, American Reality* (New York: Hill and Wang, 1980), 259.

17. Nathan O. Hatch, "The Christian Movement and the Demand for a Theology of the People," *Journal of American History* 67 (December 1980): 561; see also *Encyclopedia of World Methodism*, (Nashville: United Methodist Publishing House, 1974) s.v. "pew rental"; "Pews," *American Quarterly Church Review* 13 (July 1860): 284–300; and Timothy L. Smith, *Revivalism and Social Reform* (New York: Harper, 1957), 23–24, 164.

18. Leon Horowitz, "Tuv Artsot Habrit," *Rumania Ve'Amerika* (Berlin: 1874), 6; this work has been translated by Randi Musnitsky, "America's Goodness: An Edited Translation of Leon Horowitz's *Tuv Artsot Habrit* (Ordination thesis, Hebrew Union College-Jewish Institute of Religion, 1983); for a cultural evaluation of social cleavage during this era, see Neil Harris, ed., *The Land of Contrasts* (New York: George Braziller, 1970), esp. pp. 16–19.

19. Grinstein, *The Rise of the Jewish Community of New York,* 538, n11. See also Solomon Jackson, "Address to Joseph Dreyfous. . . . 1829," reprinted in Solomon Solis-Cohen, "A Unique Jewish Document of a Century Ago," *Jewish Exponent,* 25 (October 1929): 8.

20. Charles Howard Hopkins, *The Rise of the Social Gospel in American Protestantism, 1865–1915* (New Haven: Yale University Press, 1961); Robert D. Cross, ed., *The Church and the City* (Indianapolis: Bobbs-Merrill, 1967); and Ronald C. White and C. Howard Hopkins, *The Social Gospel: Religion and Reform in Changing America* (Philadelphia: Temple University Press, 1976), which provides valuable background and additional bibliography. For a typical free-seating debate, see *Congregationalist* 78 (1893): 245, 255–256, 848–849. On the Social Gospel and the Jews, see Egal Feldman, "The Social Gospel and the Jews," *American Jewish Historical Quarterly* 58 (March 1969): 308–322; Leonard J. Mervis, "The Social Justice and the American Reform Movement," *American Jewish Archives* 7 (June 1955): 171–230; Bernard Martin, "The Social Philosophy of Emil G. Hirsch," *American Jewish Archives* 6 (June 1954): 151–166; and John F. Sutherland, "Rabbi Joseph Krauskopf of Philadelphia: The Urban Reformer Returns to the Land," *American Jewish History* 67 (June 1978): 342–362.

21. Hopkins, *Rise of the Social Gospel,* 154–156; William S. Rainsford, *Let Us Anchor Our Churches and Make Them Free* (New York, 1890); and Myer Stern, *The Rise and Progress of Reform Judaism* (New York, 1895), 77–78.

22. Jacob R. Marcus, ed., *The American Jewish Woman: A Documentary History* (New York: Ktav, 1981), 383; on Frank, see Simon Litman, *Ray Frank Litman: A Memoir* (New York: American Jewish Historical Society, 1957); and Reva Clar and William M. Kramer, "The Girl Rabbi of the Golden West," *Western States Jewish History* 18 (1986): 99–111, 223–236, 336–351.

23. *Reform Advocate,* 20 June 1896, pp. 359–360; *American Hebrew,* 28 August 1896, p. 414.

24. William Rosenau, "The Attitude of the Congregation to the Non Member," *Central Conference of American Rabbis Yearbook* 8 (1898): 65.

25. *A History of Congregation Beth El, Detroit, Michigan, Volume 2, 1900–1910* (Detroit: Winn & Hammond, 1910), 35–40, 80; Minutes, 5 April 1904, Temple Beth El Minute Book, Box X-6, American Jewish Archives, Cincinnati, Ohio. For other brief accounts, see Irving I. Katz, *The Beth El Story* (Detroit: Wayne University Press, 1955), 99–101; Robert Rockaway, "The Progress of Reform Judaism in Late 19th and Early 20th Century Detroit," *Michigan Jewish History* (January 1974), 17; and idem, *The Jews of Detroit* (Detroit: Wayne State University Press, 1986), 124.

26. *Constitution and By-Laws of Congregation Beth El* (Detroit: 1892), 7, 11–12; Minutes, 8 September 1903–27 April 1904, Beth El Minute Book; *History of Beth El* 2: 38.

27. Leo Franklin, "A New Congregational Policy," Beth El Scrapbook, Box X-201, American Jewish Archives. See also *American Israelite* 17 (November 1904): 4.

28. Franklin, "A New Congregational Policy"; Minutes, 11 May 1904, Beth El Minute Book.

29. Minutes 11 May 1904, 8 November 1904, Beth El Minute Book; newspaper clipping, 15 February 1905, Beth El Scrapbook.

30. Ibid, and Minutes, 18 September 1905, Beth El Minute Book.

31. Gordon S. Wood, *The Creation of the American Republic* (New York: W. W. Norton, 1969), 70–75, traces the origin of this tension. See also Martin Diamond, "The American Idea of Equality: The View From the Founding," *Review of Politics* 38 (July 1976): 313–331; and David M. Potter, *People of Plenty* (Chicago: University of Chicago Press, 1954), 91–110.

32. Franklin, "A New Congregational Policy."

33. Minutes, 7 December 1905, Beth El Minute Book.

34. Ibid., 31 October 1904; and Franklin, "A New Congregational Policy," *History of Beth El* 2:39.

35. Franklin, "A New Congregational Policy"; Melvin Urofsky, *A Voice That Spoke for Justice: The Life and Times of Stephen S. Wise* (Albany: State University of Albany Press, 1982), 34–38; Julius J. Nodel, *The Ties Between* (Portland: Temple Beth Israel, 1959), 89–98; and White and Hopkins, *The Social Gospel,* 232. Leo Franklin subsequently proposed abolishing stratified dues, but his board ignored him; see Minutes, 18 September 1905, Beth El Minute Book.

36. Stephen S. Wise, "What Is A Free Synagogue?" in *Free Synagogue Pulpit* (New York: Bloch, 1908) 1:10–15.

37. Cyrus Adler to Solomon Schechter, 28 December 1910, Solomon Schechter Papers, Jewish Theological Seminary of America, New York; Rubin, *Third To None,* 253. Interestingly, Mordecai Kaplan, who also sought to "break down the social barriers which prevent Jews of different economic status from sharing their spiritual interests," did not advocate a free synagogue, but rather one maintained jointly by the Jewish community and the beneficiaries; see *Judaism As A Civilization* (1934, rpt. New York: Schocken, 1967) 427.

38. Louis Witt, "The Basis of Membership in the American Synagogue," *Central Conference of American Rabbis Yearbook,* 21 (1911), 195–212; Ernest Lee,

Temple Israel: Our First Century 1854–1954 (Memphis, Tenn: 1954), 38; Marcus L. Aaron, *One Hundred Twenty Years: Rodef Shalom Congregation* [pamphlet] (Pittsburgh, Pa.: Rodef Shalom, 1976), 8; Arthur Mann, ed., *Growth and Achievement: Temple Israel 1854–1954* (Cambridge: Riverside Press, 1954), 36; Anne Nathan Cohen, *The Centenary History: Congregation Beth Israel of Houston Texas, 1854–1954* (Houston, Tex.: The Congregation, 1954), 50; Leo M. Franklin, *An Outline History of Congregation Beth El* (Detroit: Beth El, 1940), 27; Frank J. Adler, *Roots in a Moving Stream* (Kansas City: Congregation B'nai Jehudah, 1972), 192; Marjorie Hornbein, *Temple Emanuel of Denver: A Centennial History* (Denver: Congregation Emanuel, 1974), 128–129; and Ethel and David Rosenberg, *To 120 Years!* (Indianapolis: Indianapolis Hebrew Congregation, 1979), 99. See also Leon Jick, "The Reform Synagogue," in Wertheimer, *The American Synagogue,* 99. The venerable Temple Emanu-El of San Francisco maintained "sixteen different categories of seats . . . which precisely reflected the socioeconomic stratification of the membership" into the late 1950s; democratization and the "fair share" plan were only fully implemented in the 1960s. See Fred Rosenbaum, *Architects of Reform* (Berkeley, Cal.: Judah L. Magnes Museum, 1980), 91–92, 167.

39. Heilman, *Synagogue Life,* 36–39.

40. See also my introduction to Alexandra S. Korros and Jonathan D. Sarna, *American Synagogue History: A Bibliography and State-of-the-Field Survey* (New York: Markus Wiener, 1988). Discussions regarding whether to introduce a "democratized" synagogue polity and a "progressive" income-based dues structure seem to me to fall into the same structural category of reforms; the subject requires further investigation.

41. Nathan Glazer, *American Judaism,* 2d ed. (Chicago: University of Chicago Press, 1972), 138; cf. White and Hopkins, *The Social Gospel,* xii, 230, and items cited in note 20.

42. Murray Friedman, *The Utopian Dilemma* (Bryn Mawr, Pa.: Seth Press, 1985), 89–92.

10

Religious Divisions and

Political Roles:

Midwestern Episcopalians,

1860–1920

A central characteristic of the new religious history is its attention to the powerful connections between religion and other aspects of American life. Among the most important ideas is that religion was the primary basis for politics during the nineteenth and early twentieth centuries. Critics have questioned how any religious outlook in this era could have supported a general political perspective. They have also argued, using behavioral evidence, that some denominations divided rather evenly in party affiliation and that religious beliefs were often not politically salient. This essay explains how and why religious views were connected with politics by focusing on the Episcopal church in the Midwest. It shows that political divisions in this church actually reflect important differences over religious beliefs and that the Episcopal church played a critical role in political competition and especially political leadership in this era.

BEGINNING IN THE 1950S, religious history was reestablished as a legitimate subfield of American history by valuable studies on theologians and broad, national trends. However, these works generally treated religion as an isolated subject, as if the religious perspectives of most persons were not connected to their social, economic, and political lives.[1] The major advances in connecting denominational and national perspectives and in linking religious and secular concerns came primarily from scholars analyzing the social bases of politics. Initially suggested by Lee Benson and Samuel P. Hays, this ethnocultural analysis of politics reached mature expression in studies of the Midwest during the late 19th century by Paul Kleppner and Richard Jensen.[2] These authors identified three ways in which religion influenced politics. First, they analyzed two politically salient religious belief systems—an evangelical, pietist perspective and ritualist approach that emphasized liturgy and traditional creeds. Second, they explained how religious communities functioned as positive reference groups for their members, reinforcing a particular political perspective. They also showed how certain groups (e.g., Catholics) served as strong negative referents for others (e.g., Scotch-Irish Presbyterians).[3] Finally, they noted that denominations or congregations occasionally took specific political stands.

Many political historians disagreed with this interpretation, convinced that debates on national economic questions were more important than disputes over moral issues like the sale and use of liquor. Some argued that the views of leaders deserved more attention than the actions of voters, but even some analysts of voting behavior disagreed with the emphasis on religion. Part of the debate has been methodological, with ethnocultural historians focusing on rural townships or urban wards with homogeneous populations, while their critics have championed the virtues of ecological regression analysis of county data. Both approaches have advantages and disadvantages. In fact, it is much more accurate to use data on individuals rather than on any geographical area, but such information is difficult to obtain and time consuming to analyze, even for a relatively small sample.[4]

Although these methodological arguments were also substantive, the major objections to the ethnocultural interpretation reflect a skepticism that religion could ever have been so important. These critics clearly overreacted, for ethnocultural historians did not claim that religion (and culture) were the only factors—just the most important, to most people, at most times. Thus, one issue involves measuring the relative and possibly varying importance of religion. A second, substantive concern is further explaining how religion could have been such a dominant influence.

Some of the explanation may be that during the nineteenth century primary, personal identification was shaped by fewer influences than is the case today. Because of rural residence, limited access to information and other people, constraints on travel, and an emphasis on tradition, people were socialized by fewer associations, groups, and individuals. Because family, church, culture, and political party overlapped as communities and values, people's basic loyalties to them ran deeper.

While an analysis of personal socialization helps to explain how religion functioned socially and as a value system, using the "church-sect typology" clarifies the similarities between religious groups and the reasons why religious and political beliefs were connected. The doctrine of redemption is the analytical starting point in this typology, for it defines the relationship between God and man, the meaning of revelation, and the nature of the church. A religious group's position on these issues shaped its perspective on human nature, on the organization of society, and on the relationship between church and state.[5] Far from being only marginally connected to politics, religious beliefs created for their adherents a general approach to politics and required them to adopt strong positions on particular political issues.

Studies have shown that the membership of many denominations heavily favored one major party or the other.[6] But if the political salience of religion is clear for denominations having roughly 90 percent affiliation with one party (such as the Catholic, Congregational, Quaker, or Swedish Lutheran churches), or even 75 percent (like the Methodists), how should one understand the connection of religion and politics in denominations like Presbyterians, Baptist, and Episcopalians, whose party preferences were more evenly distributed? Perhaps these denominations simply had more members whose political views were primarily influenced by nonreligious factors, such as wealth or occupation. It is true that church leaders, who typically identified more strongly with their church, were more united in party affiliation than were other members of their denomination.[7] However, this does not necessarily mean that members were not also influenced deeply by religious factors.

Did these divided churches simply demand less of their members? In fact, declining membership requirements were common during the late nineteenth century and not uniquely characteristic of politically divided churches. Furthermore, churches such as Baptist or Disciples of Christ were more strict than the politically united Roman Catholic or Congregational denominations. Finally, one might argue that whatever the standards, some churches were more inclusive, while others were more exclusive. This can be measured to some extent, for sources from Iowa and Canada at the turn of the century note the number of people claiming simply to be adherents, not members, of a denomination. One can calculate, then, the ratio of adherents to members for each church, but examination shows no relationship between these ratios and the degree of political unity in a church.[8]

It is also possible that the basic beliefs of these divided churches were not politically relevant—that they had no view of government's proper role or of the nature of society. Yet even a brief reading in the history of these churches shows the inaccuracy of that notion. In fact, their beliefs were politically salient and their political divisions reflected internal religious conflicts.[9]

One source of these differences was church polity, for churches with a congregational polity, such as the Disciples or the Baptists, contained considerable variation. Even a church with more structure, however, could include diversity. The omnipresent Methodist, for example, attracted members whose first-choice church was unavailable in their area.

Churches that had formed from merger or reunion were even more likely to show political divisions. Thus, the Old School/New School split among Presbyterians was papered over in favor of a sectional division in the mid nineteenth century, but the deep religious differences remained and were reflected in political perspectives and party affiliation.

A final and most instructive example of internal division—in both religious and political perspectives—is the Protestant Episcopal church.[10] This was not a church created by merger or reunion. Nor had church polity encouraged division, for this was a hierarchical organization in which bishops and church councils made policy for congregations. Nor had this church attracted disparate members by being the earliest church in an area: Unlike Methodists, Episcopalians typically came later and only to certain areas.

It is commonly assumed that the Episcopal church grew because it attracted upwardly mobile persons who considered the church more socially appropriate. Although logically flawed and resting on scanty, impressionistic evidence, this notion is generally accepted, and its failings must be noted. The belief that the elite was disproportionately Episcopalian is largely based on an impression of conditions in large, eastern cities. Not only was there no national elite in most periods of American history, there was also great diversity of places and conditions in the country. With so little systematic research on medium or smaller sized cities, we cannot be precise, but we do know that the religious characteristics of the elite varied widely from place to place.[11]

Shifting from the religions of the elite to the status of church members, even if the entire elite had become Episcopalian in this era, that would only account for a small part of the increase in church membership. One might also question the direction of the causal relationship: Were the wealthy becoming Episcopalians or were Episcopalians becoming wealthy? Finally, the assumption that people belonged to this church primarily for socioeconomic reasons slurs the piety of Episcopalians and represents a simplistic view of religion. While Episcopalian membership was secondarily influenced by nonreligious factors, this was also true for the membership of virtually all other churches.[12]

Thus, the Episcopal church was certainly distinctive in some ways, but it was not unique. Its internal differences resembled those of other divided churches, and they stemmed in part from the same cause: the evangelical movement of the early nineteenth century. The Episcopal church differed in that except for one very minor defection (the Reformed Episcopal church in 1873) it remained united throughout this period. It was able to contain these differences mainly because all Episcopalians believed that theirs was the one true church. This particularism was not unique, for many other churches made the same claim, but where other churches separated in order to remain pure, the Episcopal church saw its mission as unifying all Christians on common, basic principles.[13] Given this sense of mission and its internal division, the Episcopal church serves as an especially good case for studying the basis of religious divisions and their connection with political perspectives and behavior. Furthermore, since some of its members were of higher social status, it is also quite useful for examining the nature of political leadership.

FROM A POSITION of major importance in the eighteenth century, in numbers and as a legally established church, the Episcopal church declined significantly after American independence. By the 1850s it finally regained momentum, and its membership nearly doubled from 532,000 in 1890 to 938,000 in 1910 (an increase well above the percentage gains of Methodist, Baptists, and Presbyterians). Despite this growth, its proportion of the American religious population declined from 4 to 2.7 percent, and it ranked seventh—just ahead of the Congregationalists and somewhat behind the Disciples of Christ and Presbyterians.[14]

The distribution of Episcopalian churches and members around 1900 still reflected the church's early history. It was strongest in the Tidewater and Chesapeake Bay areas, from eastern Pennsylvania to New York city, and in southern New England. It was also visible in northern New England and in the Midwest. The church was also distinctly urban. Nationally, in both 1890 and 1906 approximately half of the membership resided in cities of over twenty-five thousand. Among major denominations this was equaled only by Catholics, it was twice the proportion of urban Presbyterians and Lutherans, and it far exceeded the 15 percent level for Baptists and Methodists. This urban concentration was especially evident in Baltimore, Philadelphia, New York, and Boston, but the church was also visible in smaller Eastern cities. Similarly, to the west—from Rochester (10.6 percent Episcopalian) to Toledo (6.5 percent) to Omaha (6.2 percent)—the church flourished best in urban climates. Its strength in the urban Midwest grew so that by 1906 Detroit and Minneapolis-St. Paul totaled more members than Baltimore or Boston. Thus, despite its base in large eastern cities, the church was vibrant in medium-sized cities and in the Midwest, and those areas require analysis.

Within the region, Michigan and Indiana offer interesting and manageable cases to study. Although they ranked highest and lowest in their proportion of Episcopal members, the gap between them was only several percent. More significant, they were fed by two different population streams—from the border South and Tidewater into Indiana, and the southern New England–Yankee-Yorker migration into Michigan. These groups reflected regional differences that connected with conflicting religious perspectives.

Both Michigan and Indiana had originally been single dioceses, but each had been divided by 1900. Michigan had split into eastern and western dioceses in 1876. By 1905, the Western Michigan Diocese had grown to twenty-nine churches, thirty missions, and nearly six thousand communicants. Indiana split into northern and southern dioceses in 1899, and by 1905 the Indianapolis diocese included nineteen churches, twenty-five missions, and 4,402 communicants.[15] The distribution of those members demonstrates two important aspects of the church. First, as shown in Table 10.1, a clear majority of churches had less than two hundred members. Second, a sizable minority of the members belonged to churches in the diocesan seat: 28.3 percent in Grand Rapids and a slightly higher proportion, 36.4 percent, in Indianapolis. Thus, both dioceses had a large number of relatively small churches, many of them in small communities. However, in each diocese a sizable minority of members lived in the largest city (Indianapolis or Grand Rapids), which also contained the two largest congregations.

Episcopalians in Michigan and Indiana, as well as elsewhere in the nation, shared common perceptions of the church and its role, especially

TABLE 10.1.   Size of Episcopal Congregations in 1905

Size of church (# Members)	Number of congregations by diocese	
	Western Michigan	Indianapolis
Over 400	4	3
200–399	5	3
100–199	8	8
50–99	6	3
Under 50	6	2

SOURCE: *Journal of the Proceedings of the Convention of the Diocese of Western Michigan, 1905:* 156–57; and *Journal of the Proceedings of the Convention of the Diocese of Indianapolis, 1905:* 92–93.

NOTE: these figures refer only to established congregations, not missions. None of the missions in either diocese had over 100 members, and most had less than 50.

a belief that it was unique. In the words of the Michigan bishop in 1899, they claimed "a higher position historically, a greater nearness to Apostolic rule and sanction, [as well as] more edifying services and better culture of the divine life through sacramental means and priestly offices."[16] A key element in this perspective was how they understood the church's historic role. As one author phrased it, "The present Church of England was not founded in the sixteenth century," but was actually the former church continued in slightly different form. "The same church remained, having essentially the same worship and sacraments, preserving without a break the ancient episcopate, retaining its property and Church buildings, and claiming to retain the Catholic faith and religion, freed only from what were regarded as mediaeval additions."[17] By the early twentieth century the church had increased its traditional concern with its reputation, creating a Committee of Defense to correct the "common bias" against the church in history books and to pressure school administrators and publishers.[18]

Because of this perception of its distinctive role and history, the church remained somewhat distant from ecumenical activities. Although it had joined the first interdenominational societies in the early nineteenth century, by the 1840s the church had left them and formed its own organizations. Episcopalian clergy could not participate in interdenominational services; and nonchurchmen could address an Episcopalian congregation only with a bishop's permission and only in exceptional circumstances.[19] The church was also ambivalent about the Federal Council of Churches, hesitating before sending a delegation to the 1905 organizing convention and choosing affiliation rather than membership in 1908. In essence, it accepted limited cooperation but not federation. Because they believed in their church's unique role as the only continuous apostolic church, Episcopalians also considered their church as the home to which individuals and prodigal denominations should return. And in the late nineteenth and early twentieth centuries, they saw increasing signs that this reunification was about to occur.[20]

The church was also notable for emphasizing theology and particular beliefs. Besides its views of original sin, redemption, and discipleship, a major source of distinctiveness was its definition of the church as the recipient and guardian of God's revelation and the dispensor of the sacraments. In general, the church remained committed to this perspective on belief, especially when confronted by the threats of modernism.[21] Thus, catechetical training was provided in Sunday school and was required for church membership. In clear contrast to the way many other Protestant churches regarded Sunday School, theology, and the Bible, Episcopalians emphasized not general religious sentiments, but "faith as declared in the creeds and supported and illustrated by the Bible."[22]

While this regard for theology and religious education encouraged an interest in Christian literature and reading, far more important were the implications for Episcopal views of public education and proper role of government. Recognizing that denominational differences prevented public schools from teaching a single religious view, the Michigan church argued confidently that "we need have no apprehension of evil from the secular nature of these schools, if Christianity shall only prove faithful to herself in the sacred relations of the Family and the Church." This position reflected a belief that state, church, and family had separate responsibilities and that fulfilling these would yield harmony and success. Rather than demanding that government enforce their views and morality, they stressed the wisdom and primacy of church and family action. Both dioceses also established several parochial schools, but their support and interest in such activities were quite limited.[23]

Episcopalians valued not only theology, but also liturgy, ritual, and imagery. Far more than other churches, Episcopal leaders stressed the tradition and importance of these elements of religion. In fact, it was a revived tradition, for beginning in the 1830s at Oxford University, the Tractarian movement had sparked a desire to return to a more elaborate and symbolic liturgy. Besides appreciating the form and language of worship as laid out in The Book of Common Prayer, Episcopalians uniquely emphasized the role and quality of music in worship services. Every church desired a musical instrument, and acquiring an organ, or replacing it with a better instrument, provoked much interest and even boasting.[24] Trained choirs were also considered very necessary, and excellence—not just sincerity—was the guiding principle. Churches sought to organize mens, boys, and mixed choirs; vestries pondered the music to be sung and even discussed what robes should be worn.[25] Thus, both form and content of all aspects of the service had major importance. The exterior of the church drew similar attention from members, for the Gothic church architecture, the spires and crosses, and the bells and chimes, all held symbolic importance as signs of "the supernatural manifesting itself to the senses."[26]

ALTHOUGH EPISCOPALIANS nationally and in these two dioceses shared these basic values, they were also at odds on many issues. In brief, they split into High Church and evangelical Low Church factions, with High Church forces being dominant. Their primary differences concerned liturgy, theology, and church structure, but these also reflected various social and political issues. Adding more complexity and tension to the division was that the bishops of both dioceses, and to a lesser extent the clergy, were more sympathetic to Low Church ideals.

Liturgy was the most frequently debated issue, especially by the bishops. The use of incense, carrying a cross, and most notably the method of celebrating Holy Communion aroused special controversy and were denounced as "Anglo-Catholicism." Indianapolis Bishop John White sharply criticized both clergy and laity who "continue to indulge their taste for fanciful and questionable ritualism." Some members of the bishop's own Indianapolis congregation who opposed his Low Church views broke away to form a parish with a more formal liturgy. Given such division, the church decided in 1898 to carve out a separate and hopefully more congenial diocese in northern Indiana for the bishop. His successor, Bishop Francis, was more conciliatory but no High Church partisan. "I love as much as anyone magnificent churches, and beautiful services, and well-trained choirs, and the like, but these are of secondary importance." Second, he felt, to the church's missionary focus. Francis periodically reiterated this position, and he later expanded it to criticize the advertising of musical services.[27]

In Michigan, debates over music had begun in mid-century, with the Great Tune Book War in St. Mark's church, and continued in diocesan debates and a vote on whether to criticize High Church practices. By the 1890s, like his counterpart in Indiana, this bishop was complaining that "there is sometimes the indication that the music of the Church has come to be regarded as its chief duty and attraction." He further condemned as "almost profane" the advertising of music and singers, and he particularly denounced the substitution of music services for normal Sunday evening worship. This position won relatively little support, however, for at the same time St. Mark's decided to pay several choir members who were being courted by other churches, and they authorized the choirmaster to hire special singers to "promote large attendance" at the evening music services.[28]

A second major issue, particularly in Michigan, that divided congregations was church finance. While the use and amount of funds were always matters of interest, it was the method of financing that caused dissatisfaction during this era. Traditionally, churches had raised their basic operating expenses by the annual sale or rental of pews, using voluntary offerings to pay for additional, special needs. The main alternative, which developed in the early nineteenth century, was to use envelopes for weekly contributions, with members determining the amount.

One ingredient in the debate over these methods was economic: The annual rental made church budgeting more predictable, while the envelope system relied on budgeting by individuals. The accountability of members was a second element, for the envelope system rejected a fixed and public fee in favor of private contributions determined by an individual's wealth and convictions. In addition, free seats were expected to enable the poor to attend. A final consideration was that church law restricted the qualified voters in any parish using the pew system to males who owned or rented all or part of a pew. This did not necessarily disfranchise many people, since members were expected to rent and most churches had few free pews, but that fact meant that there was relatively little space for visitors.[29] Thus, High Church partisans, who believed in traditional organization and public commitment, tended to favor pew rentals, while Low Church advocates, who emphasized individual responsibility and church expansion through missionary efforts, prefered the envelope system.

The seriousness of the issue is shown by several cases. In 1860 the Kalamazoo church split, in part because of this issue. When the two congregations reunited in 1883, adoption of the envelope system was one of the conditions.[30] The first Grand Rapids church, St. Mark's, had from its inception relied on pew rentals, but congregations organized in the late nineteenth century, notably Grace Church, used the envelope system virtually from their beginnings. From 1886 through 1888, the St. Mark's vestry fought over whether to end or amend the system. Although the records do not report the debates, the pattern of the struggle and the identity of the participants indicate that the heart of the controversy involved evangelical concerns about the openness of the church and the role of emotion. After considerable turmoil, the vestry enacted only minor changes.

This situation continued until 1911, when the issue finally came to a head. The problem was that the new rector made the elimination of the system a condition of his taking the position. Facing this ultimatum and after considerable debate the vestry finally agreed. In truth, however, the system was probably doomed by the changing demands of church expenditures, for in the previous decade St. Mark's expenses had gone up considerably, and it had been obliged to institute an envelope system to raise the necessary money.[31] Nor was St. Mark's alone in this position. As Table 10.2 shows, both the proportion of western Michigan churches with a pew rental system and the proportion of money raised by this system had declined significantly by 1911.

The nature of church leadership and decision making marked another but related difference. There was no formal limit on tenure in office, and

TABLE 10.2.   Church Financing Systems in Western Michigan

| | Finance system | | | | |
Year	Pew rental	Envelope	Both	Neither	Mean percent revenue from pew rental*
1880	25.0%	8.3%	0.0%	66.7%	68.0%
1890	16.7	41.6	4.2	37.5	50.2
1899	28.0	44.0	0.0	28.0	40.3
1911	9.7	48.3	9.7	32.3	36.3

SOURCE: *JPWM, 1880:* 109–157; *1890:* 125–159; *1899:* 81–134; *1911:* 93–140.
*This refers to the percentage of income from pew rentals for all churches using this and not the envelope system. Including churches that also used the envelope system would lower the level in 1911, for example, to 29.5 percent.

when such a limit was proposed at St. Mark's in 1888, it was voted down. Although the records are almost silent on this issue, it is clear that the supporters of this measure were the same Low Churchmen who pressed for changing the pew-rental system. The vestry's decision reflects a belief that there should be no limits on service and that leaders should remain in office indefinitely. As further evidence, most of those who resigned, or attempted to resign, from the vestry, were asked to reconsider their decision, and many did so.[32]

In fact, most vestrymen at St. Mark's did serve a long time. Some remained in office for over twenty years, and very few failed to be returned at least several times. Excluding seven dissenters from the 1880s, each of whom served only a single term (and most of whom left for other congregations), the average length of service for the twenty-eight vestrymen at St. Mark's was ten years. Unfortunately, the information for Grace Church vestrymen is inexact, but even a liberal reading of this data shows that the average vestry service was much briefer in this Low Church.

A second position, that of delegate to the diocesan convention, demanded much less time, but this office also yielded meaningful differences in leadership selection. Most Grand Rapids and Indianapolis churches usually chose at least one person with experience as one of their several convention delegates. But though all churches had some veteran leaders, delegates from the High Churches (St. Mark's Church in Grand Rapids and St. Paul's Church in Indianapolis) had more continuity from year to year and generally more experience than did men from the Low Churches (Grace Church in Grand Rapids and Christ Church in Indianapolis). This pattern reflects an important difference in how people viewed the church, and even society. High Churchmen generally took a traditional view of the institution, were concerned about continuity and the past, and emphasized leadership, while Low Churchmen focused on representation and change.[33]

The two factions were also at odds to varying degrees over a series of perennial moral issues that troubled most Protestant churches. The liquor question caused much less strife than it did in many other denominations, yet it separated Episcopalians from other churches, and it did create some internal divisions. In 1881, the Michigan bishop reported complaints about the use of wine at Holy Communion. Although not sympathetic to prohibition legislation, he did promote the organization of a church temperance society, and the diocese created a temperance committee. Six years later he was warning the clergy and laity of "the fearful evils of drinking habits" and urging them to "denounce the demon of drink."[34] Such admonitions apparently fell on deaf ears, and he neglected the issue for a number of years. After 1910, Grace Church took up the issue again, criticizing the use of liquor and discussing substitutes for the saloon. Hoosier Episcopalians were no more sympathetic to the cause of temperance, and neither bishop, clergy, nor laity even raised the issue at the annual diocesan conventions.[35]

Misuse of the Sabbath provoked some complaints from a Michigan committee dominated by Low Churchmen. They criticized poor church attendance, which they contrasted with the "unwholesome" interest in various social functions. The bishop was more explicit, denouncing not only public ball games and picnics, but also Sunday dinner parties by church members.[36] Most Episcopalians saw no harm in amusements such as card playing, dancing, and theatre going, but using them to raise funds for the church prompted some dissent. The bishop of Indianapolis warned that this was "degrading [the church] in the eyes of the world." The Michigan bishop went much further, denouncing them as an "appeal to purely animal gratification."[37]

Thus, Episcopalians knew of these social-moral issues, but they were not agitated about them as were other denominations. One reason was their view of original sin and human nature, but another major influence was their perception of the proper roles of church, family, and the state. Like all churches in this era, Episcopalians declared the family to be the basis of society and civilization. But while some denominations demanded government regulation of morality, Episcopalians viewed this as the responsibility of the family and church and not a legitimate function of government. Differences between Episcopalians primarily concerned the degree of responsibility to be held by church or family, but by the early twentieth century some Low Churchmen, who were very worried about "moral decay," began supporting some state intervention.[38]

Questions about the proper role of government, church, and family were even more central in discussions about the social and economic problems created by urbanization and industrialization. Urban members were often aware of the problems in rural areas, particularly because of the difficulties facing rural churches, but church members from small towns or rural areas were less familiar with conditions in cities. This, plus the fact that social problems were traditionally handled by local churches, meant that in both Grand Rapids and Indianapolis congregations began dealing with urban problems on their own. Later action by dioceses followed their initiative and direction.[39]

One approach by the church was to organize separate churches to minister to certain "problem" groups. St. Beda's Church in Grand Rapids ministered to the deaf, as did St. Albans in Indianapolis. Although neither attracted many members (the former peaked at forty-one in the 1890s, and the latter reached thirty-five), they did represent a unique mission to a disadvantaged group.[40] More striking were the missionary efforts among blacks. The Michigan diocese created a committee in 1906 to evaluate the prospects, while the Indiana diocese accepted a proposal to choose black bishops, or at least ministers, to assist in missionary efforts. In both cities the church established mission churches that attracted a stable and self-supporting membership.[41] Episcopalians undoubtedly believed that, in one way or another, church membership led to social and economic benefits for members, but they perceived the primary value of these churches as being religious.

More direct efforts to ameliorate social problems were followed in both cities, but the types of efforts—and the perspectives they reflected—varied considerably and changed over time. In Grand Rapids during the 1850s, St. Mark's established a sewing school for poor children, as well as providing some money and clothing to the poor. Other socially active groups associated with the church included the Industrial Band and the Helping Hand. In the 1870s the church began providing some lodging for persons who were aged or homeless and child care for working mothers. Within a few years, this project was transformed into a hospital, and in 1902 the church relinquished all authority over the institution. In the same year, St. Mark's established a "parish house," followed a few years later by Grace Church, which initially provided libraries and recreation.[42]

Concern over social problems increased after 1910, when the national convention of the denomination called each diocese to organize a social service Commission. In Indiana the immediate effect was to generate support (albeit temporary) for a residence for working girls. The diocese also created a Social Service commission which studied the social services of each parish, recommended sermon topics, and wrote pamphlets. It examined the conditions of jails and workhouses, and urged each parish to do the same. Finally, beginning in 1914, it operated an employment bureau.[43]

The Indianapolis congregations differed substantially in how they approached these issues. Some had only hospital guilds or a Girls Friendly Society, while other churches more directly assisted the poor, and some helped care for the sick or even bury the dead. The most extensive effort came from St. George's Church, which represents the "institutional church" approach. In 1914, it was offering sewing and gym classes; it had a loan officer and an employment bureau; it provided coal, food, and rent money; and it operated a free dispensary and a day nursery.[44]

The Social Service Commission of the Michigan diocese observed that the "improvement of social, economic, [and] industrial conditions has become an absorbing pursuit," and proclaimed that "the Church as a unit is committed to Social Service as this is the inevitable expression of the first and great commandment." The commission took a narrow view of its responsibilities, confining itself to encouraging local organization and, unlike its Hoosier counterpart, not even surveying the results. A notable case in Grand Rapids was the work of Grace Church, located just south of the downtown area. The clergy contributed greatly to these efforts. Rev. Francis Godolphin arrived in 1906 and "was a believer in the institutional church and was cordially supported by the vestry and his parishioners."[45] His replacement in 1913, Rev. George Sargent, carried this program much further. During the next five years, the church operated a free kindergarten and a gym; offered classes, clubs, a prenatal clinic, and an infant-feeding clinic; provided pool tables, sponsored Boy Scouts and Camp Fire Girls, supported work in prisons and a fund for widows and orphans, and ran a study group on social issues.[46]

An interest in social problems existed throughout the church and during this entire era, but the perspective and concerns changed over time. During the mid to late nineteenth century, the focus was on charity activities, specific "good works," and individual efforts. By the turn of the century, there was a growing sense that social problems were increasing, because of new industrial and urban circumstances, and that new approaches might be necessary. The resulting emphasis on structure, control, and efficiency accompanied the shift from High to Low Church domination of the church's social efforts. Thus, while St. Mark's had a
f resurgence of social activity in 1912 and 1913, following the denomi-

national directive, this lapsed after a few years. At Grace Church, besides its supervised programs, the Social Service Guild spent much time "learning the scientific methods of investigation" and attending many lectures on current social problems. Rev. Sargent envisioned the guild as "a School of Philanthropy to study conditions and be able to help in a scientific, yet friendly way." He hoped that when the women "completed their training and are experts" that they would do good for the church and themselves. In fact, while this probably "raised the social consciousness" of the members, it did little directly to ameliorate existing social problems.[47]

This Low Church approach was also weakened by the traditional emphasis on the spiritual aspect of religion. After an initial enthusiasm, both bishops began talking about subordinating social activity to the spiritual mission. United States involvement in World War I also diminished any interest in social problems. As a result, by 1918 neither diocese displayed much support for social programs. The Indiana Social Service Commission reported that "no business of importance was transacted and no definite work undertaken. The Social Service Commission, as such, has accomplished nothing during the year."[48] In Grand Rapids, war support became virtually the sole social interest of Grace Church, and the Social Service Guild abandoned a regular meeting time by December 1918. By the 1920s, it had a tiny membership compared with other guilds, and there was no evidence of any interest in social problems.[49]

In general, Low Churches and Low Church men and women displayed the greatest interest in social causes. Grace Church in Grand Rapids and Christ Church in Indianapolis provided the most clerical and lay leadership, as well as demonstrating the greatest commitment. In Indiana, the leading social activist—the longest serving member of the Social Service Commission, the man who suggested and supervised studies of jails and workhouses, the man who ran the employment service out of his office—was Low Churchman Judge James Collins. This connection is further evidenced in the 1886–1888 controversy in St. Mark's Church, where the dissenting (and Low Church) vestrymen included William Innes (former state railroad commissioner) and Fred Maynard (future state attorney general)—both Republicans.[50]

As the foregoing analysis of social and religious differences reveals, the High Church-Low Church split within the denomination reflected substantial differences over the importance and role of spirituality and religious enthusiasm, the moral strictures on behavior, and the responsibility of the church in society. Those latter views in particular, concerning the relationship of church and state, had significant implications for party identification and political activity. During the late nineteenth and early twentieth centuries, a majority of the denomination was High Church and Democratic, but these overall divisions were not mirrored identically in all congregations. Instead, congregations demonstrated a relatively strong preference for either High or Low Church religion, which therefore produced congregations with different partisan preferences. Grace Church and Christ Church were Low Church and their leaders were mostly Republican, while St. Mark's and St. Paul's were High Church and had Democratic leaders. Perspective rather than context determined these relationships, for even in High Churches the Low Churchmen were Republicans, while High Churchmen in Low Churches were still Democrats.[51] It was not just leaders, of course, who fit this pattern, but the evidence regarding membership is much more difficult to obtain. In Indianapolis, however, the partisan character of the churches was well known. St. Paul's was formed during the Civil War era by Democrats seceding from Christ Church, which was strongly Unionist and Republican. Despite the passage of decades, this division and an awareness of it continued.[52]

Episcopalians played different but vital roles in both parties. Because of their limited numbers they had little importance as voters, but they were very influential officeholders and political leaders. This was not simply a consequence of their social status, for not all Episcopalian politicians were eminent, nor was the socioeconmic elite in either city exclusively—or even predominantly—Episcopalian. Instead, this results from their willing involvement, a political commitment based on their religious perspective. In Indianapolis, all four Democratic candidates for mayor from 1889 to 1913 (three were elected) were Episcopalians and members of St. Paul's. One of them—Thomas Taggart—actively dominated city politics for over a decade, guided the state party for twenty-five years, and was influential in national party politics, even serving a term as national party chairman. Episcopalians were less numerous among Republican leaders, but they included such notables as Judge Collins and former Congressman William E. English.[53]

In Michigan, various Episcopalians belonged to the Democratic State Committee, such as Isaac Weston, who served as treasurer from 1882 to 1886 and chairman from 1886 to 1890. Church members were also notable as office seekers, including the gubernatorial candidate in 1896, Charles Sligh. Episcopalians were even more influential in the city politics of Grand Rapids. Two of the eight Republican mayors from 1859 to 1917 belonged to the church. Even more striking, eleven of the thirteen Democratic mayors were Episcopalian, and nine of them served as vestrymen at St. Mark's.[54]

These men became politically active because of their religious perspective; they succeeded because of their personal characteristics and the structure of urban politics. As shown in Table 10.3, all vestrymen of the two main Grand Rapids churches held at least middle-class occupations, over half were businessmen, and a number were associated with major economic concerns in the city. They were, in brief, men of prominence and position.[55] But while such economic status and citywide visibility were useful if not essential for service as mayor, it was obviously less necessary, or even desirable, for aldermen. Of the sixty-eight aldermen who served in the years 1850, 1860, 1870, 1880, 1890, or 1900, only six were Episcopalians, and five of them served in 1850 or 1860.

The basis of this pattern is apparent from Table 10.4, which summarizes and contrasts the occupations of aldermen and mayors. While nearly half of the mayors were merchants, and another third were manufacturers or bankers, alderman had only a third as many men in those occupations. Instead, some ward representatives held low white-collar jobs, and, most strikingly, the greatest number were workers. Examining aldermen who served in 1890 or 1900 sharpens the contrast.

TABLE 10.3.   Occupations of Grand Rapids
                Vestrymen, 1877–1915

| | Church | |
Occupation	Grace	St. Mark
Business		
Employee	18.8	7.0
Owner	15.7	15.8
Officer	34.3	15.8
Merchant	6.3	10.5
Banker	3.1	7.0
Lawyer	18.8	38.6
Doctor	3.1	5.3
Total	100.0	100.0

SOURCE: See note 54, ch. 10.
NOTE: Business Employee includes auditor, bookkeeper, cashier, agent, and clerk. All data are given in percentages.

TABLE 10.4.   Occupations of Grand Rapids Politicians, 1850–1906

	Aldermen (n = 49)	Mayors (n = 26)
Merchant	18.4	42.4
Manufacturer	10.2	19.3
Banker	0.0	11.5
Own business	10.2	3.8
Manager	10.2	7.7
Professional	14.3	15.4
Low white collar	8.2	0.0
Worker	28.6	0.0
Total	100.0	100.0

SOURCE: See note 54, ch 10.

NOTE: This table includes all aldermen serving in 1850, 1860, 1870, 1880, 1890, or 1900; it includes all mayors serving 1859–1917. The "n" figures refer to the number of individuals for whom occupational information was found. The other data are given in percentages.

Merchants and manufacturers comprised only 20 percent of this group, while workers and low white-collar workers made up 42.9 percent, and the category of "worker" included not only skilled worker but also "machine hands."

These occupational differences help explain why Episcopalians were often mayors but were virtually absent from the ranks of aldermen. Their social standing and contacts benefited them in citywide contests, but these same factors—and their likely lack of interest—kept them from other posts. In the mid-nineteenth century, when Grand Rapids was still small and had few wards, Episcopalians did serve on the city council. During the next fifty years, however, the pattern changed. As the city and the number of its wards increased, Episcopalians were concentrated in a proportionally decreasing part of the city and in relatively few wards. In addition, as in other cities across the nation, men of this status withdrew from neighborhood politics, repelled and defeated by working-class politicians (like the Irish-born Thomas Doran in Grand Rapids).[56]

By the turn of the century, the continuing changes in the nature of the city's economy, plus the size and composition of its population, led to a further shift in the balance of power and the end of the sociopolitical system in which Episcopalians had prospered. "Boss" George Ellis, first elected in 1906 and reelected till 1916, put together a coalition of various working-class, business, and ethnic voters, much like Hazen Pingree's efforts in Detroit a decade earlier. In reaction to this, a new coalition pressed successfully in 1916 for a new charter, instituting a nonpartisan commission-manager government with only three wards. This reflected and confirmed the power of a different combination of businessmen and professionals, many of whose leaders belonged to the theologically "liberal" Fountain Street Baptist Church. Even though one last Episcopalian, a vestryman at St. Mark's, was elected city commissioner and mayor in 1917, the dominance of this downtown church and this style of politics was finished.[57]

Episcopalians were less important as leaders in the Republican party for several reasons. First, more of them were businessmen, especially in Indianapolis, and they were typically less interested in holding office. By contrast, more of the Democratic Episcopalian leaders were lawyers, a profession which routinely involved them in politics and often brought them officeholding experience. Even more important than the character of Episcopal leaderhip was the composition of the electorate, especially in the Democratic party. Catholics made up a sizable portion of the population in both cities—49 percent in Grand Rapids and 40 percent in Indianapolis—and the substantial majority of Democratic voters. Given anti-Catholic sentiment, the need for candidates with relatively high social standing, and the limited number of other Protestant Democrats of equal status, Episcopalians were the obvious choice.[58]

Focusing on Episcopalians also helps to explain the dwindling fortunes of the Democratic party in these cities. In Indianapolis, the party encountered serious trouble over religion in 1909. To the consternation of both Catholic and non-Catholic politicians, Democratic voters in the 1909 primary chose Catholic candidates for mayor and all but two of the other citywide offices, which resulted in complete defeat in the general election. This began a slide that left the party substantially weaker and vulnerable to the anti-Catholic, Ku Klux Klan-dominated Republican party in the 1920s. Only a backlash against the KKK and political corruption in 1929 brought Democrats back to power.[59] In Grand Rapids the party declined sooner and permanently—by roughly the turn of the century. Understanding the connection of party and the church helps to explain the precipitous decline. The change might appear simply a minor shift in the balance of power to Republicans, since all of the Democratic candidates who lost to Ellis were Episcopalians. In fact, as noted above, these losses to a progressive Republican who attracted some immigrant and lower class voters represent a basic transition in the economy and politics of the area.[60]

Nearly every Episcopal Democrat who was politically active in 1896 affiliated with the breakaway Gold Democratic Party. They were, in fact, a sizable and influential part of the movement, and they included state party chairman William Shelby, a warden at St. Mark's for an extraordinary thirty-three years, from 1877 to 1910. After the election most of these men returned to the party, but its changing focus left them uninterested and increasingly uninvolved. The shift is further apparent in that two of the four Democrats who ran for mayor after 1904 were prominent leaders in Grace Church, most notably Charles Sligh, a former Republican who joined the party in 1896 to run as the silver fusion candidate for governor.[61]

THE CHANGING CONDITION of the Episcopal church in these two areas significantly affected the relationship of religion and politics. Internal divisions in the early nineteenth century reflected the conflict between the evangelical and Tractarian movements. Each position was supported by cultural groups from certain geographical areas. The more traditional, liturgical perspective dominated in the Chesapeake region, as well as the Ohio and Hudson valleys; while the more modern, evangelical religion was most influential in southern New England and western New York. Migrants to the Midwest carried their views with them and, when possible, formed churches with like-minded persons. Their cultural backgrounds and religious beliefs were the basis of their political views and attachments.

These conditions were complicated by the social, economic, and political developments beginning after the Civil War. In both Grand Rapids and Indianapolis, economic growth, especially in manufacturing, drew additional population, which substantially altered the distribution of occupational, ethnic, and religious groups. This shift had various political consequences, including far fewer opportunities to hold elective political office for middle-class Anglo-Americans—a category including most Episcopalians. Other forms of population mobility also disrupted religious patterns. Migrants whose former denomination was absent from these cities had to choose a new church, while others used the move as an opportunity to change churches.[62] Similarly, some immigrants wishing to assimilate changed their church membership. Because of the religious backgrounds of these new members and the evangelicals' emphasis on missions, new members more often belonged to Low Churches and supported that perspective within the denomination.[63]

The evangelical wing of the church also benefited greatly from clerical support. Despite limited information on the views of most clergy, various sources reveal a clear evangelical preference. A sign from early in this era is an 1874 vote in the Michigan diocese: Most western clergy voted for an evangelical position and were opposed by a majority of the laity.[64] Over the years, bishops in both dioceses consistently advocated evangelical views on missions and behavior, at the same time criticizing "excessive" ritualism. The clerical-lay differences are all the more interesting because the laity controlled the selection process. Perhaps doctrinal issues were ignored in hiring decisions, but it is more likely that, for whatever reason, more eligible clergymen were evangelical. A third and vital influence was personal connections. The vestry minutes of St. Mark's suggest that such considerations were important in choosing clergy. Rector Sargent of Grace Church also hinted at the general role of such connections when he noted that evangelical Bishop White of Northern Indiana had known him from childhood.[65] The clergy's power was limited, but as spokesmen for the church, and sometimes as major financial contributors, they could set a general direction. Furthermore, in their public statements and community activities they represented the church.[66]

The church's position in politics changed during the early twentieth century. Economic and demographic shifts, which had reduced political officeholding by its members, also stimulated political debates over the nature of government. Traditional Episcopal beliefs in the responsibilities of church and family and in limited government authority had long been widely appealing. However, in an age of labor strife, unemployment, poverty, and other socioeconomic problems—problems that could be ameliorated by private charity but whose solution seemed to require government action—traditional views came under attack. Differences within the church were not unimportant, but they fell within certain limits, and the Episcopalian view of their denomination as the mother church was a vital factor in preventing division. Despite declines in political prominence and changing views of society, the Episcopal church, like other churches, spoke to the central issues of the human condition, the nature of the church, and the role of the state. Analyzing intra- as well as inter-denominational differences reinforces an understanding that the basic connection of religious perspectives with political beliefs and behavior remained.

NOTES

1. For the revival of religious history, see, for example, James Ward Smith and J. Leland Jamison, eds. *The Shaping of American Religion* (Princeton: Princeton University Press, 1961); Henry May, "The Recovery of American Religious History," *American Historical Review* 70 (February 1964): 79–92; and Winthrop S. Hudson, *Religion in America: An Historical Account of the Development of American Religious Life* (New York: Scribner, 1965). Some social analysis was done, for example, by H. Richard Niebuhr, *The Social Sources of Denominationalism* (Cleveland: World Publishing, 1929); Whitney R. Cross, *The Burned-over District: The Social and Intellectual History of Enthusiastic Religion in Western New York, 1800–1850* (New York: Harper & Row, 1950); Will Herberg, *Protestant-Catholic-Jew: An Essay in American Religious Sociology,* rev. ed. (Garden City, N.Y.: Anchor Books, 1960); Robert Doherty, "Social Bases for the Presbyterian Schism of 1837–1838," *Journal of Social History* 2 (Fall 1968): 69–79; and Martin Marty, *Righteous Empire: The Protestant Experience in America* (New York: Dial Press, 1970). However, all of the systematic analysis, except for Doherty's essay, was done by sociologists.

2. Paul Kleppner, *Cross of Culture: A Social Analysis of Midwest Politics, 1850–1900* (New York: Free Press, 1970); and Richard Jensen, *The Winning of the Midwest: Social and Political Conflict, 1888–1896* (Chicago: University of Chicago Press, 1971). See also Ronald P. Formisano, *The Birth of Mass Political Parties: Michigan, 1827–1861* (Princeton: Princeton University Press, 1971); Kleppner, *The Third Electoral System, 1853–1892: Parties, Voters, and Political Cultures* (Chapel Hill: University of North Carolina Press, 1979); and Philip R. VanderMeer, *The Hoosier Politician: Officeholding and Political Culture in Indiana, 1896–1920* (Urbana: University of Illinois Press, 1985).

3. See especially Kleppner, *Third Electoral System,* passim.

4. See, for example, James E. Wright, "The Ethnocultural Model of Voting," *American Behavioral Scientist* 16 (May–June 1973): 653–674; Richard L. McCormick, "Ethno-Cultural Interpretations of Nineteenth-Century American Voting Behavior," *Political Science Quarterly* 89 (June 1974): 351–378; Dale Baum, *The Civil War Party System: The Case of Massachusetts, 1848–1876* (Chapel Hill: University of North Carolina Press, 1984); and Allan J. Lichtman, "Political Realignment and 'Ethnocultural' Voting in Late Nineteenth Century America," *Journal of Social History* 16 (Spring 1983): 55–82.

5. See the discussion and references in VanderMeer, *Hoosier Politician,* 97–109; and VanderMeer, "Religion, Society, and Politics: A Classification of American Religious Groups," *Social Science History* 5 (Winter 1981): 3–24.

6. See the sources in note 4.

7. VanderMeer, *Hoosier Politician,* 116–119.

8. See the data and discussion in Jensen, *Winning the Midwest,* 86; and Henry K. Carroll, *The Reilgious Forces in the United States,* rev. ed. (New York: Scribner, 1912), xxxiv.

9. For information on the history and characteristics of various churches, see Carroll, *Religious Forces;* F. E. Mayer, *Religious Bodies of America,* 4th ed. (St. Louis: Concordia Publishing House, 1961); Phillip Schaff et al., eds. *American Church History Series,* 13 vols. (New York: Scribner, 1893–1897); Sydney E. Ahlstrom, *A Religious History of the American People* (New Haven: Yale University Press, 1972); and VanderMeer, *Hoosier Politician,* 97–120.

10. Besides the sources in note 9, see also E. Clowes Chorley, *Men and Movements in the American Episcopal Church* (Hamden, Conn.: Archon Books, 1961); Raymond W. Albright, *A History of the Protestant Episcopal Church* (New York: Macmillan, 1964); and Robert Bruce Mullin, *Episcopal Vision/ American Reality: High Church Theology and Social Thought in Evangelical America* (New Haven: Yale University Press, 1986).

11. For example, despite its merits, E. Digby Baltzell, *Philadelphia Gentlemen: The Making of a National Upper Class* (Glencoe, Ill.: Free Press, 1958) exhibits this seriously flawed view of the church. Notable among the few systematic studies is Richard Jensen, "Quantitative Collective Biography: An Application to Metropolitan Elites," in Robert P. Swierenga, ed., *Quantification in American History: Theory and Research* (New York: Atheneum, 1970).

12. Notions about changes in church membership were misdirected by Robert W. Doherty, "Sociology, Religion, and Historians," *Historical Methods Newsletter* 6 (September 1973): 161–169. See, for example, Harry S. Stout and Robert Taylor, "Sociology, Religion, and Historians Revisted: Towards an Historical Sociology of Religion," *Historical Methods Newsletter,* 8 (December, 1974): 29–38. Contrary to stereotypes, the western Michigan bishop claimed that Episcopalians were joining other churches for business or social reasons. *Journal of the Proceedings of the Annual Convention of the Diocese of Western Michigan* (hereinafter *JPWM*), *1899:* 72. Ethnicity and race have had the most important influence on church membership, followed by class. One should note, however, that class identification could send people in a variety of directions. Furthermore, the obvious connection between class and "style" could translate into ritual and liturgy in religious terms, which often reflects important religious values.

13. For example, the Disciples of Christ, Landmarkean Baptists, and Synodical Conference (Missouri Synod) Lutherans.

14. This discussion of the size and distribution of church membership is taken or calculated from statistics reported in Carroll, *Religious Forces,* xxxvii–lxxv, 379–461; and from the U.S. Census, *Census of Religious Bodies, 1906,* 1: 380–400. In calculating church rank, Methodist and Lutheran divisions are ignored to highlight the basic pattern.

15. The Western Michigan diocese began in 1876 with thirty-three churches, seventeen missions, and roughly three thousand communicants. When the Indiana diocese split, the north took fifteen churches, eleven missions, and 2,067

communicants, while the Indianapolis diocese retained twenty-one churches, seventeen missions, and 3,483 communicants.

16. *JPWM, 1899:* 72–73.

17. "The English Church and the Reformation: A Statement of Facts," *Grace Church Bulletin* 1 (December 1913): 11 (bound volumes in possession of Grace Episcopal Church, Grand Rapids, Michigan).

18. For Indiana, see *Journal of the Proceedings of the Annual Convention of the Diocese of Indianapolis* (hereinafter *JPI*), *1908:* 29–30, *1911:* 29–30, *1912:* 25, and *1913:* 17–18; and in Michigan a Committee on School Histories, noted in *JPWM, 1911:* 52–53.

19. Albright, *Episcopal Church,* 250–251; *JPI, 1908:* 47–49; and Winthrop S. Hudson, *American Protestantism* (Chicago: University of Chicago Press, 1961), 108–109.

20. J. A. Hutchinson, *We Are Not Divided: A Critical and Historical Study of the Federal Council of Churches* (New York: Round Table Press, 1941), 33; Charles S. MacFarland, ed. *The Churches of the Federal Council* (New York: Fleming H. Revell, 1916), 3; Albright, *Episcopal Church,* 170–174, 348–349; Mayer, *Religious Bodies in America,* 275; Peter Mode, "Aims and Methods of Contemporary Church-Union Movements in America," *American Journal of Theology* 24 (April 1920): 224–251; *JPWM, 1905:* 54–55, *1908:* 67; and *Grace Church Bulletin* 4 (February 1916): 6 (May 1916): 3.

21. *JPI, 1905:* 55; *JPI, 1906:* 40–41; Albright, *Episcopal Church;* and Mayer, *Religious Bodies in America.*

22. Quotation from *JPWM, 1906:* 24. Marriana C. Brown, *Sunday-School Movements in America* (New York: Fleming H. Revell, 1901), 124, 132; Eli Lilly, *History of the Little Church on the Circle: Christ Church Parish Indianapolis, 1837–1955* (Indianapolis: Lakeside Press, 1957), 105; Sarah S. Pratt, *Epsicopal Bishops in Indiana: A Churchwoman's Retrospect* (Indianapolis: Pratt Poster Co., 1934), 29; *JPI, 1914:* 17–18; and *JPWM, 1896:* 76.

23. Quotation from *JPWM, 1881:* 46. Also *JPWM, 1884:* 81. On Indiana parochial schools, see Lilly, *Little Church,* 77; and lists in Indiana State Superintendent of Public Instruction, *Biennial Report, 1887–1888* (Indianapolis, 1889), pt. 2, pp. 489–490 (two schools had died by 1900 and the third was a military academy). On Michigan, see e.g. *JPWM, 1895:* 54–56, *1896:* 75–76, *1907:* 49–50, *1906:* 24–25. St. Mark's started a college in 1850, but it only lasted a few years. Franklin Campbell Smith, *The Diocese of Western Michigan: A History* (Grand Rapids: Diocesan Historical Commission, 1948), 68–70.

24. *JPWM, 1896:* 74–75; Edgar W. Hunting, *History of Grace Church, Grand Rapids, Michigan, Diocese of Western Michigan* (Grand Rapids: n.p., 1922), 4–5; Roger Allen, *The Story of St. Mark's: A Century of Christian Witness in Grand Rapids, Michigan* (Grand Rapids: St. Mark's, 1936), 22–25; Smith, *Diocese of Western Michigan,* 99–100; Lilly, *Little Church,* 60, 134; and *JPWM, 1906:* 82–84.

25. St. Mark's Vestry minutes, 5, 12, 17 September 1883, in "Records of St. Mark's Church," vol. 1, St. Mark's Episcopal Church, Grand Rapids, Michigan; Charles W. Calkins, "History of St. Mark's Parish," copy in St. Mark's, "Rec-

ords," vol. 1, 8 October 1886; and Lilly, *Little Church,* 234, 246, 270. On music generally see Leonard Webster Ellinwood, *The History of American Church Music* (New York: Morehouse-Goreham, 1953), esp 75–76, 134–139; and Albright *Episcopal Church,* 293.

26. Quotation Lilly, *Little Church,* 132–133.

27. Quotations from *JPI, 1898:* 32, and *JPI, 1907:* 52. See also *JPI, 1898:* 35–36, *1902:* 89, *1910:* 38–39, *1914:* 54–55; Pratt, *Episcopal Bishops,* 44–45; and Albright, *Episcopal Church,* 277–286, 293, 297.

28. Quotation from *JPWM, 1893:* 86. Smith, *Diocese Western Michigan,* 101, 178–179; Franklyn Morris, "St. Mark's: A Michigan Ministry," *Cathedral Age,* 28 (Spring, 1953): 10–13; Allen, *St. Mark's,* 22–23; and St. Mark's, "Records," vol. 2, 4 October 1898; 7 February 1899.

29. The problem of payment was often serious. Grace church reported in 1914 that only 250 of the 800 members had pledged. *Grace Church Bulletin* 1 (May, 1914): 5. Timothy L. Smith discusses free seating in a general context in *Revivalism and Social Reform: American Protestantism on the Eve of the Civil War* (1957; rpt. New York: Harper & Row, 1965), 23–24, 164. The Episcopal law ruling is quoted in St. Mark's, "Records," vol. 1, 12 March 1887. See the discussion of the rental policy and the description of rental units and amounts in ibid., 15 February and 22 March 1888.

30. Smith, *Diocese of Western Michigan,* 78–79, 297–298.

31. The revenue and means of raising it are listed, for each church, in the "Parochial Reports" printed in *JPWM,* 1876–1918. St. Mark's "Records," vol. 1, 11 April, 7 September, 5 October, 9 November 1887; 4 January, 15 February, 22 March 1888; vol. 2, 1 March 1898; vol. 3, 14 September, 6 November 1911.

32. St. Mark's, "Records," vol. 1, 9 November 1887; 4 January, 15 February, 7 March, 4 May 1888.

33. The service of vestrymen at St. Mark's was calculated from their presence in the "Records," vols. 1–3. For Grace Church, the names of vestrymen and some dates of service are reported in Hunting, *History of Grace Church,* 4–7. Lists of wardens and delegates to diocesan conventions were compiled from data reported in *JPWM,* 1871–1918, and *JPI,* 1890–1920. On patterns of leadership, see the insightful comments of Richard J. Jensen, "Modernization as a Framework for American History," paper presented to the Organization of American Historians, Detroit, 2 April 1981.

34. *JPWM, 1887:* 97, 98.

35. *JPWM, 1881,* 72–73, 59–60; *Grace Church Bulletin* 4 (October 1916): 3, (December 1916): 5, 5 (May 1917): 4; Lilly, *Little Church,* 103.

36. *JPWM, 1889:* 59–60, 73–74.

37. *JPI, 1903:* 51; *JPWM, 1896:* 78. See also Lilly, *Little Church,* 121–122, 197; *Grace Church Bulletin* 4 (March 1916): 6, (June 1916): 2.

38. For example, the discussion of morality and public education in *JPWM, 1907:* 50.

39. *JPI, 1906:* 89–90, *1909:* 31, 45; *1911:* 34, 49–51; *1915:* 41; *Grace Church Bulletin* 5 (October 1917): 7.

40. Jacob Piatt Dunn, *Greater Indianapolis,* 2 vols. (Indianapolis: B. F. Bowen, 1912), 1: 613; *JPWM, 1895:* 229, *1900:* 145.

41. The churches were St. Phillip's in Indianapolis and St. Paul's in Grand Rapids. *JPWM, 1906:* 51; *JPI, 1904:* 30, 51, *1905:* 28; *Grace Church Bulletin* 4 (March 1916): 5; Dunn, *Greater Indianapolis,* 1: 613. St. Mark's contributed money to the Home Mission to Colored People in the 1870s. *JPWM, 1876:* 138. By 1914 there was a black Episcopalian minister in Indianapolis. *JPI, 1914:* 52–53.

42. Smith, *Diocese of Western Michigan,* 72–73, 449–450; Calkins, "History of St. Mark's Parish"; "From St. Mark's Church Home to Butterworth Hospital, 1873–1902," Dedicatory Address, 21 May 1925, Butterworth Hospital, Grand Rapids, Michigan, in Box 2, Collection of the Protestant Episcopal Church in the Diocese of Western Michigan, Bentley Historical Library, University of Michigan (hereinafter PEWM); "St. Mark's Centennial, 1836–1936," typescript, p. 24, in Box 2, PEWM; *JPWM, 1876:* 134–135; *JPWM, 1880:* 164–165; Hunting, *History of Grace Church,* 6.

43. *JPI, 1912:* 26, 48, *1913:* 18–22, 49–51, *1914:* 21–23.

44. *JPI, 1913:* 19–22. See also ibid., *1904:* 51.

45. Quotations from *JPWM, 1913:* 52; *JPWM, 1912:* 47; Hunting, *Grace Church,* 6. See also Smith, *Diocese Western Michigan,* 429.

46. *Grace Church Bulletin* 2 (October 1914): 2, 5; 2 (November 1914): 4–5; 4 (April 1916): 7; 4 (Oceober 1916): 4; 5 (February 1917): 5.

47. Quotations from *Grace Church Bulletin* 2 (December 1914): 13, 12; 2 (November 1914): 7; and 2 (December 1914): 4. Also see e.g. ibid. 4 (February 1916): 6–7. On St. Mark's see Smith, *Diocese Western Michigan,* 433–434.

48. Quotation from *JPI, 1918:* 36. *JPI, 1914:* 54–55.

49. See the *Grace Church Bulletin* for these years, especially 6 (December 1916): 2, and 9 (March 1921): 10.

50. On Collins see *JPI, 1914:* 21–22; and the biographical sketches in Dunn, *Greater Indianapolis,* 2: 1162; *Indianapolis News,* 4 December, 1946. Collins was also an important member of the Charity Organization Society and the Immigrant Aid Society. For sources on Innes and Maynard, see note 54.

51. The Republican-Democrat party balance among the leaders in these churches was eight to two in Grace Church and ten to zero in Christ Church, compared with eight to nineteen for St. Mark's and seven to eighteen for St. Paul's. Although I found party affiliation for fewer Low Church leaders, this pattern is consistent with their political perspective, reflecting less interest in elective public office. Lists of religious leaders were compiled from sources in note 33. Biographical information on Indianapolis leaders comes from various sources, including Dunn, *Greater Indianapolis; A Biographical Directory of the Indiana General Assembly (BDIGA),* 2 vols. (Indianapolis: Select Committee on the Centennial History of the Indiana General Assembly, 1980–1984); county and city biographical collections and histories listed in Carolynne L. Wendel, *Aids for Genealogical Searching in Indiana* (Detroit: Detroit Society for Genealogical Research, 1962); Ann McKenzie, ed., *The Greater Indianapolis Blue Book* (Indianapolis: Bowen-Merrill, 1899); and the biographical files in

the Indiana Division, Indiana State Library: the Indiana Biography Series and the George S. Cottman Collection. For sources on Grand Rapids leaders see note 54.

52. Lilly, *Little Church*, 147, 185, 206; Dunn, *Greater Indianapolis*, 1: 612.

53. Even a glance through city and county histories reveals the religious diversity of those prominent in politics, economics, or social activities. In Grand Rapids, for example, many such persons belonged to the First Presbyterian or Park Congregational churches; the prominent churches in Indianapolis included First Presbyterian, Plymouth Congregational, and Meridian Street Methodist Episcopal, and most Republican mayors were Methodist or Presbyterian. See the sources in notes 51 and 54. For a complete list of Indianapolis mayors see Dunn, *Greater Indianapolis*, 1: 644. Taggart is discussed in Philip R. Vander-Meer, "Bosses, Machines, and Democratic Leadership: Party Organization and Managers, Indiana, 1880–1910," *Social Science History* 12 (Winter 1988): 420–421; and John B. Stoll, *History of the Indiana Democracy 1816–1916* (Indianapolis: Indiana Democratic Publishing Co., 1917), 1034–1038. For basic information on English see *BDIGA*.

54. Religious information was missing for four Democratic and four Republican mayors. Grand Rapids mayors and aldermen are listed in Dwight Goss, *History of Grand Rapids and Its Industries*, 2 vols. (Chicago: C. F. Cooper & Co., 1906), 1: 266–279. Biographical sketches of most mayors (including Weston) are found in Ernest Fisher, *Grand Rapids and Kent County, Michigan*, 2 vols. (Chicago: Robert O. Law Company, 1918), 1: 171–179, 452–453. Additional biographical information on mayors, aldermen, and religious leaders was collected from Albert Baxter, *History of the City of Grand Rapids, Michigan* (Grand Rapids: Munsell & Company, 1891); A. W. Bowen & Co, *City of Grand Rapids and Kent County, Michigan* (Logansport, Ind., 1900); Franklin Everett, *Memorials of the Grand River Valley* (Chicago: Chicago Legal News Company, 1878); Z. Z. Lydens, ed., *The Story of Grand Rapids* (Grand Rapids: Kregel Publications, 1966); *Grand Rapids City Directory, 1903* (Grand Rapids, 1903); George Reed, *Bench and Bar of Michigan* (Chicago: Century Publishing and Engraving, 1897); *Michigan Manual* (Secretary of State: Lansing, 1880–1920); and St. Mark's, "Records."

55. The status and occupations of members were, of course, different, but unfortunately no membership lists have survived. In lieu of this, I compiled a list of Grace Church members who were listed in the 1914 *Grace Church Bulletin* as belonging to a church society. Only a third were managers, professionals, or manufacturers; nearly half were clerical or sales; but still only 12 percent were workers, and they were typically skilled.

56. One elite withdrawal see Samuel P. Hays, "The Politics of Reform in Municipal Government," *Pacific Northwest Quarterly* 55 (October 1964): 157–169; Jon C. Teaford, *The Unheralded Triumph: City Government in America, 1870–1900* (Baltimore: Johns Hopkins University Press, 1984), 15–82; and Eugene Watts, *The Social Bases of City Politics: Atlanta, 1865–1903* (Westport, Conn.: Greenwood Press, 1978). Thomas Doran was a classic urban politico, serving as city marshall from 1873 to 1876, and on the city council for eighteen years, starting in

1863 and ending in 1909. So fully identified with politics was he, that his obituary failed to list another occupation. *Grand Rapids Press,* 8 March 1917; and sources in note 54.

57. On Ellis, see Anthony R. Travis, "Mayor George Ellis: Grand Rapids Political Boss and Progressive Reformer," *Michigan History* 58 (Summer 1974): 101–130. Jeffrey Kleiman discusses the transformation in "The Rule From Above: Businessmen, Bankers, and the Drive to Organize in Grand Rapids, 1890–1906," *Michigan Historical Review* 12 (Fall 1986): 45–68; and "Creating a Reform Machine: The Grand Rapids Citizens League, 1917–1927," paper presented to the Great Lakes History Conference, 20 April 1989, Grand Rapids, Michigan. Compare the analysis of Dayton in Judith Sealander, *Grand Plans: Business Progressivism and Social Change in Ohio's Miami Valley, 1890–1929* (Lexington: University Press of Kentucky, 1988). On Pingree, see Melvin G. Holli, *Reform in Detroit: Hazen S. Pingree and Urban Politics* (New York: Oxford University Press, 1969).

58. In Indianapolis, 75 percent of the Democratic leaders were lawyers, but only one of the twelve Republicans. In Grand Rapids, 57.1 percent of the Democrats and 47.1 percent of the Republicans were lawyers. The percentage figures for Catholics represent the proportion of the religious population and are calculated from *Census of Religious Bodies, 1906,* 1: 380–400.

59. Dunn, *Greater Indianapolis,* 1: 433. Ironically, the victorious candidate in 1929 was Reginald Sullivan, son of former mayor Thomas Sullivan and, like his father, a member of St. Paul's church. See the discussion in James H. Madison, *Indiana Through Tradition and Change: A History of the Hoosier State and Its People, 1920–1945,* vol. 5 of *The History of Indiana* (Indianapolis: Indiana Historical Society, 1982), 26–75, especially 73–74.

60. For an analysis of the campaigns and some electoral analysis, see Travis, "Mayor George Ellis."

61. Philip R. VanderMeer, "Political Crisis and Third Parties: The Gold Democrats of Michigan" *Michigan Historical Review* 12 (Fall 1989): 61–84 discusses the party. Western Michigan men are listed in *Lansing Weekly Journal,* 31 July 1896; and biographical information came from sources listed in note 54. On Sligh and especially the 1896 campaign, see the Sligh Family Papers in the Michigan Historical Collections, Bentley Library, University of Michigan.

62. Of course various forms of population mobility had different consequences. See Mode, "Aids and Methods of Church-Union Movements."

63. E.g., in Grace Church, 20 percent of the officers of the women's Guilds in 1914 were Dutch. Calculated from *Grace Church Bulletin* 4 (October 1914): 2–3.

64. Vote calculated from Smith, *Diocese of Western Michigan,* 178–179.

65. On bishops, see the discussions above; also *JPWM, 1881:* 66–67; James E. Wilkinson, "Reminiscenses," in Box 2, PEWM; and *Grace Church Bulletin* 6 (May 1918): 5.

66. As an example of financial contribution see the thanks to Rev. Bruille for his "munificent donation" in St. Mark's, "Records," vol. 1, 21 December 1885. Clerical leadership is noted in *Grace Church Bulletin* 4 (March 1916): 9.

CONTRIBUTORS

TERRY D. BILHARTZ is an associate professor of history at Sam Houston State University. His publications include *Francis Asbury's America* (1984) and *Urban Religion and the Second Great Awakening* (1986). His current project is a social history of the historical profession in the United States.

CATHERINE A. BREKUS is a graduate student in American studies at Yale University and is completing a dissertation entitled "Female Preachers and Evangelical Religion in America, 1740–1840."

GERALD F. MORAN is professor of history at the University of Michigan-Dearborn. His publications include articles in *The Journal of Social History, William and Mary Quarterly, Journal for the Scientific Study of Religion,* and *The Encyclopedia of Adolescence.* His forthcoming book is entitled *The Puritan Saint: Church Membership and Society in Connecticut, 1636–1800.*

LINDA K. PRITCHARD is an associate professor at the University of Texas at San Antonio and currently convener of the Religion and Society Network of the Social Science History Association. Her most recent article is "A Comparative Approach to Western Religious History" in *The Western Historical Quarterly* (November 1988). She is currently completing a monograph entitled *Evangelical Environments: The Social Context of Evangelical Religion in the Upper Ohio Valley, 1790–1860.*

JONATHAN D. SARNA is the Joseph H. and Belle R. Braun Professor of American Jewish History at Brandeis University. He has written, edited, or coedited eleven books, including *JPS: The Americanization of Jewish Culture, 1888–1988; The American Jewish Experience;* and *Jacksonian Jew: The Two Worlds of Mordecai Noah.*

HARRY S. STOUT is professor of religious history and master of Berkeley College at Yale University. Besides his numerous articles, he has written *The New England Soul* (1986). At present he is working on a history of the First Congregational Church of New Haven, which is part of the University of Chicago's multi-volume *The Congregation in American Life.*

ROBERT P. SWIERENGA is professor of history at Kent State University. He is editor of *The Dutch in America: Immigration, Settlement, and Cultural Change* (1985) and author of many books and articles on American immigration, ethnicity, and land history. He is currently completing a book-length manuscript entitled *The Forerunners: Dutch Jewish Immigrants in Nineteenth Century America.*

MARGARET SUSAN THOMPSON is an associate professor at Syracuse University. Se his the author of *The "Spider Web": Congress and Lobbying in the Age of Grant* (1985) and numerous articles in Catholic feminist history. Her forthcoming book, *The Yoke of Grace: American Nuns and Social Change, 1808–1917,* will be published by Oxford University Press.

PHILIP R. VANDERMEER, associate professor of history at Arizona State University, is the former convener of the Religion and Society Network of the Social Science History Association. He is the author of *The Hoosier Politician: Officeholding and Political Culture in Indiana, 1896–1920* (1985) and various articles in political history. His current project is a study of the transformation of the legal profession in the Midwest, 1850–1920.

MARILYN J. WESTERKAMP received her Ph.D. from the University of Pennsylvania and is an assistant professor at the University of California at Santa Cruz. The author of *Triumph of the Laity: Scots-Irish Piety and the Great Awakening* (1986), she is presently working on a study of Anne Hutchinson.

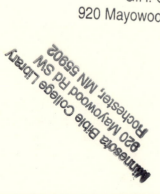